TURKEY'S FOREIGN POLICY IN THE 21ST CENTURY

To all the friends of ECCMES at EMU

Turkey's Foreign Policy in the 21st Century:

A Changing Role in World Politics

Edited by
TAREQ Y. ISMAEL
University of Calgary
MUSTAFA AYDIN
Ankara University

Routledge
Taylor & Francis Group
LONDON AND NEW YORK

First published 2003 by Ashgate Publishing

Reissued 2019 by Routledge
2 Park Square, Milton Park, Abingdon, Oxon, OX14 4RN
52 Vanderbilt Avenue, New York, NY 10017

Routledge is an imprint of the Taylor & Francis Group, an informa business

A Library of Congress record exists under LC control number:

ISBN 13: 978-1-138-70790-0 (hbk)
ISBN 13: 978-1-138-70788-7 (pbk)
ISBN 13: 978-1-315-19873-6 (ebk)

Contents

List of Contributors

Bülent Aras is assistant professor of International Relations at Fatih University (Turkey) where he is Chair of the Department and serves as Director of the Institute of Social Sciences. His latest books include: *Emerging Black Sea Area: Politics, Security and Economy* (2002); *New Geopolitics of Eurasia and Turkey's Position* (2001); *Oil and Geopolitics in Caspian Sea Basin* (1999); and *The Palestinian-Israeli Peace Process and Turkey* (1997).

Mustafa Aydın is associate professor of International Relations at the Faculty of Political Science, Ankara University; as well as at the National Security Academy, Ankara. He was Research Fellow at the Center for Political Studies, University of Michigan, Ann Arbor (1998), and a Fulbright Scholar at the John F. Kennedy School of Government, Harvard University (2002). Among others, he is the author of *Turkish Foreign Policy During the Gulf War* (1998), *Turkish Foreign Policy Towards the Year 2000* (1998, in Turkish); *New Geopolitics of Central Asia and the Caucasus: Causes of Instability and Predicament* (2000); and editor of the *Turkish Yearbook of International Relations;* the *Review of International Affairs*; and *Ankara Papers,* as well as *Turkey at the Threshold of the 21st Century* (1998); *Greek-Turkish Relations in the 21st Century: Escaping from the Security Dilemma in the Aegean* (forthcoming, with K. Ifantis); *Turkish-American Relations; 200 Years of Divergence and Convergence* (forthcoming, with Ç. Erhan).

Tozun Bahcheli is professor of political science at King's College in London (Canada). His most recent book is *Greek-Turkish relations and U.S. foreign policy* (1997) and his *Greek-Turkish Relations Since 1955* (1990), is regarded as the definitive analysis on the subject of Greek-Turkish relations. He is currently writing a book on ethnic conflict in Cyprus.

Tareq Y. Ismael is professor of political science at the University of Calgary (Canada). He is president of the International Centre for Contemporary Middle East Studies at Eastern Mediterranean University (TRNC) and was a founder and past president of the International Association of Middle Eastern Studies (IAMES). Author of more than twenty-five books his most recent titles include: *The Arab States of Africa: Contemporary Government and Politics* (forthcoming); *The Communist Movement in the Arab World* (forthcoming); *The International Relations of the Middle East in the 21st Century: Patterns of Continuity and Change* (2001); *Middle East Politics Today: Government and Civil Society* (2001); and *The Communist Movement in Syria and Lebanon* (1997).

Eric L. Knudsen is professor of International Relations and Director of Research at the International Center for Contemporary Middle East Studies at Eastern

Mediterranean University (TRNC). He is author of *Great Britain, Constantinople and the Turkish Peace Treaty 1919-1922* (1987) and has contributed articles to the *Journal of South Asian and Middle Eastern Studies* and *Diplomacy and Statecraft*. He is currently working on a book dealing with Syria and the Baath party.

Ozay Mehmet is professor of economics at The Norman Paterson School of International Affairs at Carleton University (Ottawa, Canada). His most recent publications include 'Promoting a Fair Global Market Place: Is it Time for a Progressive Canadian Agenda?' in *Canadian Foreign Policy* (forthcoming); *Water Balances in the Eastern Mediterranean* (edited with David Brooks, 2000); *Westernizing the Third World, The Eurocentricity of Economic Development Theories* 2nd edn. (1999) and Towards A Fair Global Labour Market: avoiding a new slave trade (with Errol Mendes and Robert Sinding, 1999).

Sabri Sayarı is the executive director of the Institute of Turkish Studies and a research professor in the School of Foreign Service at Georgetown University. His most recent books include: *Political Leaders and Democracy in Turkey* (with Metin Heper, 2002); *Politics, Parties, and Elections in Turkey* (with Yılmaz R. Esmer, 2002) and *Turkey's New World: changing dynamics in Turkish foreign policy* (with Alan Makovsky, 2002).

A. Seda Serdar is a researcher at the Centre for Eurasian Strategic Studies at the department of European Studies. She received her MA from the University of Amsterdam on Turkish-EU relations. Currently a PhD student at the Middle Eastern Technical University in Ankara, she is working on European integration and the concept of security within this process.

Oktay F. Tanrısever is a Lecturer in International Relations at the Middle East Technical University, Ankara, Turkey. His research interests cover Russian politics, Russian foreign policy and theories of international relations. He has published several articles, including 'The Battle for Chechnia: Russia Confronts Chechen Secessionism', *METU Studies in Development* (Autumn 2000), and 'The Impact of the 1994 Tatar-Russian Power Sharing Treaty on the Formation of Post-Soviet Tatar National Identity', *Slovo* (2001).

Dan Tschirgi is professor of political science at the American University in Cairo (Egypt). His most recent publications include: *Origins and Development of the Arab-Israeli Conflict* (with Ann Mosely Lesch, 1998) and *Development in the Age of Liberalization: Egypt and Mexico* (1996).

Nuri Yurdusev is Associate Professor of International Relations at the Middle East Technical University, Ankara. In addition to numerous articles on International Relations theory, Turkish foreign policy and Turkish-European relations, he is the author of the forthcoming book *International Relations and the Philosophy of History*, to be published by Palgrave. He is also editing a book on *Ottoman Diplomacy* for Palgrave.

Preface

The idea for an edited book on *Turkey's Foreign Policy in the 21st Century: A Changing Role in World Politics* emerged at the Third International Conference organized by the International Center for Contemporary Middle Eastern Studies, (ICCMES) held at Eastern Mediterranean University (North Cyprus) in April 2000. That conference was the beginning of this project, as well as the genesis of the ideas presented in this volume. The stimulating presentations and ensuing discussion led to a greater understanding for all of the challenges facing Turkey in the new millennium. Due to the subsequent dramatic changes in domestic Turkish politics and alterations in the regional and international political order, the contributions to this volume were solicited for this book in the spirit of the conference.

There are many systems of transliteration from the Turkish and Middle Eastern languages, and no particular standards prevail. In an effort to aid the reader's recognition of names and places the system of transliteration used in this book follows popular usage in the media rather than a particular formal system.

Many individuals contributed to making this endeavor successful. I would like to extend my gratitude to the faculty and staff at Eastern Mediterranean University for their hospitality and scholarly excellence in hosting and participating in the April 2000 conference; to those scholars who visited the Cyprus campus in 2000, both for their contributions and for the discursive effect those presentations and the ensuing discussions had on all those involved in the project; to the authors, who drew from the conference itself, as well as from their own scholarly expertise, to pursue this subject matter in the format of an edited collection. It would be remiss of me not to thank Doreen Neville, who typeset the entire manuscript through countless revisions, and John Measor who kept the project on track, sometimes in spite of the editors. Finally, I would like to thank Mustafa Aydın for his patience and tireless efforts in seeing this project through to completion. His determination to see the assorted contributions through to the finish was a contribution I will not soon forget.

Tareq Y. Ismael
Calgary, Alberta,
Canada

Introduction

Tareq Y. Ismael

The organization of this volume reflects the effort to situate events in the context of a theoretical analysis of Turkey's foreign policy as well as its relationship with the West and with its regional neighbours. The first chapter attempts to provide a complementary analytical framework for the analysis of Turkey's foreign policy. In the next three chapters, Turkey's relationship with, and aspirations for, membership in the Western 'club' of advanced capitalist liberal democracies are examined; while in the following seven chapters Turkey's relations with regional neighbours is considered.

In chapter one, 'Twenty Years Before, Twenty Years After: Turkish Foreign Policy at the Threshold of the 21st Century', Mustafa Aydın focuses on the challenges posed to Turkish policies in the light of the dramatic alterations to the international political landscape immediately before and following the end of the Cold War. Aydın examines how Turkey, once a distant outpost of NATO on the European periphery has emerged as an important actor, poised to play a leading role across a vast region extending from Eastern Europe to western China. The burden of expectations placed on Turkish policy-makers is examined in terms of the tensions generated between Turkey's evolving national on the one hand, and the unstable regional context on the other. Presupposing that any country's foreign policy is a product of the interplay between its domestic and external imperatives, Aydın considers the internal and external determinants of Turkish foreign policy since 1980 in an attempt to project a probable future 'road map' for Turkey.

Aydın also explores how throughout the Cold War, Turkey's geostrategic 'value' was largely determined by its role within the Atlantic Alliance. This provided Turkey with a familiar and somewhat stable environment in its external relations. However, this environment has been altered since 1980 as a result of three important developments. First, the military takeover in 1980 resulted in a shift in Turkish foreign policy whereby the economy was opened up and integrated with the world at large. Second, in the aftermath of the takeover, many issues that Turkey had previously considered to be internal affairs became issues in its relations with other states, especially those of Western Europe. The third factor was the dynamism that was brought into Turkish domestic and foreign policies by new politicians who emerged following Turkey's return to multiparty democracy.

Aydın then turns his attention to the effects on Turkish policy-makers of changes in international politics occurring in the 1990s. He argues that in the emerging new world order – or disorder – 'perhaps no other country outside the former Soviet block has seen its strategic position more radically transformed than

Turkey.' As a result, the country is facing tremendous opportunities and potentially new hazards in a newly-restructured environment. Examining Turkey in the light of such events, Aydın postulates four sets of factors that have the potential to affect Turkey's foreign policy in the coming decades: the nature of the political regime in the country and external reactions to it; the basic needs of Turkey's economy and the possible sudden alterations in its economic preferences; the current structure and alternative policies available in the foreign policy decision-making system; and, changes in regional and international structures.

In chapter two, 'Turkey and the United States', Sabri Sayarı examines Turkey's relations with its principal ally since the end of the Second World War: the United States of America. Sayarı details how the alliance between the United States and Turkey originated in their shared perception of a Soviet threat in the aftermath of the Second World War. As a consequence, during the Cold War the military, political, and economic ties between the two countries expanded rapidly despite the strains that were imposed on the bilateral relationship by the political eruption in Cyprus and Greek-Turkish disputes within the Aegean Sea. Sayarı elucidates how, following the collapse of Soviet power in 1991, the agenda of US-Turkish relations expanded significantly. Finding that the two countries have cooperated on a broad range of issues including regional security problems in the Middle East, the Balkans, and the Caucasus, energy development in the Caspian region, and international terrorism, Sayarı lays out the principles according to which the relationship will develop in future.

Sayarı also analyses how US and Turkish policies have tended to diverge on several issues, most notably regarding Saddam Hussein's rule in Iraq. He details events that in 2001 had an effect in both countries, principally Turkey's financial crisis in February and the terrorist attacks on the United States in September, arguing that they have underscored the importance of the bilateral ties connecting both Turkey and the United States.

In chapter three, 'Turkey and the European Union: A Troubled Relationship', Ozay Mehmet analyses EU-Turkish relations in the aftermath of the Helsinki decision to grant Turkey formal candidate status. Mehmet argues that while this decision has the potential of being an historic turning point in Turkish-EU relations, it may also create major hurdles for policy-makers in both Ankara and European capitals. The chapter is organized into four parts. Following an introductory overview, Mehmet focuses on the potential obstacles on the road to full Turkish membership in the EU, utilizing the Copenhagen Criteria (CC) to summarize and highlight the potential sticking points on both sides. Part three is devoted to a discussion and evaluation of the benefits of an 'historic partnership' between Turkey and the EU while the final section offers analysis and conclusions.

In chapter four,. 'The New European Security Architecture and Turkey', A. Seda Serdar examines the importance of Turkish-EU security coordination and cooperation while recognizing that relations have often proved awkward in the past. Serdar examines the contentious political and economic aspects of the liaison and also discusses technical military issues. She points out that formalized Turkish-EU relations have been maintained for four decades, without a satisfactory resolution to the problems outlined. On the contrary, high tension has come to characterize the relationship, endangering future liaisons between Turkey and EU member states. Serdar then examines security issues, which are deemed especially delicate since they involve multiple actors, including regional states not affiliated with the two negotiating sides. In this way she predicts how the transatlantic dimension of the European Security and Defense Identity will be discussed in the future by examining the positions of Turkish, EU and US policy-makers.

In chapter five, 'Perceptions and Images in Turkish (Ottoman)-European Relations', Nuri Yurdusev discusses the role of the 'identity question' in Turkish-European relations and reexamines the established opinion that the identities held by Europeans and Turkish policy-makers are incompatible. Yurdusev posits that the gap between European identity and Turkish identity is not as wide as is commonly assumed. He argues further that the question of identity is not the only determining factor in Turkish-European relations, despite the central treatment it receives in the literature. Yurdusev asserts that what is significant is not the difference in identity itself, but the respective understanding of identity. He also suggests that *raison d'état* has been equally significant in determining Turkish-European relations. Yurdusev finds that the result is neither an outright negation nor a ready affirmation of the other, but rather a policy of managing the other. The Europeans and the Turks cannot simply ignore one other. His article deals mainly with the European perception of the Turk as 'the other', the role of Turkey in the making of the modern European identity and the policy of managing 'the other'.

In chapter six, 'Turkey and the Arab World in the New Millennium' Dan Tschirgi examines the overall pattern of Turkish-Arab relations that have prevailed following the establishment of the modern Turkish state. He then explores the alterations that marked the 1990s, and the significance of September 11, and the ensuing US-led War on Terrorism, for Turkish-Arab relations. Tschirgi outlines the tensions placed upon this relationship in lieu of three interrelated problems: the US military campaign against Afghanistan's Taliban regime; Washington's declared intention to bring about the fall of Saddam Hussein's regime in Iraq; and the deterioration of the situation in Palestine to a point that by the spring of 2002 had threatened to provoke a wider conflict between Israel and the Arab states. Tschirgi frames the tensions within Turkey's own longstanding war against terror and popular Turkish sentiments disapproving of a Western military response that was directed solely against Muslim peoples in Central Asia and the Middle East.

Tschirgi notes that the Turkish government, however, promptly showed it had overcome its initial inhibitions against a close identification with the US effort and was soon prepared to embark on a policy sharply at variance with the prevailing regional outlook. He finds that the Western campaign post-September 11 provided Turkey with an opportunity to achieve victory in Turkey's own ongoing struggle with various streams of terrorism and to strengthen its alliance with the United States. Thus the development of Turkish policy toward Afghanistan after September 11 demonstrated that Ankara accorded far higher priority to maintaining and nurturing its relations with the West than to cultivating ties with the Arab world. Using a February 2002 joint meeting in Istanbul between the Organization of the Islamic Conference (OIC) and the European Union (EU) as a bridge between the West and the Muslim world, Turkey saw itself as a facilitator of understanding as opposed to simply having turned its back on the Arab world. However, Tschirgi observes that Turkey's post-September position between the Arab world and the West increasingly resembled that of a strained link between two objects that were inexorably drifting apart than a bridge between the two communities, largely due to the uncertainties surrounding the future of Iraq and Palestine.

Chapter Seven, 'Turkey and the Russian Federation: Towards A Mutual Understanding?' by Oktay Tanrısever, seeks to examine the emerging patterns in Turkey's relations with Russia in the post-Cold War era. In addition, it aims to explore the opportunities and the limitations of developing closer relations between Turkey and the Russian Federation. Tanrısever convincingly demonstrates that Turkish-Russian relations could be understood better by exploring the changing positions of these states in the international system than by focusing on their foreign policy actions. From this point of view, Tanrısever argues, the structural opportunities and limitations in the international system significantly affected the pre-1997 geopolitical rivalry and the post-1997 rapprochement between these two states. The article starts by exploring the positions of both Turkey and the Russian Federation in the aftermath of the Cold War. It then investigates the problematic nature of the post-Soviet reform process in Russia and its impact on Russia's relations with Turkey by looking at the geopolitical rivalry between the two states. Tanrısever then examines the rapprochement between Turkey and the Russian Federation through the convergence of the two states' positions in the international system, and their cooperation in the fields of economic and security policy since 1997. Finally, the chapter concludes with an exploration of the opportunities for a 'strategic partnership' between Turkey and the Russian Federation, the existing structural limitations of their relations and the emerging trends in Turkish-Russian relations.

In chapter eight 'Between Euphoria and *Realpolitik*: Turkish Policy towards Central Asia and the Caucasus', Mustafa Aydın examines the emergence of eight independent states to Turkey's northeast following the Cold War. Aydın argues that the challenges posed possible enlargement of Turkey's role in the world while opening Turkey's eyes to a vast territory inhabited largely by fellow Muslim Turkic-speakers. This presented Turkey with a historical opportunity, ending the years of claustrophobia, and emphasizing Turkey's common cultural, linguistic, and religious bonds with the newly independent states of Central Asia and the Caucasus. The truth of the matter is that Turkey of the 1990s faced tremendous opportunities and potential risks in Central Asia and the Caucasus, which collectively posed extraordinary and complex challenges.

While the century-old Soviet/Russian threat to Turkey's security has disappeared, Aydın argues, the vacuum created by this departure in the Central Asia and the Caucasus has become the breeding ground on Turkey's borders for potential risks and threats for regional security because of the deep tensions between mixed national groups, contested borders, economic difficulties, and competition of outsiders for influence. In this unstable environment, Turkey was cited as an important stabilizing actor, because of its strong historical, cultural, ethnic and linguistic bonds with the newly independent states. Thus, the positive role Turkey may play in this region has been extensively discussed not only within

Turkey but also in the West, whose fear that radical Islam might fill up the power vacuum created by the collapse of the USSR, led to strong encouragement to these states to adopt a 'Turkish model' of secular democracy combined with liberal economy. While Turkey has traditionally avoided such involvement in regional politics, it has already been unavoidably drawn into the volatile new politics of the Caucasus. Thus, we can now clearly foresee that Turkey is currently undergoing a dramatic shift away from its traditional policy of isolationism, and that Turkish foreign policy in the future will increasingly focus on Central Asia, alongside the Balkans, and the Middle East.

The emergence of independent Turkic republics in Central Asia and the Caucasus represented a turning point in Turkey's regional role and policies. Turkey has become one of the important players in a region where it previously had only a marginal influence and no active involvement. Although economic and political conditions in the region are unlikely to stabilize for some years, it is almost certain that Turkish policymakers will continue with their efforts to create new networks of interdependency between Ankara and the regional capitals. Also, it is without doubt that other regional players, especially Russia and Iran, will continue to view these policies with suspicion and challenge them.

In chapter nine, 'Cycles of Tension and Rapprochement: Prospects for Turkey's Relations with Greece', Tozun Bahcheli outlines the long-running disputes over the maritime boundaries in the Aegean, and the Cyprus issue, which have brought Turkey and Greece to the brink of war on three occasions in recent decades. Bahcheli delineates how these dangerous confrontations have usually prompted the two neighbors to explore diplomatic avenues to stabilize their relations while also seeking to find solutions to their bilateral problems, though as yet without success. As a case study, Bahcheli cites the Davos initiative of 1988-89, which failed to yield a diplomatic breakthrough due to domestic factors in both countries. He details the vital Turkish interests at stake in both the Aegean and Cyprus, and notes that Ankara has been deeply mistrustful of Athens due to the latter's policies aiming at weakening Turkish interests. However, Bahcheli is not jaundiced by past relations between the two states, as he points out that the emerging rapprochement between Turkey and Greece beginning in late 1999, and the prospect of Turkey's accession to EU membership during the first decade of the new millennium, have created additional incentives for settling Turkish-Greek differences. Bahcheli's chapter explores the elements of a compromise settlement between the two countries, and evaluates the future prospects of Turkey's relations with its important neighbor.

Chapter ten, 'Turkey's Relations with Iran in the Post-Cold War Era', by Bülent Aras, examines the hurdles described by Turkish academics and the media that are preventing a more positive bilateral relationship between Turkey and Iran. This chapter outlines the nature and causes of these problems, and critically analyzes their severity. Aras notes as especially critical the extent to which domestic pressures have been influential in the development of Turkey's foreign policy towards Iran. As such he questions whether Turkish decision-makers define their rivals on the basis of intrinsic national interests, or whether they merely react to images projected by self-interested politicians and external actors.

Further, Aras explores the question as to whether Turkey is drifting into a potentially dangerous rivalry without sufficient reason to see Iran as a primary opponent. In his chapter, Aras argues that Turkey's policy towards Iran has become hostage to the worldview of Turkey's governing elite, one that has demonstrated itself to be increasingly unable to successfully cope with political change at domestic, regional, and international levels. After analyzing bilateral, regional, and international contexts, he argues that Turkey has drifted into an unproductive rivalry without having actually decided that Iran represents a prime opponent.

Furthermore, Aras finds a cyclical pattern of ruptures in Iranian-Turkish relations, characterized by severe crises involving ideologically-driven incriminations, and at times the recall of diplomats, generally followed by periods of pragmatic interactions. Aras argues that if both states' foreign policy-makers could move beyond a mere reaction to images projected by self-interested politicians, and formulate a new policy paying attention to changing domestic, regional and international politics, this pattern might be overcome.

In chapter eleven, 'Syria, Turkey and the Changing Power Configuration in the Middle East: An Analysis of Political, Economic and Regional Differences', Erik L. Knudsen outlines the past half century of Syrian-Turkish diplomatic relations. Knudsen argues that these have been marked by suspicion, mistrust and at times outright hostility which have nearly resulted in armed confrontation. Knudsen attempts to explain why Damascus and Ankara have formulated policies that have resulted in such tense relations. Past territorial disputes, the impact of Turkey's pro-Western orientation, and Syrian support of elements within Turkey that are critical of the Turkish government's policy are examined. Knudsen then focuses on the contemporary issues which have exacerbated insecurity on both sides of the Syrian-Turkish border, such as Ankara's decision to sign a strategic agreement with Israel, attempts by the Damascus government to politically move closer to real or potential regional enemies of Turkey, as well as disputes over the sharing of water resources.

PART I: TURKISH FOREIGN POLICY IN A NEW CENTURY

Chapter 1

Twenty Years Before, Twenty Years After: Turkish Foreign Policy at the Threshold of the 21st Century

Mustafa Aydın

We are witnessing momentous changes in the international system. None, perhaps, was so greatly welcomed as the end of the Cold War. As the Berlin Wall crumbled, the Eastern Europeans took their future into their own hands and the Soviet Union disintegrated, the Cold War was declared over and the World anticipated the dawn of an unprecedented era of peace, stability and democracy. Today, unfortunately, the wisdom of these anticipations is questioned. The initial optimism and euphoria have been silenced by extremely grave problems that have subsequently developed. The community of nations was either ill prepared to recognise such problems or simply too slow in preventing them. However, if one thing is certain today, it is the 'change' that the international system has experienced and continues to be influenced by.

Amidst the dust created by the important systemic changes that we have experienced since the end of the Cold War in 1989, Turkey, once a distant outpost of NATO on the European periphery, has emerged as an important actor, poised to play a leading role across a vast region extending 'from eastern Europe to western China'.[1] This change in Turkey's status, however, was not accidental, but due to wider changes experienced within and around Turkey during the 1980s.

Today, Turkey is a country on the move. The roots and dynamics of this lie in the changes that affected her throughout the 1980s and 1990s, changes without which she could not have expected to benefit from her new role as it emerged in the international arena after the end of the Cold War. It is not exactly certain where this movement will take Turkey. However, taking into account general principles of foreign policy making in Turkey together with recent developments that force change, we may project the possible future paths for her external relations.

In today's world, while interdependence is being intensified with mind-blowing speed, 'change' is the most pronounced word that has become a byword for development and progress. This of course makes prediction a difficult business in international relations. It also increases the suspicions and concerns about the expectations and capabilities of the countries that could be influential within their sub-regions, which are not yet stabilised within the 'new world order' context, and thus makes their realistic analysis imperative for world security and peace in general.

Turkey is one of the most affected countries from the cyclical systemic changes in world politics. Another important attribute of Turkey that makes her interesting to our analysis is that her internal political system as well as socio-economic dynamics is changing in parallel to the international system. Sure enough, 'change' is one of the consistencies of Turkish daily life. Since the military *coup d'état* of 12 September 1980, Turkey has experienced fundamental changes in every field. Her political structure, her economic system, social strata, cultural patterns, religious expressions, and of course her foreign policy, have all had their share of fast evolving developments. Turkey at the end of the decade was a largely transformed country and the impetus for change is still visible. At the same time, while the constant change became the rule within the country, Turkey, from a reverse angle, is considered a stability factor within her surrounding unstable and insecure region. Therefore, as a country expected to play an important role in regional and global politics in the coming years, analysis of Turkey's security and foreign policies are important not only for the understanding of the said country but also for world peace and stability.

Balance of Last 20 Years in Turkey and the World

While the collapse of the Berlin Wall in 1989 signified the beginning of the end for the system that the international community had become used to during the Cold War, for Turkey it introduced new difficulties in her foreign and security policies. During the Cold War, Turkey's foreign policy was conducted within well-know parameters and with age-old policies. Even though the nuclear bipolarity carried within it the dangers of a possible global catastrophe, it also provided a stable, balanced, well known and thus a 'secure' environment for countries like Turkey. Within this system, Turkey, entrusting her security to NATO membership and the USA's nuclear umbrella, was occupied in her foreign policy with well-delineated problems such as the Aegean and Cyprus.

In this context, Turkey, with the principles developed since the establishment of the republic, followed a foreign policy known for its high degree of rationality, sense of responsibility, long-term perspective and 'realism found in few developing nations'.[2] What's more, the governments, like most of the Turkish people during the 1970s, were engulfed with a struggle for survival while the leftist and rightist groups continuously killed each other on the streets, and thus refrained largely to take a new initiative in foreign policy

This picture has changed because of two important developments, one internal and the other external. The internal development was the 12 September 1980 *coup d'état* and the dilemmas that it brought for the country. Externally, the end of the Cold War and the collapse of the international system that we had become so used to sent shock waves throughout the Turkish foreign policy-making structure necessitating a re-evaluation. The September 12 coup unleashed number of forces that had long-term implications for Turkish foreign policy.

i) First of all, upon takeover, the military decided to promote Turgut Özal to the post of state minister responsible for economics. Before the takeover, he was part of the technical team that prepared the 'January 24th Economic Austerity Measures'. This decision showed that the military intended to follow the economic policies that had been introduced by the previous civilian government. This had a number of important implications for Turkey's foreign policy.

While the January 24 decisions opted for structural change for the country's economic system, it rested on three pillars: more exports, more foreign capital flow towards Turkey, and more foreign borrowing. The significance of these for foreign policy is that, in addition to Turkey's willingness and perseverance, all three were dependent on the willingness of other states to comply with Turkey's wishes: that is, their willingness to buy more Turkish goods, to invest more in Turkey, and to supply more aid to Turkey. This, on the one hand, forced the internationalisation of the Turkish economy leading to increased vulnerability, while on the other hand,it brought about a new concept for Turkish foreign policy making: economy-politic or political economy.

This meant that Turkey could not conduct her foreign policy with only a 'security' dimension as she had done previously. The Foreign Ministry, in addition to its other duties, was forced now to follow worldwide economic trends and to contribute to the economic development of the country with an 'active' foreign policy. Hence, the parameters of foreign policy making in Turkey was expanded, and diplomats and politicians became actively involved in promoting Turkey's and its businessmen's economic priorities in the international arena.

ii) Another important aspect of the September 12 coup for Turkish foreign policy-making was that it brought up allegations of torture and the country's human rights record indicating a failure of democratisation in general, which moved to the top of the political agenda both inside and outside the country. This process that started with the *coup d'état* forced the internationalisation of Turkey's domestic politics. Then, the institutionalisation of this practice with the transformation of the Helsinki Process, first to CSCE and later on to OSCE along with the recognition of Turkey's full membership status in the EU, indicated a new area that Turkey did not have to dwell on during the Cold War: Internationalisation of Turkey's domestic political problems. This has created a constant restraint on governments, and as such had effects both on the country's domestic political evaluation and on her foreign relations as well.

iii) Another effect of the September 12 coup on Turkish foreign policy came with the decision to force out all the former politicians from active politics. This enabled new faces to enter politics with new ideas. These 'new faces', starting with Turgut Özal and continuing with Murat Karayalçın, Mesut Yılmaz and Tansu Çiller, promoted an 'active foreign policy' discourse for Turkey, trying to emphasise their differences with past political leaders. While the discussion of the positive and negative outcomes of this discourse, which was a natural reaction in part to the inactivity of Turkish foreign policy during the 1970s, is beyond the scope of this paper, it is obvious that this new discourse brought about a newfound dynamism to Turkish foreign policy.

While these events were happening within Turkey, forcing the country to new openings, the decade that started with the September 12 coup in Turkey, ended with a new development outside Turkey: The Cold War suddenly ended and the bipolar international system disappeared, leaving behind an uncertain and vague international structure.

It is stated above that Turkey struggled with known problems within well-known parameters during the Cold War. The international system that made possible this policy was the stable character of the Cold War. Everything was rather easy while we knew where and how the threat came. The end of the Cold War, however, has changed this. The game that we played for 45 years ended and was replaced by a new game, the rules of which were not yet known. Therefore, while the new era suddenly signified the emergence of new problems for Turkey, it became clear that Turkey could not follow the foreign polices that were formulated under the tranquillity of the Cold War.

i) First of all, the abandonment of the Communist regime and attempts for democratisation of politics within Russia and other newly independent states of the former Soviet Union, improved the possibility of global cooperation transcending the enmities of the Cold War. However, since then, in the absence of clearly defined mechanisms for preventing regional conflicts in the post-Cold War era, perpetual instability within the new states, and tensions among them, have created a serious risk of interstate military clashes and widespread civil war in the heart of Eurasia, where Turkey is situated.

ii) Additionally, the political implosion of the Soviet system has undermined the international alliances originally designed to counter Soviet expansionism and has created a major risk of socio-political instability extending far beyond former Soviet territories into the nearby countries of Europe, the Middle East and Asia.

iii) Moreover, many former Soviet regions and nationalities that once seemed of marginal significance for an understanding of international relations have become critically important. The model that these people should emulate in their quest for national identities, political and economic development, and new international alliances has became a source of controversy not only within these republics but also among the nearby countries and global actors, more so because some of the former Soviet Union's nuclear capacity was inherited by the newly independent, and yet unstable, states.

iv) Furthermore, a somewhat natural extension of the end of the Cold War has been the diminishing importance of old East-West division of the international system, being replaced with a new line dividing North and South. In such an emerging division, where bi-polarity of the Cold War era had disappeared, it seems inevitable that regional concerns will play a more important role in determining the course of the international relations in the foreseeable future than the 'interests and restraints related with global concerns'.[3] Thus, a struggle between aspiring regional hegemons for supremacy within the various sub-systems of the international system, including the Balkans, the Middle East, Central Asia and the Caucasus, seems to be the likely order of the day.

With these general observations in mind we may suggest a working proposition of the following factors as contributing to Turkish foreign policy formulation during the first quarter of the 21st century: the nature of the domestic political regime and external perceptions and reactions towards it; Socio-Economic dynamics; the structure and composition of the policy-making system; and external environmental circumstances.

Structure of the Political System and its International Reflections

In any political system domestic issues have an important bearing on the formulation and substance of foreign policy, though the extent and nature of this influence varies with a nation's political system.[4] There are differences between parliamentary democracies; guided democracies (of which Turkey was an example during the second half of 1980s); authoritarian governments (as the military regime of 1980-1983 could be categorized); and totalitarian regimes. In democracies, the government has to contend with political parties, the interests these parties represent, the desire to further improve standard of living, traditions, ethics, religion, and a multitude of pressure groups. Moreover, in democracies, the very nature of democratic multiplicity of interests rarely, if ever, permits unanimous approval of a policy. Thus to maintain political equilibrium, democratic governments must rule by compromise. They have to trade one principle against other. Consequently, democratic administrations may make internal concessions to gain endorsement for foreign policies or, vice-versa, sacrifice foreign policies in order to carry out domestic measures.

The political system of a country is also significant in terms of the decision-making process and responsibilities, and it determines powers, focus and the mechanisms of decisions in foreign policy.[5] The institutional structure in a country, at a minimum, 'determines the amount of the total social effort which can be devoted to foreign policy'.[6] Aside from the allocation of resources, the domestic structure crucially affects the way the actions of other states are interpreted. Without denying the importance of other factors, the actual choice of policies within states are determined to a considerable degree by the interpretation of the environment by their leaders and their conception of alternatives. Their understanding of the nature of their choice in turn depends on many factors, including their experience during the rise to eminence, the structure in which they must operate, and the values of their society.

Moreover, in the contemporary period, the very nature of the governmental structure introduces an element of rigidity that operates more or less independently of the convictions of statesmen or the ideology it represents. Daily issues are usually too complex and relevant facts too manifold to be dealt with on the basis of personal intuition. Therefore, a vast bureaucratic mechanism emerges within the states to aid the leaders to choose between options. In today's society, there are few government offices that do not contribute to foreign policy-making in one form or another. While doing this, however, in time, they, too, develop a momentum and a vested interest of their own, and certain governmental influences may be brought to bear upon the administrators of foreign affairs. When this happens, of course, bureaucracy becomes an obstacle to policy-makers and thus they may try to overcome it.

In the modern world, the political leadership in most societies acts in order to maintain the security of their national state,[7] so much so that foreign and security policies have merged to the point where statesmen and military strategists must collaborate closely.[8] Therefore, it goes without saying that military leaders are needed for expert advice, and it is possible that their considered opinion can strongly influence policy decisions. However, it is the responsibility of the decision-makers to determine, if they can, 'how much influence the military may be permitted to exert on foreign policy decisions and whether military personnel should be permitted to state conflicting views in public'.[9] Whether the influence of military leaders can be kept within bounds by a civilian government will always be crucial to a nation's position in international affairs and to its own internal politics. Since Turkey was under outright military dictatorship between 1980-1983 and even after 1983 the military was effective in determining policies in the country, the civil-military relationship and the foreign policy-making of the military regime are important aspects of this paper.

During the 1980s, Turkey passed through different regimes. The decade started with a period of multi-party democracy, which was entrapped by mounting terrorism and rampant economic disasters, and which was abruptly interrupted by the September 12 *coup d'état*. What followed was three years of outright military dictatorship and a transitional period that finally gave way once again to a multi-party parliament, if not full democracy. Thus, from the outset, it might seem that Turkish politics ended the decade where it had originally started. However, appearances are mostly deceptive in the social sciences. Thus, the Turkey of December 3, 1990, when the Chief of Staff, General Torumtay, resigned because the governing framework at the top clashed with his 'principles and understanding of what the state should be',[10] or the Turkey of February 28, 1997, when the Generals, who thought that the survival of the Turkish state was at stake, chose to work within the system cooperating with the President and the Prime Minister through the National Security Council, were fundamentally different from that of September 12, 1980, when the then Chief of Staff, General Evren, led a junta to dislodge the elected government because 'the state had been rendered unable to function...and the political parties have failed to bring about unity and togetherness'.[11]

The difference between these actions for the Turkish foreign policy can be inferred from the reactions and resultant complications she faced in her relations especially with European democracies following the September 12 *coup*. In general terms, the nature of the political regime of a country and its composition affects its foreign policy for mainly two reasons.[12] Firstly, the political regime has the power to define the broader framework of any country's overall political philosophy, which, in the final analysis, constrains, if not conditions, its choices in the international arena, since it determines how the regime sees itself *vis-à-vis* other regimes or state groupings. Secondly, the nature of political regime in a country also creates images outside the country and any change in the 'established' political regime of a country tends to attract reactions from other countries, which, again in the final analysis, might result in pressures for change.[13]

Accordingly, it is one of the arguments of this paper that during the 1980s, being governed by a military dictatorship or a transitional democracy at best, circumscribed Turkey's options in the foreign policy arena and put constraints on her already existing relationships. Specifically, this effect manifested itself in Turkey's relations with western European countries, mainly because of the nature of her existing linkage patterns with those states. Especially the western Europeans, who were non-committal in their early reactions towards the *coup*, in time became hostile towards it because of what they perceived as the impossibility of condoning a military dictatorship, with its deteriorating human rights record and torture allegations, and especially of accepting it within the European 'democratic club'. On the other hand, due to the presence of a linkage area between Turkey and Europe, the European countries chose to pressurise Turkey instead of pushing her out of the European system, and thereby their sphere of influence. However, the 'ever-lasting' foreign (read: European) pressure created a counter-reactive attitude in Turkey, forcing her to look for alternative options to Europe. In this context, president Evren's reminder that Turkey was 'a Middle Eastern country as well as a European one' was indicative of where Turkey's search for new partners could lead her.

In this context, it should be emphasised that Turkey's attempts since the 1960s to follow a 'multi-dimensional', 'active' or 'regional' foreign policy has been unsuccessful in creating alternatives to Turkey's European connection. It is rather difficult to sever all her links that have been created over the last 50–60 years. Besides, there is no other formation within Turkey's vicinity with which she could identify. Cooperation within the Middle East based on common religion is far from satisfying Turkey's military, political, economic and ideological needs. Indeed, Turkey's experience, over the in last 100 years makes such company rather impossible.

On the other hand, a grouping in Central Asia and the Caucasus based on common culture and language is also beyond reach because of Turkey's limited potential, tendency of the regional countries to emphasise their distinctiveness and the strong opposition from Russia to such a gathering. Furthermore, organisations based on emotional rather than rational concerns do not usually succeed. While Turkey-USA-Israel, Turkey-RF, BSEC, ECO or D8 are beneficial groupings and should be followed as new dimensions in foreign policy, they are not capable of answering all of Turkey's needs alone.

Another important aspect of the connection between Turkey's domestic political situation and external perceptions and also reflections of it, was that the effects of the democratic nature of Turkish politics on her foreign policy gain meaning primarily in the context of Turkey's Western vocation, and external pressures are only effective so long as the subject state is receptive to them. It is clear that the internationalisation of Turkey's domestic politics has created a constant restraint on governments, and as such had effects on both the country's domestic political evaluation and on her foreign relations. The crucial factor in this connection has been Turkey's receptivity towards external, that is European, pressures due to the existence of political, economic, military and ideological linkages between itself and Europe. While these linkages enabled Europeans to pressurise Turkey on certain aspects of her internal politics, especially over her human rights record and the democratisation process, Turkey's own identification with Europe at the same time made it susceptible and responsive to such pressures.

Approached from this angle, it becomes easier to understand why successive Turkish governments have reacted harshly when faced with European criticism, and why they attributed such importance to the opinions of an otherwise marginal European organisation, i.e. the Council of Europe. Turkey's membership of the Council was an institutionalised proof of her Europeanness for the Turkish westernising elite, and their ideological and indentificational linkages demanded being part of that community of nations, namely Europeans.

The strength and importance of Turkey's linkages with western Europe was amply demonstrated by the fact that even during the worst period of European criticisms, the Turkish leadership chose to stay and faced the criticisms instead of taking the country out of the European realm. Thus, during the 1980s, European attempts to influence were strongly felt in Turkey and, whatever the political rhetoric to the contrary, were responded to. Although this response usually manifested itself in publicly defiant attitudes, most of the time the governments were quietly engaged in diplomatic and propaganda campaigns in western states both to 'explain' Turkey's policies and to curtail further public criticisms.

In the process, however, Turkish foreign policy, especially *vis-à-vis* Western Europe, became dependent both on domestic political developments and on European reactions to them. The latter, in turn, were an important input in determining domestic political developments, as well. Although it is difficult to ascertain the exact proportion of the effectiveness of European pressures on Turkey's democratisation process, it is pretty clear that Turkey's 'western vocation' and her long history of westernisation affected this transition to a considerable extent.[14] On the other hand, during the process, Turkey and the European countries grew apart, both because of the Turkish people's disappointment with the Europeans who 'let them down in their hour of need' and also because of considerable coolness of European public opinion towards Turkey, created by what appeared as yet another demonstration of the Turk's inability to sustain a workable democracy and by a constant barrage of criticism directed toward her which highlighted her deficiencies *vis-à-vis* Europe and as such built up the 'otherness' of Turkey.

Thus the external, that is mostly European, criticisms and hostile international, i.e. European, environment faced by Turkey after 1980 forced the hands of her leaders to look for new foreign policy patterns and were also instrumental in Turkey's openings towards the Middle East and former Eastern Block countries.

All this, of course, denies neither the role of domestic actors and internal factors, nor the effects of systemic changes in general in reformulation of Turkish foreign policy. But the emphasis here, in contrast to the official Turkish view, is on the existence of a linkage pattern between international pressures and Turkey's domestic political developments, a connection that ultimately affects her foreign policy as well.

Turkey's European connection is not only important for her external relations but also important for her domestic political development and democratisation. Despite frequent rhetoric to the contrary, Turkey is receptive and responsive to external pressures. Turkish foreign policy especially became vulnerable towards domestic political development of the country and the European criticism levelled against it. Similarly, Turkey's internal developments became linked with her external connections. Thus, a Turkey that has to move away from Europe, might see repercussions in her domestic politics, as well as her external relations. It is quite conceivable that anti-secular and anti- democratic forces and tendencies may grow stronger in such a Turkey.

Socio-Economic Dynamics

The political system of a country is not, of course, strictly limited to 'politics' *per se*. It also includes the country's economic policies, its cultural affinities, ideological inclinations, and its arrangements for social order. In this context, it is clear that Turkey's international affinities have affected her economic policies. Especially, Turkey's move towards a liberal economy in early 1980s which had much to do with her links with, and aspirations to be part of, the western political system.[15] Turkey's partnership in the western political system and her essential role within it for western security interests, on the other hand, provided her with much more foreign aid and help during her economic transition than any other country that tried to do the same thing. Therefore there came into existence yet another link between Turkey and its Western vocation thorough her transition to a liberal economy.

Furthermore, once Turkey had made her switch, her new liberal economic system demanded a certain set of political actions and international connections. The common attribute of the programme that introduced the liberal economy to Turkey on 24 January 1980, and other austerity programs introduced since than with the backing of IMF and the World Bank for the recovery of the Turkish economy, is that they all necessitated huge amounts of net foreign currency inflows into the country. The ways to generate the necessary amount included heavy borrowing from abroad, persuading foreigners to invest in Turkey, and increasing and diversifying Turkey's export potentials. However, the crucial point to all the economic measures aimed at obtaining the above-mentioned results is that they all, in one-way or another, depend on the willingness of other countries to respond in a way that would favour Turkey. Since it is clear that the success of such programmes depend largely on the availability of foreign assistance, it can easily be imagined how Turkish foreign diplomacy has to exert itself to maintain contact with the various assisting governments and organizations.

Therefore, both during the 1980s, as the Turkish economy progressively integrated with the world economy, and during the 1990s, while it became part of global economics, the foreign ministry became increasingly concerned with obtaining necessary foreign loans, opening up markets for Turkish goods, and striking deals with foreign governments and, sometimes, even with private companies, in order to bring more investment into the country. Thus, as the foreign policy of the country needed to be in tune with its economic programmes, economic necessities also became an important variable of Turkish foreign policy making.

As a result, as Turkey's need for fresh markets was growing, so her political efforts to find openings in the Middle East and Eastern Block also increased. However, at the same time, realization of the fact that the huge sums needed by the Turkish economy could come only from Western sources demanded a continuation of Turkey's links with the West. Any severing of political relations would have dealt a blow to her economic transformation as well. The end of the Cold War and the subsequent break up of the Soviet Union, opened new economic opportunities for Turkey in both the former Soviet republics and Russia itself because of economic reforms in the latter. Further, the cultural affinity of the Central Asian republics towards Turkey is also a factor worth considering for future economic attempts in the region.[16]

On the social side, too, Turkey had experienced important changes during the 1980s. The repression of the liberal and left-wing intelligentsia by the military regime, and also their efforts to promote orthodox Islam as an antidote to extremism in society, have led to the perhaps not totally unexpected, but unforeseen, result of growing visibility of Islam in Turkish society, which was also affected by the world-wide Islamic revival.

Although many high level and influential Motherland Party members were branded as 'Islamist', at least partial to Islam, by the secular Turkish intelligentsia, it is difficult to find particular instances during the 1980s where they used their influence to get, and obtained, policy changes in foreign relations. Making allowance for the difficulty of separating the possible influence of Islam from other motivating values, and also of distinguishing between Islam's motivating and/or justifying roles, a possible explanation for this subdued role of the 'Islamists' within the Motherland Party, could be that the 'Islamic faction' of the party was pre-occupied most of the time with a power struggle against the 'idealist' and 'liberal' factions. At the same time, the leader of the party, Turgut Özal, who controlled the party completely, had strong foreign policy ideas of his own and thus, thanks to his delicate balancing between various factions of the party, did not allow any one faction to dictate his policy-making. Moreover, most of the time, the presence of ever-watchful President Evren against 'Islamic' manifestations within Turkish politics, was also a restraining factor for Islamic influences on foreign policy.

As a result, especially up to 1989, the Islamic revival within the country had not particularly affected Turkey's foreign policy-making – provided that there was a desire and pressure for change from the 'Islamists' since this is, save sporadic demands for closer relations with the Islamic countries, also difficult to pin down. Therefore, one of the actions that the Islamists were supposed to oppose strongly, that is Turkish application to the EC membership, went smoothly without significant opposition.

However, since 1989, the effects of the Islamic affinities, in connection with the ethnic and historic sentiments, seemed to be on the rise. Yet again, it was still very difficult to ascertain whether the Turkish public's outcries regarding the Karabakh and Bosnian conflicts were the results of Islamic connections, or rather originated from what was perceived, by the public at large, as attempts to wipe out Turkish ethnic brethren in the East and Ottoman legacy in the West. The support displayed by the Turkish public in general to the Coalition war effort during the Gulf War indicates the dominance of the latter – although it could be argued that the Turkish public's support could be seen within the context that the Islamic countries themselves were divided about the issue. It may be sufficient to point out that even within those Islamic countries that sided with the West there were strong anti-Western sentiments in contrast to Turkey where most of the opposition came from the outlawed left-wing Revolutionary Youth, and callings from the Islamic extremists failed to mobilise Turkish public in general.

In conclusion, therefore, it could be argued that the role of Islam in Turkish foreign policy during the last 20 years was mostly confined to the justification of the policies for which the government opted for other reasons. Also, Turkey's reorientation towards the Middle East during the 1980s was the result of a combination of factors, among which the Islamic revival in Turkey occupied a small part – as indicated by the fact that Turkey turned towards the Western Europe and the Soviet Union (later on former Soviet Republics) when the political and economic incentives for closer cooperation with the Middle East declined after 1985.

This discussion, then, brings us to the question of the Turkish public's role in the changing patterns of Turkish foreign policy during the 1980s. As elaborated elsewhere, all the channels of public expression were ruthlessly suppressed under the military regime (1980-83) to the point that the role of public opinion in foreign policy-making was minimal. Its effects, if there were any, during this period were only indirect in that the military regime was anxious to keep the public on its side. Thus the military leaders might have taken decisions, which, they thought, would go well with the public, although, due to nature of the regime, there was no apparent domestic pressure on the military government.

Even after the return of the civilian government, the recovery of public freedom of expression was slow as a result of various restrictions formulated by the new Constitution and other related laws. Under the new laws, the activities of the various groupings, through which public opinion could be related to the government, were restricted to non-political areas, which by definition also excluded the foreign policy-making. Thus, most of the 1980s, the governments got an 'easy-ride' in foreign policy-making as far as public pressure was concerned.

However, as Turkish public opinion became a progressively important factor in the policy-making process, paralleling the increasing democratisation of society especially after 1989, the Turkish government had to resist particularly strong pressures over its policies towards the Karabakh and Bosnian conflicts.

From the government's point of view, both of these conflicts represented no-win situations. As far as the Karabakh conflict was concerned, Turkish public opinion sided heavily with Azerbaijan, and the government was under pressure not to sit on the sidelines so long as the fighting continued. Non-intervention by Turkey only stirred up public opinion and also gave Iran an opportunity to steal the lead from Turkey and play protector to Azerbaijan. Intervention, on the other hand, would have been extremely costly for Turkey in her future relations in the Caucasus, and in her relations with Russia, NATO, and the United States. Hence, in her official approach to the conflict in Nagorno-Karabakh, the Turkish government faced difficult policy choices between domestic pressures, stemming from the sympathy of the Turkish public for the Azeris, who they regarded as victims of Armenian aggression, and its desire to remain neutral and play a moderating role. Moreover, the complacency with which Armenian military advances had been received in the West did not help the severely embarrassed government, which was not only pro-Western but did its best to remain on good terms with Armenia as well as Azerbaijan. Thus, it seems that this conflict firmly underscored the dilemma that would face Turkey in its future efforts to maintain strict neutrality regarding ethnic conflicts in the former Soviet republics.

Moving across from the former Soviet Central Asia and Caucasus to the Balkans, we come to yet another manifestation of growing nationalism in world politics after the end of the Cold War, which aroused great interest in the Turkish public, that is the bloody struggle between Serb, Croat and Muslim forces over Bosnian territories. Though Bosnia is several hundred miles from Turkey's borders and the Bosnian Muslims are not ethnic Turks, it seems that Turkish public opinion has developed a feeling of kinship and responsibility for the Muslims left behind by the retreating Ottoman Empire from the Balkans after around five hundred years of domination.[17] Moreover, the existence of substantial numbers of 'Boshnaks', Turkish citizens of Bosnian origin, about four to five million, in Turkey further increased the identification of Turkish people with the Bosnian Muslims.

What is important for future Turkish involvement in the region is that the importance of religious and historical links, alongside ethnic bonds, seems to be on the increase in Turkey,[18] and the Turkish government, as in the conflict between Armenia and Azerbaijan, seems to be caught in between domestic pressure and what are considered by decision-makers as sensible and responsible policies. Thus, while the Turkish government in its official response to the crisis, had been trying to be extremely restrained and had followed a policy aimed at creating coordinated policies with other states through international organizations, such as the UN, NATO, the CSCE and the ICO, in order to avoid charges that Turkey pursues pan-Ottomanist policies in the region, Turkish public opinion, increasingly frustrated by the inactivity of the West, became very critical of what they perceived as the passivity of their government.

Although the Turkish government has so far resisted public pressure and avoided direct military involvement in either of the conflicts, the increased importance of religious and historical bonds may yet result in increased public pressure on the governments to act if new conflict emerges in or spreads to areas where Turkish minorities live. Thus Turkey may still get involved in situations where neither her security nor her national interests are directly threatened.

Moreover, there are much wider and maybe in the longer-term more important aspects of these conflicts for Turkish foreign policy. Most notably, a reassessment among the vast majority of Turkish people about the 'real face' of the 'western values' and the status of Turkey *vis-à-vis* the West took place. Especially in connection with the Bosnian conflict, while the long Western inactivity towards Serbian aggression interpreted as 'Western complacency' towards Serbian atrocities, questions were raised about whether the West would have allowed the Serbs to conduct their so-called 'ethnic cleansing' if the victims were Slovenians or Croatians, that is Christians instead of Moslems. Thus speculations that Serbian attacks were in fact part of a new 'crusade' aimed at expelling the last remnants of the Ottomans from Europe were also aired.

The events in the Balkans, when viewed together with the Karabakh issue, where, as mentioned earlier, Turkish public opinion again saw a Christian solidarity against Muslim Azerbaijanis, resulted in the questioning of both Turkey's Western orientation and the desirability of her further integration into Europe. In the meantime, pan-Turkist and neo-Ottomanist ideas advanced among at least right-leaning intellectuals.[19] Although it is not clear yet where these discussions will eventually lead Turkey, it would seem that, coupled with the frustration felt as a result of 'European rejection' of Turkey, the above mentioned developments in the Balkans and the Caucasus are putting Turkey, into a process of yet another reassessment of her self-identity in the early 21st century.

Structure of the Decision-Making Mechanism

The 1982 Constitution, prepared by the military regime, gave priority to a strong state and a strong executive within that state; and, moreover, favoured the president against the Cabinet, as reflected in the strong positions taken both by President Evren, and later, by President Özal, in their relations with the different governments. This eventually had a spill over effect on foreign policy, as well as domestic policies, an area that hitherto governments had tended to leave to experts and foreign ministry bureaucrats. Thus, the new system has enlarged the decision-making system and brought the President and the National Security Council effectively into the process. Therefore, we should expect that future presidents, equipped with political background, strong powers and charismatic leadership, will put their imprint, as they had during the last 12 years, on Turkish foreign policy.

Although current president, Necdet Sezer is more likely to use his powers with more restraint than his predecessors –Turgut Özal and Süleyman Demirel– the powers and the institutional structure for forceful presidential domination over Turkish politics, both domestic and external, exist within the constitution for future aspirants. Therefore, this aspect of Turkish politics should be kept in mind when considering Turkey's future foreign policy moves. These powers would enable presidents with a political background and strong convictions about the country's place in the world to impose their 'vision' on the foreign ministry, possibly against what the latter considered as the 'national interests' of the country. Since obtaining a consensus on what constitutes the 'national interest' of a country is a difficult, if not impossible, task, this aspect of Turkish politics, with its foreign policy overtures, could create extreme tensions within the decision-making bodies of the country and among public opinion in general, as exemplified in Turkey during the Gulf Crisis of 1990-1991.

Another aspect of the decision-making process in Turkish foreign policy that should be kept in mind is the composition and powers of the National Security Council and the place of the Turkish military in Turkish political life. In a country like Turkey where the military normally plays a larger role in determining what is in the 'national interest' of the country than in the liberal western democracies, a clash between the opinions of the executive and the General Staff always carries dangers of another possible attempt to dislodge those who opposed the military's vision. Although Turkey of the 21st century is very different from earlier periods, and another outright military intervention in Turkish politics is highly improbable, it cannot be entirely disregarded that the possibility is still there and one can conceive various possible future scenarios where the military might find it extremely difficult to resist intervention. The developments in Turkish domestic politics since 1997 are proof of this. It is difficult of course to predict the possible outcomes of another *coup d'état* in Turkish domestic and foreign policies if it was to occur. However, if the past is in any way indicative of the future, it could be argued that yet another military intervention in Turkey, even if it was to keep unitary, secular and pro-western Turkey intact within the western political system, could have devastating affects on Turkey's European relations and its leaders might, ironically, end up severing Turkey's western connections (if she had not already been forced out) because of the impossibility of sustaining them in the face of mounting criticisms and extreme pressures from Europe.

Changes in balance of power within the policy-making body can also affect a country's foreign policy. In connection with this, it is obvious that the inclusion of hitherto obstructed Islamic forces into the realm of decision-making bodies after 1980 smoothed, if not directly called for, Turkey's openings towards the Middle Eastern Islamic countries. Along the same line, the dominance of economically minded administrators, led by the then premier Özal, within the government led to the 'economy first' principle in foreign relations, and throughout the 1980s, various political and ideological differences were disregarded for expected economic benefits. Of course, the most telling change in the balance of power within the policy-making system during the period was the gradual concentration of power in the hands of late President Turgut Özal. Turkey's 'untraditional' approach to the Gulf War clearly demonstrated the effects of concentration of power within President Özal's hands.

Systemic Changes

The importance of the external environment, especially regarding Western European reactions to the military coup and the subsequent evolution of Turkish democracy, has already been elaborated above. Towards the end of the 20th century, another impetus for change, originating in the external environment, came to dominate Turkish foreign policy-making and forced her to reconsider her place and standing in the world. This was the transformation of Eastern Europe and the dismemberment of the Soviet Union, which had an enormous impact both on Turkish foreign and security policies and on the Turkish worldview in general.

It has been argued that 'perhaps no other country outside the former Soviet block has seen its strategic position more radically transformed by the end of the Cold War than Turkey'.[20] Throughout the Cold War, Turkey was a distant outpost on the European periphery, a barrier to Soviet ambitions in the Middle East, and a contributor to the security of Europe. Turkey's geostrategic 'value' was largely limited to its role within the Atlantic Alliance and, more narrowly, its place within NATO's southern flank.

By the end of the Cold War, however, all these were altered by the appearance of new zones of conflict on three sides of Turkey which arguably enlarged Turkey's role in the world. Although the emergence of six independent Muslim states to its Northeast opened Turkey's eyes to a vast territory inhabited by fellow Muslim Turkic-speakers which presented Turkey with an unprecedented historical opportunity, at least potentially, to utilise for political, economic and psychological gains,[21] the fact that the new situation also presented challenges to her created a lukewarm attitude in Turkey regarding the end of the Cold War. The mainstream analysts came to an understanding that the collapse of Soviet power and the disintegration of the Soviet Union have been a mixed blessing for Turkey.

While the century-old Soviet/Russian threat to Turkey's security has disappeared, the vacuum created by this departure in Transcaucasia and Central Asia has become the breeding ground on Turkey's borders for potential risks and threats for regional security because of the deep tensions between mixed national groups, contested borders, economic difficulties, and competition of outsiders for influence. Under the prevailing atmosphere of euphoria following the collapse of the Soviet Union, Turkey's common cultural, linguistic, and religious bonds with the newly independent Central Asian and Caucasian republics were frequently mentioned, both within and outside Turkey, and she was presented as an economic and political model for these new states.[22] Even limited pan-Turkist ideas were circulated freely. In return, the Turks and Muslims of the former Soviet Union turned to Turkey to help them achieve momentum, consolidate their independence, and gain status and respect in the world.

It was not long, however, before this euphoria become tempered by reality, and it soon became clear that Turkey's financial and technological means were too limited to meet the immense socio-economic needs of the underdeveloped former Soviet republics. Turkey also gradually discovered that the links between the Central Asian republics and Russia, in some cases forged over centuries and reinforced by need and dependency, were far more solid than originally suspected. While optimism was gradually replaced by disillusionment, there emerged a suspicion that earlier enthusiasm had been merely an empty pretence, 'that in reality Turkey [was] too weak to have more than a marginal impact on these republics'.[23]

Moreover, as a country that attributes utmost importance to stability and constancy, Turkey has always been sensitive against attempts to change the existing equilibrium within its surrounding region to the extent that the preservation of the current balance is usually considered as part of the Turkish national interest. In this context, the disintegration of the Soviet Union and the constant evaluation of the former Eastern Europe in the recent past have affected both Turkey's foreign and security polices, and its world-view in general. In a similar pattern, Iran-Iraq and the Gulf wars in the Middle East, Bosnia-Herzegovina and Kosovo crises in the Balkans, and the conflicts over Nagorno-Karabakh, Chechnya and Abkhazia in the Caucasus, all took place within the immediate vicinity of the country and presented Turkey with the dangers of involvement into such regional conflicts that do not represent immediate threats to her borders.

The concerns that emerged from the possibility of setting up an independent Kurdish state in Northern Iraq after the Gulf War, as well as the effects of Nagorno-Karabakh, Bosnia-Herzogovina and Chechnya conflicts over the radicalisation of certain groups within Turkish society, have evidenced emergent public pressure within Turkey for a more interventionist policy on behalf of ethnic minorities within Turkey's vicinity; and the discussion over the new European security architecture that might leave Turkey out, may substantially affect Turkey's orientation and possible openings in her foreign policy in the near future.

Particularly, as a result of discussion, especially among the western Europeans about the relevance of NATO in the 'new world order' and attempts to move towards a new defence arrangement without Turkey, she suddenly found herself in a situation where she felt threatened, both by the lingering uncertainties regarding her immediate neighbourhood and by the fact that her western security connection, the anchor of her European vocation, was fundamentally damaged by the end of the Cold War, which hitherto provided her with a relative safety and stability in the region. The realization that she may find herself facing military threats virtually all around her without the possibility to evoke the western security umbrella for protection, shook the very foundations of Turkish security thinking and policy, and the need to reassess its post-Cold War situation *vis-à-vis* potential threats was alarmingly expressed at the highest levels.

Turkey has traditionally avoided involvement in regional politics and conflicts. However, international developments, as well as the evolution of Turkish domestic policies, compel her to concern herself more with regional events, and to attempt for a prominence in international politics and a higher profile in the Middle East and Muslim/Turkic areas of the former Soviet Union. She has already been unavoidably drawn into the volatile new politics within the Caucasus (especially Nagorno-Karabakh conflict), the Balkans (Bosnia-Herzegovina and Kosovo), and the Middle East (Kuwait-Northern Iraq), where she has been forced to take sides and follow an 'active' foreign policy. For its part, Turkey, mindful of the disruptive impacts of sub-nationalism and ultra-nationalism, has been eager to promote the positive aspects of national formation around its environs. However, the hopes for creating a form of Turkic Commonwealth able to accommodate most of the new states in Central Asia and Caucasus, which would have countered more ugly manifestations of nationalism and related problems, proved unrealistic, at least, in the short or middle term. Moreover, it is also clear by now that a transitional arrangement based on Islam, or political pan-Turkism will not materialise either in the foreseeable future, although a Turkic belt of influence stretching from the Caspian Sea to China may still emerge. Accordingly, Turkey has already made clear that such transitional concepts are not part of her policy in her external relations.

In the mean time, a new and ever-deepening Turkish rivalry with Iran is emerging over influence in the new states of Central Asia and especially Azerbaijan. If the independence of the former Soviet Azerbaijan threatens in the future to stimulate a parallel separatist movement in northern Iran, it could bring two rivals into a severe conflict with each other – even if Ankara do not seek to provoke it. On the other hand, if Russia comes to believe that Turkey's moves in the region are serving towards some sort of Central Asian Turkic unity, it will certainly lead to confrontation in the region between Turkey and Russia, especially if Russia perceives that Turkey is willingly undermining its territorial integrity by playing with the existing tendencies in the Northern Caucasus for separation from Russia.

Moreover, the recent developments in the Russian 'near abroad', in general, and in the southern Caucasian republics of Georgia and Azerbaijan, in particular, have shown that Russia would have the willingness and capability to overwhelm buffers if it resolved to do so. Thus, Russian behaviour close to the Turkish border, since the collapse of the Soviet Union, has not left Turkey in any doubt about the future intentions and behaviour of the Russian Federation, especially if it sees Turkey as an agent of the West or as a barrier to its ambitions in the region. On the other hand, under the more optimistic scenarios, Turkey, as a moderate secular state, could help direct the newly independent Turkic states of the former Soviet Union in a moderate and secular direction, and thus would indeed play a moderating role in the Muslim regions of the former USSR, support secular government, and seek closer ties with Russia as well as with the Turkic republics. It should not be forgotten that Turkish-Russian mutual interest in maintaining peace in the Caucasus and Central Asia, and in regional cooperation in the Black Sea is considerable, and Turkey's trade relations with Russia is still larger than all of the former Soviet republics put together.

Finally, dramatic changes in Turkey's traditional policy of isolationism from regional conflicts and her increasing active participation in regional issues have, on the one hand, provided her with the potential to fulfil its economic and political expectations, while on the other hand, brought about new challenges and security problems. Moreover, the success of her newly emerging posture and her influence in its region is limited by its own modest economic and industrial resources, and will depend on her success in dealing with ethnic issues within Turkey.

Expectations and Concluding Remarks

With these general observations in mind we can now come up with several indicators regarding the orientation of the future Turkish foreign policy.

i) It is clear by now that Turkey's ambition to become a full EU member will dominate her foreign policy in near future. It is imperative that related domestic and external issues will preoccupy Turkey for a considerable period. In this context, Turkey will continue to follow pro-Western policies in the foreseeable future. Despite Turkey's other involvements, the full membership of the EU still remains as one of the fundamental objectives of her foreign policy. Whatever the extent of Turkey's current disappointments and frustrations with Europe, it should not be forgotten that none of the areas that are presented as alternatives to Turkey's Western vocation, would be able to satisfy Turkey's economic, security and ideological needs. Thus, so long as Turkey is permitted to enjoy cooperation with the West (not necessarily in the form of EU membership) she will remain pro-Western in her attitudes. However, one could easily speculate about the implications of an Islamic regime on Turkey's foreign policy. Although such an eventuality seems highly questionable, it is obvious that a regime based on Sharia law would have a worsening affect for Turkey's Western orientations in favour or more 'Eastern' options. On the other hand, a more plausible scenario could be the one that presents a situation where Turkey's Western orientations may be weakened, if not altogether annulled, as a result of the interactions of certain domestic developments with a combination of frustrations, retreats, and defeats on the western front as well as the open estrangement of Turkey's links from the West by the Western states.

In view of the broad consensus among the major centre left and right political parties regarding foreign policy, the question of which of these parties holds power in the longer term is likely to be an insignificant factor with respect to basic values, objections and instruments of Turkish foreign policy. In this context, it should not be forgotten that even the pro-Islamic Virtue Party openly stated its willingness to support Turkey's EU membership after the Helsinki Summit.

ii) Economic factors may still be expected loosely to shape Turkish foreign policy in the coming years. The procurement of foreign credits is also likely to remain a task of Turkish diplomacy for the middle to long-term and depend on the evolution of Turkey's relations with foreign countries. As in the past, the biggest part of foreign aid is expected to come from the West. In this context, under the pressures to procure more foreign aid, the Turkish government will not be unwilling to accept assistance from other sources, such as Middle Eastern petroleum-rich Arab countries and Japan.

On the other hand, Turkey's growing need for export markets may emerge as a new source of tension between Turkey and her western allies, especially if the rising protectionism against Turkish products and Turkey's disadvantageous position *vis-à-vis* EU after the conclusion of the Customs Union at the end of 1995, continues.

iii) The nature of the political regime in Turkey will remain influential in Turkey's relations, especially with European countries. It should be expected that allegations of human rights abuses and torture would eventually affect Turkey's acceptability as a European state. In this context, ethnic issues, such as Kurdish separatism remain explosive and could play an important role in determining Turkey's future. It is obvious that containment of the Kurdish problem within domestic politics and attempts to prevent it from becoming a poisonous international issue will remain one of the preoccupations of the Turkish foreign ministry as long as the problem endures. Therefore, in coming years, Turkey will have to try to prevent her Western allies from intervening into this issue, while at the same time trying to forestall the developments in Northern Iraq to develop into such a stage that would be conducive to establish a Kurdish state there.

As long as Turkey is not in full control of the domestic situation, her freedom of movement in foreign and security policies will be necessarily subjected to and limited by the requirements of the Kurdish issue. The problem also clouds Turkey's further movement towards greater democratic freedoms, which in turn threatens to jeopardise relations with Western Europe. It is also quite obvious that a country with a domestic problem as such Turkey's Kurdish issue could not convincingly claim to be a role model for stability and democratic-liberalism to anybody, as Turkey aspired to play throughout the Caucasus and Central Asia.

iv) In the realm of defence, Turkey will most likely to continue to adhere to NATO and try to widen her strategic relationship with the U.S. in the absence of an institutionalised security linkage with Europe. Turkish-American relations may be expected to continue pretty much in the same mould as today unless changes in the region suddenly force the U.S. to change its attitude.

As Turkey is situated in the very centre of the three most insecure areas of the post-Cold War era, security issues are expected to dominate Turkey's foreign policy formulations during the coming years as well. Therefore, taking into account the current unstable and insecure environment she is in, Turkey has to continue with modernisation of her military capacity. In this context, in the absence of a new institutional security arrangement with Europe, Turkey's only other alternative to her U.S. connection would be to seek security through associations with neighbouring states. Given that her relations with most of them are inherently problematic, this does not seem either a desirable or feasible option. In this context, though the Turkey-U.S.-Israel triangle serves for Turkey's short-term security needs in general, it is imperative that this will continue to affect her relations with the Arab world. If Turkey wishes to play a greater role in the Middle East, she should also take care of the sensibilities of regional countries and should try to follow a balanced political role in Middle Eastern affairs. In this context, Turkey's more active participation in the Israeli-Palestinian Peace Process would enhance her standing in the region in general.

v) It is now clear that Turkish foreign policy in the near future will have to focus increasingly on three bordering areas; The Caucasus, the Balkans, and the Middle East. While Turkey has traditionally avoided involvement in regional politics, 'the international environment has changed and the bloc system ended.

Turkey has to accept, against her will, that she is a regional power'.[24] In other words, it is almost inevitable that she will need to concern herself more with regional events as regional developments will undoubtedly compel her to do so, as already witnessed in Turkey's unavoidable involvement during the Gulf War and in the Karabakh and Bosnian conflicts.

In this context, while keeping her traditional pro-Western orientation intact, Turkey, since early 1980s, despite a series of odds, has added new components (The Caucasus, the Balkans, and the Middle East) to the substance of her foreign policy. As the balance of relations was being re-ordered to make room for new actors, Turkey's multi-dimensional setting was emphasised once more and her role in bridging different cultures and geographical settings was underlined, without, however, losing sight of her Western vocation.

vi) Finally, it should be mentioned that, in the absence of a driving and forceful leadership like Turgut Özal, exercising a decisive influence in foreign policy, it is likely that the main principles and areas of emphasis in Turkish foreign policy should be expected to continue to exist both in the external and domestic environments during the coming years, unless dramatic international changes necessitate widespread reconsideration of its pillars. As far as domestic impetuses for change are concerned, separatist ethnic movements, possible serious economic difficulties, and political Islam should be watched as likely factors inhibiting the smooth functioning of Turkish foreign policy in the near future.

Notes

1 For the analysis of Turkey's newly-found self-reliance on its external relations at the end of the Cold War see Aydın, M. (1996), 'Turkey and Central Asia; Challenges of Change', *Central Asian Survey*, vol. 15 (2), pp. 157-77; Gürel, Ş.S. and Kimura, Y. (1993), *Turkey in a Changing World,* Institute of Developing Economies, Tokyo.

2 Rustow, D.A. (1989), *Turkey; America's Forgotten Ally*, Council on Foreign Relations Press, New York, London, p.84.

3 Gürel, Ş.S. (1993), 'Turkish Foreign Policy in a Changing World' in Gürel and Kimura (eds.), *Turkey in a Changing World,* p. 1.

4 London, K. (1965), *The Making of Foreign Policy: East and West,* Lippincott, New York, p.56.

5 Gros, F. (1954), *Foreign Policy Analysis*, Philosophical Library, New York, p. 118.

6 Jacobsen, H.K. and Zimmerman, W. (1969), *The Shaping of Foreign Policy,* Alherton Press, New York, p. 141.

7 Macridis, R.C. and Thompson, K.W. (1962), 'The Comparative Study of Foreign Policy' in R. C. Macridis (ed.), *Foreign Policy in World Politics,* 2nd edn, Prentice-Hall, Englewood Cliffs, p. 12.

8 London, *The Making of Foreign Policy,* p. 73.

9 London, *The Making of Foreign Policy,* pp. 100-101.

10 Quoted from the resignation letter of the Chief of Staff General Torumtay in *Facts on File*, 14 December 1990, p. 935. 'Military Chief Resigns'.

11 'Military Communiqué No. 1', text in General Secretariat of the NSC, (1982), *12 September in Turkey; Before and After,* Ongan Kardeşler Printing House, Ankara, p. 221.
12 Sezer, D. (1989), 'Turkish Foreign Policy in the Year 2000' in Turkish Political Science Association, *Turkey in the Year 2000,* Dünya Publication, Ankara, p. 65.
13 Goldman, K. (1988), *Change and Stability in Foreign Policy; The Problems and Possibilities of Détente,* Harvester Wheatsheaf, New York, London, p. 4.
14 Similar views held by many observers of Turkish politics. Among them, see particularly, Hale, W. (1988), 'Transition to Civilian Governments in Turkey: The Military Perspective' in M. Heper and A. Evin, (eds.), *State, Democracy and the Military: Turkey in the 1980s,* Walter de Gruyter, Berlin, New York, pp. 161-2; Steinbach, U. (1988), 'Turkey's Third Republic', *Aussenpolitik (English Edition),* vol. 19 (3), p. 248. For opposing views see Özbudun, E. (1988), 'Development of Democratic Government in Turkey: Crises, Interruptions and Reequilibrations' in E. Özbudun, (ed.), *Perspectives on Democracy in Turkey,* Turkish Political Science Association, Ankara, p. 45; and Turan, İ. (1984), 'The Evolution of Political Culture in Turkey' in A. Evin (ed.), *Modern Turkey: Continuity and Change,* Schriften den Deutschen Orient-Institutes, Leske, p. 55. Both emphasise the importance of the existence of Turkish democratic political culture and downplay the role of external factors in determining Turkey's political regime. They also argue that foreign pressures were usually counter-productive.
15 This linkage was clearly demonstrated in Aydın, M. (1994), *Foreign Policy Formation and Interaction Between Domestic and International Environments; A Study of Change in Turkish Foreign Policy, 1980-1991,* unpublished PhD Thesis, Lancaster University, Ch. 7: Foreign Policy and the Revitalisation of Turkish Economy.
16 The economic possibilities opened for Turkey to pursue in the new world order were discussed in *The Economist,* 'A Survey of Turkey', 14 December 1991, pp. 1-22.
17 For recent analysis of the Turkish position in the Balkans see Winrow, G. (1993), *Where East Meets West; Turkey and the Balkans,* Institute for European Defence and Strategic Studies, European Security Study No. 18, Alliance Publishers, London.
18 Winrow, *Where East Meets West,* p. 25.
19 For representative examples of such views see the special issues of the Turkish journal *Türkiye Günlüğü,* no. 19, Summer 1992; and no. 20, Autumn 1992.
20 Mortimer, E. (1993), 'Active in a New World Role' in *Turkey, Europe's Rising Star; The Opportunities in Anglo-Turkish Relations,* published for the Turkish Embassy, by Lowe Bell, London, p. 44.
21 The then Turkish president, Turgut Özal, in his opening speech of the Turkish Grand National Assembly 1 September 1991, described the situation created by the end of cold war and breaking up of the former Soviet Union as an 'historic opportunity' for the Turks to became a 'regional power', and urged the Assembly not to 'throw away this change which presented itself for the first time in 400 years'. See *Minutes of the TGNA,* Term: 19-1, vol. 1, no. 3, p. 25.
22 As the then Turkish Prime Minister Süleyman Demirel put it, 'we share a common history, a common language, a common religion and a common culture. We are cousins cut off from each other for over a hundred years, first by the Russians under the Czars, and then by the Communist regime'. See M. Hussain, (1993, February 19), 'Iran and Turkey in Central Asia; Complementary or Competing Roles?' *Middle East International,* p. 19. Also see 'Turkey; Central Asia's Dominant Power', *Newsweek,* 28 January 1992.

23 See Robins, P. (1993), 'Between Sentiment and Self Interest; Turkey's Policy Toward Azerbaijan and the Central Asian States', *Middle East Journal,* vol. 47, no. 4, p. 595.

24 Quoted in Fuller, G.E. (1993), 'Turkey's New Eastern Orientation' in Graham E. Fuller and Ian O. Lesser, *Turkey's New Geopolitics; From the Balkans to Western China*, A RAND study, Westview Press, London, p. 67, from *Los Angeles Times*, 16 March 1991.

PART II: TURKEY AND THE WEST

Chapter 2

Turkey and the United States: Changing Dynamics of an Enduring Alliance

Sabri Sayarı

The alliance between Turkey and the US that was formed in the immediate aftermath of World War II has remained in effect for more than half a century, easily qualifying it as one of the longest lasting international alliances in the history of modern Turkey. The US-Turkish alliance was born out of the mutually shared concern of the two countries about the threat posed by the Soviet Union. It grew into a close politico-military relationship during the Cold War years, and remained strong during the uncertain international environment of the post-Cold War era. Along this developmental path, the alliance witnessed both high degrees of cooperation as well as serious strains. By the end of the 20th century, what had begun more than 50 years ago as a relatively simple bilateral arrangement that was based on the American desire to contain the Soviet Union, and Turkey's wish to find an effective deterrent against the Soviet threat, had developed into a highly complex relationship that included a broad spectrum of issues ranging from regional security problems in the Middle East, the Balkans, and the Caucasus to Caspian energy development and Turkey's domestic politics.

Despite the major changes that have taken place in its international and domestic contexts since the late 1940s, the US-Turkish alliance has proven to be enduring and, for all practical purposes, reasonably strong. Turkey's strategic location has traditionally been the most important reason for Washington's interest in promoting close military and political ties with Ankara. During the Cold War period, the US viewed Turkey as a key NATO partner in Western defense strategies against the perceived Soviet threat. Developments in the aftermath of the Cold War underscored Turkey's continuing geostrategic importance for US national interests and security concerns in the Middle East, the Balkans, and the Caucasus. For Turkey, the bilateral alliance with the US has meant, first and foremost, military aid and assistance to meet its security and defense requirements. Additionally, Turkey has valued close military and political ties with the US for its economic and political implications. Until the early 1990s, Turkey was the third largest recipient of US economic aid after Israel and Egypt. A long-lasting alliance with the world's leading power has also provided Turkey with an important political and diplomatic asset in the conduct of its foreign policy and international economic relations.

Despite the emergence of numerous minor and several major problems in bilateral relations over the years, both countries have maintained their basic commitment to preserving and strengthening the US-Turkish alliance. Events in the early 2000s once again dramatically revealed the importance of their bilateral ties to both Turkey and the United States. The deep financial and economic crisis that struck Turkey in February 2001 underlined the extent to which support from the US in international financial organizations such as the IMF and the World Bank had become essential for Turkey's economic viability. Similarly, when the US sought to retaliate against the perpetrators of the deadly terrorist attacks in New York and Washington a few months later in September of that year, the importance of Turkey's cooperation and support became evident, particularly regarding the use of Turkish airspace and the Incirlik airbase in southeastern Turkey for US military operations in Afghanistan.

The Legacy of the Cold War

The principal source of close bilateral cooperation between the United States and Turkey during the Cold War period was the basic symmetry in their security perceptions.[1] Both shared the view that the Soviet Union posed a major security threat to the West and that Moscow was bent on expanding its territory, political role, and ideology beyond its borders. Turkey had a deep sense of mistrust regarding the Soviets that stemmed from several centuries of wars and conflicts between the Ottoman Empire and Tsarist Russia. This established view was rejuvenated with even greater force when Stalin demanded territory in Eastern Turkey and Soviet control over the Turkish Straits at the end of World War II. Stalin's designs on Turkey played a major role in Turkey's departure from the neutral stand it had maintained during the war and in its search for an effective deterrent against the perceived Soviet threat. Turkey's efforts coincided with the deterioration in America's relations with the Soviet Union and Washington's endorsement of a policy that aimed at containing possible Soviet expansionism in Europe and elsewhere. Turkey's location as a country that had long land and sea borders with the Soviet Union made it an ideal candidate to play a major role in this new American strategy.[2]

The congruence of their security perceptions enabled the US and Turkey to develop close military and political ties within a short period after the onset of the Cold War and the East-West polarization in world politics. Beginning with the Truman Doctrine in 1947 that provided military and economic aid to Greece and Turkey, the alliance that was formed between the two countries led to Turkey's participation in the Korean War in 1950, followed by its entry into the North Atlantic Treaty Organization (NATO) two years later. The 1950s witnessed a significant enlargement of the American military presence in Turkey that included numerous bases and installations around the country where nearly 30,000 US servicemen were stationed. This was accompanied by large-scale military and economic aid to Turkey and programs for the training of Turkish military officers in the US. By the end of the 1950s, as East-West tensions continued to dominate world affairs, the US-Turkish bilateral ties had blossomed into an extensive network of military, economic, and political relations that had the full support of policy makers in both Washington and Ankara.[3]

During the next three decades, the US and Turkey continued to share a similar security perception concerning the potential threat posed by the Soviet Union. The relaxation of the Cold War tensions, and the beginning of a rapprochement in East-West relations did not fundamentally alter the Turkish view regarding Moscow's policies. It did, however, lead to an improvement in diplomatic and economic relations between the Soviet Union and Turkey. However, events such as the Soviet invasion of Afghanistan in 1979 only served to reinforce the traditional Turkish security perceptions and led Turkey to maintain a strong defense posture *vis-à-vis* its neighbor in the east and across the Black Sea. This meant, first and foremost, the continuity of close bilateral relations with the US and strong support for multilateral security arrangements through NATO. Within NATO itself, Turkey was the staunchest supporter of American leadership among all member states and played a key role in NATO's Southern Flank.[4]

However, US-Turkish relations also encountered serious strains during the 1960s and 1970s. Their main source was the Cyprus problem which created a major conflict between two NATO allies across the Aegean Sea, Greece and Turkey.[5] Washington's efforts to lower the tensions between its two NATO allies averted a potential war but led paved the way for the rise of anti-American sentiments in both Greece and Turkey. In Turkey, the so-called 'Johnson letter' incident proved to be the spark that ignited anti-Americanism, especially among the country's newly emerging leftist movements. In his letter to Prime Minister Inonu in 1964, President Johnson warned the Turkish leadership that NATO would not defend Turkey if the Soviet Union attacked it during a Turkish intervention to protect the Turkish Cypriot minority from the communal violence spearheaded by the Greek Cypriot majority. The 'Johnson letter' created shock waves among the Turkish policymakers and general public and it seriously undermined Turkey's trust in the US regarding Washington's commitment to the defense of Turkey against a possible Soviet incursion. The effects of the ill-conceived 'Johnson letter' have proved to be long lasting on generations of Turkish security officials.[6] The perception that the US had sided with Greece over the Cyprus issue and had undermined Turkey's national interests also played a major role in the growth of anti-Americanism on Turkish university campuses, among the leftist intelligentsia, and radical left-wing organizations during the latter part of the decade.[7]

The flare-up of the Cyprus crisis in 1974 proved to be even more damaging to the US-Turkish alliance. Ankara's decision to send troops to the island in response to an attempt by Athens to change the constitutional status quo in its favor initially met with tacit US support. However, as the Turkish military expanded its territorial control and settled for a long-term presence in the island, the US position changed. Mobilized by the powerful Greek lobby in Washington, the US Congress passed a resolution in 1975 that imposed an arms embargo on Turkey. The change in Turkey's status from a trusted ally to a sanctioned friend met with a predictably strong reaction from Ankara. The Turkish government suspended the Defense Cooperation Agreement of 1969 and terminated the activities of all the American bases in the country with the exception of those that had a purely NATO function.[8] Although the US Congress lifted the sanctions on Turkey in 1978, the arms embargo inflicted considerable, though not irreparable, damage to US-Turkish relations.

Several developments in the 1980s helped to put the bilateral relationship back on stronger footing. First, both countries were concerned about the security and regional stability implications of the Soviet invasion of Afghanistan and the rise of a fundamentalist Islamic regime in Iran in 1979. The similarity in their threat perceptions regarding the Soviet actions and radical Islamic fundamentalism led to an increase in security cooperation between Ankara and Washington during the 1980s. Secondly, the US administration refrained from criticizing the 1980 military coup in Turkey, thereby tacitly supporting the generals' decision to intervene and restore political stability. The US position contrasted sharply with that of Turkey's European NATO allies which sought various means to show their opposition to the military takeover. Thirdly, President Turgut Özal's rise to power in Turkey had a positive impact on US-Turkish relations. Compared to other contemporary Turkish leaders, Özal, who served as Prime Minister from 1983 to 1989 and as President between 1989 and 1993, was much more favorably disposed toward the United States and the US role in regional and international politics.[9] Irritated by European coolness toward Turkey's quest for full membership in the EU, Özal was instrumental in the development of closer economic and political ties with the US.

US-Turkey Relations in the Post-Cold War Era

The relations between the US and Turkey displayed considerable resilience and strength in the aftermath of the Cold War.[10] Despite the major changes ushered in by the disintegration of the Soviet Union and the transformation of the political landscape of Eurasia, the two countries have maintained their basic commitment to the bilateral alliance. The 1990s witnessed continued cooperation between Washington and Ankara on a number of key issues such as regional security matters and energy development. At the same time, however, the bilateral relationship also experienced strains in some other areas of mutual concern, most notably those involving US policy toward Iraq and Turkey's continued approach to the Cyprus problem.

In the post-Cold era, regional security problems have dominated the agenda of the US-Turkey relationship.[11] This has stemmed primarily from the eruption of armed conflicts and political violence near Turkey's borders in the Middle East (the Gulf War), the Balkans (Bosnia and Kosovo), and the Caucasus (Nagorno-Karabakh, Chechnya) and Ankara's efforts to pursue a new activist regional foreign policy. The American and Turkish views concerning regional conflicts and security have, on the whole, tended to coincide. Both countries emphasized the importance of regional stability and peace and opposed the expansionist policies of regional states that threatened to alter the status quo. The convergence between

Ankara and Washington in their approach to regional security problems was best displayed in the Middle East and the Balkans. In the Middle East, the 1990-91 Gulf War proved to be a critical development for the bilateral relationship. Turkey departed from its traditional policy of non-involvement in regional conflicts, took a firm stand against Saddam Hussein's regime, and participated in the US-led Allied Coalition that repelled the invading Iraqi forces from Kuwait.[12] In the aftermath of the Gulf War, the strategic cooperation between Ankara and Washington became even more pronounced with the establishment of a 'no fly zone' in northern Iraq above the 36th parallel under the protection of an allied force –Operation Provide Comfort (OPC), later renamed Operation Northern Watch (ONW)– based in southeastern Turkey at İncirlik.

Washington and Ankara have shared similar views on several other Middle Eastern regional security issues. For example, the US supported the new strategic relationship that was forged between Israel and Turkey in the mid-1990s since it brings together two of Washington's closest allies with the strongest military capabilities in the Middle East.[13] The US and Turkey also share the same strong commitment to the Palestinian-Israeli peace process and both countries view the peaceful resolution of this conflict essential to regional stability and order in the Middle East. From the US perspective, Turkey has the potential to play an influential role in the Palestinian-Israeli peace process since it is a major regional power and maintains close ties with both the Palestinians and the Israelis. The US and Turkish perspectives on the proliferation of weapons of mass destruction (WMD) in the Middle East also converge; both countries are concerned about the issue and view the development of new WMD programs as a serious threat to regional stability and peace.

The second major area of cooperation between the United States and Turkey in regional security affairs concerns the Balkans.[14] The eruption of violent ethnic conflicts following the disintegration of the former Yugoslavia seriously undermined regional stability and increased the possibility of drawing other regional states, such as Turkey, into a wider war. To contain the escalation of the conflicts and prevent the total annihilation of the Bosnian Muslims under attack from the radical Serbian nationalists, Turkey embarked on an activist diplomacy in Western capitals and international organizations on behalf of the Bosnian Muslim community. Although the Clinton administration initially appeared reluctant to become involved in the crises in the Balkans, it later took the initiative to restore peace and stability to the region, first in Bosnia and later in Kosovo. Since there was significant overlap in their policy objectives, Ankara and Washington cooperated extensively in these initiatives. With US support and backing, Turkey participated in the NATO Enforcement/Stability Force (IFOR/SFOR) that was established to enforce the provisions of the Dayton Peace Agreement. Later Turkey joined NATO's Kosovo force and deployed a small contingent of F-16s in Italy during NATO's air campaign against the Milosevic regime. In addition, the cooperation between the US and Turkey for regional security in the Balkans involved the 'equip-and-train' program for a new military force for the Bosnian Muslim-Croat Federation whereby officers from Bosnia-Herzegovina received training in Turkey.

Although the US and Turkey share similar perspectives regarding the need for regional order and peaceful resolution of conflicts, the 1990s have also witnessed the emergence of divergent views between the two allies on several issues. Undoubtedly, the most important of these concerns their approach to Iraq. The priorities and aims of the two countries regarding Iraq differ considerably.[15] The primary goal of the US is to oust Saddam Hussein from power and the collapse of the Baathist regime in Baghdad. To achieve this goal, the US has sought to 'contain' Iraq through the enforcement of UN-backed economic and trade sanctions, and support for Iraqi opposition groups. As part of its strategy against Saddam Hussein, Washington has also encouraged unity among rival Kurdish forces and the emergence of a new 'political entity' for the Iraqi Kurds in the north. Turkish priorities, on the other hand, are to restore trade and economic ties with Iraq to recoup the losses that Turkey has suffered from the sanctions regime and to preserve the territorial integrity of Iraq. Ankara is also concerned about the emergence of an autonomous Kurdish entity in northern Iraq because of its potential impact on Turkey's own Kurdish population. For this reason, it is wary about the US efforts to unify rival Iraqi Kurdish groups.[16]

The establishment of OPC/ONW in Turkey in the aftermath of the Gulf War to protect the northern Iraqi Kurds from an assault by Saddam Hussein's regime has been a controversial issue in Turkey.[17] The criticisms directed at the allied operation stems from Turkish concerns about its role in strengthening Kurdish political autonomy in northern Iraq. However, the operation based in Incirlik has arguably been the single most important part of the US-Turkish military relationship in the 1990s and it has provided Turkey with a valuable means to influence US policy. For example, Washington has officially continued to designate the PKK as a terrorist organization, supported Turkey in its fight against the Kurdish separatists, and engineered the capture of the PKK's leader Öcalan. Moreover, unlike Turkey's Western European NATO allies, the US has generally refrained from criticizing the Turkish military's periodic incursions into northern Iraq in search of the PKK's militants. Nevertheless, it is true that 'no problem of the past decade has created more tension in US-Turkish relations than Iraq, and no problem currently carries more potential for damage to those relations'.[18]

The US and Turkish approaches to security issues in the Caucasus region have contained the elements of both convergence and divergence.[19] In the early 1990s, Washington did not share Turkish concerns about Moscow's efforts to reassert its influence over the former Soviet Union's possessions in the region. Intent on integrating Russia into the Western community of nations and optimistic about its political and economic transformation, the US adopted a policy of benign neglect toward Moscow's effort to implement its 'near abroad' doctrine through overt and covert actions. Ankara's objections to the Russian violations of the 1990 Conventional Forces in Europe (CFE) treaty in the northern Caucasus and the restationing of Russian forces along Turkey's borders in Georgia and Azerbaijan did not receive a sympathetic hearing in Washington. However, the US has gradually modified its policy in the wake of the conflict in Chechnya and adopted a discernibly more cautious approach to Russian policies in the Caucasus. The US support for the Baku-Ceyhan pipeline project and the American-backed 'east-west energy corridor' represented this new approach which closely aligned US and Turkish policies after the mid-1990s. The only major exception to the convergence of views between Ankara and Washington was the continued US tilt toward Armenia in its conflict with Azerbaijan over the disputed territory of Nagorno-Karabakh.

On the other hand, during most of the 1990s, the US-Turkish bilateral relationship continued to be adversely affected by Greek Turkish disputes over the Aegean and the Cyprus problem.[20] As was the case during the Cold War, Greece and Turkey viewed each other as a potential threat to their national security. Efforts by Washington to mediate between its two allies often led to criticism from both Athens and Ankara. Nevertheless, the US intervention in the Imea/Kardak crisis in 1995 played a major role in averting an armed clash between the two countries and the Greek-Turkish rapprochement following the deadly earthquakes that hit both countries in 1999 has lowered the tensions in the Aegean and led to a new phase in the troubled relationship between the two countries. The US has welcomed the improved relations between Greece and Turkey. Progress towards better Greek-Turkish relations would likely remove a major irritant in US-Turkish alliance. However, there was no similar breakthrough regarding the protracted Cyprus problem despite the efforts of both the US and the UN to facilitate a negotiated settlement to the dispute. In general, the US position on Cyprus has been closer to that of the Greek Cypriot administration. Indeed, this, and Washington's efforts to influence Turkey's Cyprus policy, has created tensions in the bilateral relations for the past three decades. The prospective entry of Cyprus into the EU and Turkey's opposition to this development is likely to further increase these tensions.

Another major issue that has figured prominently in US-Turkish relations in the 1990s concerns energy development and security. In general, there has been a broad similarity of views and extensive cooperation between Ankara and Washington on Caspian energy development and security. The emergence of the Caspian region as a major source for oil and natural gas in the world has had far reaching economic and geopolitical implications. Faced with a growing demand for domestic energy consumption, Turkey has viewed Caspian oil and natural gas development as a much-needed new source to meet its energy requirements. In addition, Turkey has become actively involved in the competition concerning the routing of the new pipelines that would transport Caspian energy to Western markets. Producing states (Azerbaijan, Kazakhstan, Turkmenistan), neighboring countries (primarily Russia, Turkey, and Iran), Western oil companies, and the United States have all sought to influence the choice concerning the construction of the pipelines from the Caspian region.[21]

In this intense competition, the Turkish government has heavily promoted the Baku-Ceyhan project for the transport of Azerbaijani crude oil to Western markets. Turkey has maintained that the Baku-Ceyhan route offers an environmentally safer alternative to the northern route that has been strongly promoted by Russia and which would lead to increased tanker traffic through the Bosporus. However, geopolitical concerns have also played an important role in Ankara's efforts to secure the construction of the Baku-Ceyhan pipeline. The politics of Caspian pipeline construction have been intertwined with the competition for political and economic influence in the Caucasus and Central Asia between Russia, Turkey, and Iran. Turkey has viewed the Baku-Ceyhan route as a valuable strategic and political asset that would highlight its position as an energy bridge between the Caspian region and Western markets and as an important means to create closer ties between Turkey and Azerbaijan, Georgia, Turkmenistan, and Kazakhstan. Although the United States has, in principle, endorsed the idea of multiple pipelines, it has also provided Turkey with strong backing for the Baku-Ceyhan project. Washington's support for Baku-Ceyhan is part of the US policy of promoting an 'east-west' corridor for the export of oil and gas from the Caspian that would exclude Iran from becoming a potential transit state and also limit the Russian role and influence in the region. The US preference for Baku-Ceyhan also stems from a strong desire to support Turkey as an ally and strategically important country for the US in its bid for a greater economic and political role in Caspian energy development.

Turkey's quest to become a full member of the EU represents another area of close cooperation between Washington and Ankara in the post-Cold War era.[22] During the course of the 1990s, the US has lobbied extensively on Turkey's behalf with EU officials in Brussels as well as in other Western European capitals. Washington's efforts to secure Turkey's full membership have, at times, led to tensions in transatlantic relations since many European officials were resentful of American lobbying and pressures concerning the issue. US efforts played a significant role in the signing of a Customs Union between the EU and Turkey in 1995 and while the Customs Union agreement marked a significant new development in EU-Turkey relations, it fell short of meeting Turkey's expectations regarding the membership question. These expectations received a major setback in the decision of the 1997 EU summit in Luxembourg not to include Turkey in the list of prospective candidates for membership. The Luxembourg summit was strongly criticized both in Ankara and Washington as relations between the EU and Turkey took a turn for the worse. However, the EU modified its stand on the issue of Turkey's accession in its Helsinki 1999 summit and recognized Turkey's candidacy for full membership. Again, intensive pressures by high-ranking Clinton Administration officials on their European counterparts figured prominently in the modification of the EU's policy towards Turkey.

During the Cold War period, domestic political developments and problems in Turkey were generally not part of the US-Turkish alliance's agenda. However, this changed markedly in the course of the 1990s. In particular, the Kurdish issue, and the human rights problems associated with it, permeated all aspects of US-Turkish relations.[23] Washington, however, has repeatedly emphasized its support of Turkey's territorial integrity and its opposition to any moves that could lead to the redrawing of its existing boundaries. The US has also officially maintained its view of the PKK as a terrorist organization and has decried the campaign of violence conducted by the PKK. At the same time, however, there has been considerable pressure from Washington on Ankara to find a 'political solution' to the Kurdish problem and to implement reforms that would safeguard the human rights of all Turkish citizens.

Turkey's efforts to suppress the PKK gave rise to sharp criticisms in the US Congress and the media on the grounds that the fight against the PKK has involved major human rights violations. Unlike the Cold War years, human rights around the globe have become a major pillar of US foreign policy since the 1990s. In its annual reports on human rights issues, the US State Department devoted extensive coverage to the developments in Turkey with particular emphasis on the problems related to the Kurdish issue. Turkey's shortcomings regarding human rights issues have also become a source of criticism from various influential NGO's and the anti-Turkey ethnic lobbies in Washington.

The most important consequence of Turkey's human rights problems on the US-Turkish relations concerns the arms transfer and procurement process. Since the late 1940s when Ankara and Washington began to forge close ties, military assistance and arms transfers to Turkey have been a binding factor in the bilateral relationship. Over the years, a great majority of the weapons systems and equipment used by the Turkish military came from the United States. Although US military aid to Turkey declined sharply in the aftermath of the Cold War and came to an end in 1998, Turkey continued to depend on the US as its principal source of new weapons systems and military technology. However, in the 1990s the US Congress began to restrict arms transfers to Turkey to pressure Ankara to improve its human rights records and, in some instances, to modify its position in the Greek-Turkish disputes. The withholding of military equipment, sometimes bought and paid in advance by Turkey, was bitterly resented by Turkish officials, and especially by the Turkish military.

The challenge posed by political Islam to the Turkish state has introduced another potential irritant into the bilateral relationship in the 1990s. Turkey's Islamist parties and politicians have traditionally been vociferous critics of the West, Turkey's close ties with the US, and American foreign policy in the Middle East. As a result, the rise to power of the Islamist Welfare Party (WP), as the senior partner of a coalition government in 1996, created justifiable concerns in Washington. During its crisis-ridden tenure in government in 1996-97, the WP pursued relatively moderate policies and toned down its anti-Western rhetoric. This shift in party strategy became even more pronounced following the WP's expulsion from power under strong pressure from the secularist forces led by the military. The US refrained from taking a position on that crisis but it has increasingly tended to be critical of the sanctions imposed on Turkey's Islamist parties and politicians. Consequently, in addition to the Kurdish question, Turkey's policy toward its Islamist parties has become part of the agenda in bilateral discussions.

Domestic developments in the US have also created strains in the US-Turkey alliance. The end of the Cold War and the demise of the Soviet threat to the West emboldened the powerful Greek and Armenian lobbies in Washington. Both found greater room to maneuver in the Congress and, in addition to their traditional anti-Turkey agendas, also sought to exploit Turkey's human rights problems to undermine the relations between Ankara and Washington. The anti-Turkey ethnic lobbies enjoyed easy access to US legislators due to the fact that the Greek-American and Armenian-American voters far outnumber the Turkish-Americans.

Additionally, both lobbies provided substantial funds in election campaigns and have forged coalitions with the powerful human rights lobbies and NGO's. Although Turkish lobbying efforts in Washington received a strong boost from the Jewish lobby following the establishment of a strategic alignment between Israel and Turkey in the mid-1990s, Turkey continued to face an uphill battle in the US Congress in countering the activities the Greek and Armenian groups.

The main focus of the Greek lobby has been the Aegean and the Cyprus conflicts. On both of these issues, it has sought to create a pro-Greek tilt to Washington's policies. It has also been a sharp critic of the sale of arms and weapons systems to Turkey and in a well-publicized case, Senator Paul Serbanes, a prominent Greek-American legislator, personally held up the authorization of the transfer of two frigates to Turkey for more than two years. The recent rapprochement between Greece and Turkey has not, so far, led to a discernible change of attitudes and policies among the Greek-American diaspora. Further, the activities of the Armenian lobby have created even greater problems for the US-Turkish relationship. The well-organized and financed efforts of the Armenian lobby to get a resolution in Congress passed that would officially recognize the so-called 'Armenian Genocide' have periodically created crises between Ankara and Washington, most recently in the Fall of 2000. Had it not been for the last-minute intervention by President Clinton, H.R. 596 would almost certainly have been approved by the US Congress with potentially undesirable consequences for Turkish-American relations.

Conclusions

One of the most notable aspects of the bilateral relationship and alliance between the United States and Turkey has been its enduring strength. Contrary to the expectations of some observers that the absence of a common security perception in the aftermath of the Cold War would weaken their ties, Ankara and Washington have not significantly wavered in their commitment to cooperate on a broad range of issues in the 1990s. It is true that in comparison with the 1950s, the management of the alliance has become much more complex, and at times, outright problematic. Nevertheless, the level of interdependence between the two countries has also increased significantly during the past decade. In addition to growing trade and commercial ties, the US and Turkey have joined forces in dealing with a broad range of problems including regional conflicts, energy security, drug trafficking, and international terrorism.

That interdependence became evident, once again, in 2001 when Turkey faced a severe economic crisis and the US encountered the deadliest terrorist attack in its history. Turkey's close ties with the US played a critical role in its efforts to deal with the financial turmoil that hit the country in February. Supported by the US administration, Turkey won the backing of the IMF for a new stabilization and recovery program that provided an additional $8 billion for structural reforms and privatization measures. The strength of cooperation between the two countries was demonstrated in the aftermath of the terrorist attacks on New York and Washington as well. Turkey was one of the first countries to declare its full support to the US in its war on terrorism; and shortly after September 11, the Turkish government announced that it would permit the American military to use its airspace and the Incirlik airbase for operations against Bin Laden's terrorist organization.

The terrorist attacks on New York and Washington in September 2001 is likely to have major ramifications for US foreign policy in the first decade of the 21st century, some of which might help establish closer ties between US and Turkey. As a country that has suffered extensively from domestic and international terrorism for the past four decades, Turkey has a particular interest in its elimination and would be a strong supporter of counter-terrorist policies. The war that has been declared on terrorism by President George W. Bush could also lead to the renationalization of US foreign policy and the lessening of influence of special interest groups in the formulation of America's foreign relations.[24] This would be a welcome development for the supporters of strong ties between the United States and Turkey since it would weaken the influence of the anti-Turkey ethnic lobbies in Washington. However, new developments and shifts in US foreign policy in response to the terrorist attacks may also have adverse effects on US-Turkish relations. Possibly the most important among these would be the recasting of America towards Russia, whereby Washington would become more accommodating to Russian national interests in return for Moscow's cooperation in the fight against international terrorism. During the first Clinton administration in the early 1990s, Washington's benign neglect of Russian policies aimed at reasserting Moscow's influence in the Caucasus created strains between US and Turkey. A new tilt toward Russia in US policy could lead to the reemergence of similar strains in US-Turkish relations a decade later.

Notes

1 For analyses of US-Turkey relations during the Cold War period, see Harris, G.S. (1972), *Troubled Alliance: Turkish-American Problems in Historical Perspective, 1945-1971*, American Enterprise for Public Policy Research and the Hoover Institution, Washington, D.C.; Hale, W. (2000), *Turkish Foreign Policy, 1774-2000* Frank Cass, London, pp. 109-191; and Kuniholm, B.R. (1996), 'Turkey and the West Since World War II,' in V. Mastny and R.C. Nation (eds.), *Turkey Between East and West*, Westview Press, Boulder, Colorado, pp. 45-70.

2 See Kuniholm, B.R. (1994), *The Origins of Cold War in the Near East: Great Power Conflict and Diplomacy in Iran, Turkey, and Greece*, 2nd edn, Princeton University Press, Princeton.

3 Vali, F.A. (1971), *Bridge Across the Bosporus: The Foreign Policy of Turkey*, The Johns Hopkins University Press, Baltimore, pp. 115-64.

4 See Snyder, J. (1987), *Defending the Fringe: NATO, the Mediterranean, and the Persian Gulf*, Westview Press, Boulder, Colorado, esp. pp. 29-52.

5 On the emergence of the Cyprus conflict and its ramifications for the relations between Athens and Ankara, see Bahcheli, T. (1990), *Greek-Turkish Relations Since 1955*, Westview Press, Boulder, Colorado. See also Couloumbis, T.A. (1983), *The United States, Greece, and Turkey: The Troubled Triangle*, Praeger, New York.

6 For a recent assessment of the lasting impact of the 'Johnson Letter', see Çandar, C. (2000), 'Some Turkish Perspectives on the United States and American Policy toward Turkey', in M. Abramowitz (ed.), *Turkey's Transformation and American Policy,* The Century Foundation Press, New York, pp. 117-52.

7 See Harris, *Troubled Alliance*, 125-48.

8 Hale, *Turkish Foreign Policy*, 160-61.

9 Sayarı, S. (1992, Winter), 'Turkey: The Changing European Security Environment and the Gulf Crisis,' *Middle East Journal*, p.18.

10 For analyses of US-Turkey relations in the post-Cold War period, see Harris, G.S., 'US-Turkish Relations', in A. Makovsky and S. Sayarı (eds.), *Turkey's New World: Changing Dynamics in Turkish Foreign Policy,* The Washington Institute for Near East Policy, Washington, DC, pp. 189-202; Kirişci, K. (2001), 'US-Turkish Relations: New Uncertainties in a Renewed Partnership,' in B. Rubin and K. Kirişci (eds.), *Turkey in World Politics: An Emerging Regional Power,* Lynne Rienner, Boulder, Colorado, pp. 129-150; and Abramowitz (ed.), *Turkey's Transformation and American Policy.*

11 The following section is based largely on my 'US-Turkey Relations in the Post-Cold War Era: Issues of Convergence and Divergence,' in M. Aydın and Ç. Erhan (eds.), *Turkish-American Relations: 200 Years of Divergence and Convergence* (London: Frank Cass, forthcoming).

12 On Turkey's role in the Gulf War, see Sayarı, S. (1997), 'Between Allies and Neighbors: Turkey's Burden-Sharing Policy in the Gulf Conflict,' in A. Bennett, J. Lepgold, and D. Unger (eds.), *Friends in Need: Burden Sharing in the Persian Gulf War,* St. Martins Press, New York, pp. 197-218.

13 See Altunışık, M.B. 'Turkish Policy Toward Israel,' in Makovsky and Sayari (eds.), *Turkey's New World*, pp. 59-73.

14 On US-Turkish cooperation in the Balkans, see Uzgel, İ. (1998), 'Doksanlarda Türkiye İçin Bir İsbirliği ve Rekabet Alanı Olarak Balkanlar,' in G. Özcan and Ş. Kut (eds.) *En Uzun Onyıl,* Boyut, İstanbul, pp. 403-44.

15 See Makovsky, A., 'US policy Toward Turkey: Progress and Problems,' in Abramowitz (ed.), *Turkey's Transformation and American Policy*, esp. pp. 230-33.

16 Aykan, M.B. (1996, October), 'Turkey's Policy in Northern Iraq, 1991-1995,' *Middle Eastern Studies*, pp. 343-66.

17 See, e.g., Oran, B. (1996), *'Kalkık Horoz': Çekiç Güç ve Kürt Devleti,* Bilgi Yayınevi, Ankara.

18 Makovsky, 'US Policy Toward Turkey: Progress and Problems,' p. 230.

19 On Turkey's approach to the Caucasus, see Winrow, G., 'Turkish Policy Toward Central Asia and Transcaucasus' in Makovsky and Sayarı (eds.), *Turkey's New World*, pp. 116-130; and Hale, 'The Foreign Policy of Turkey', pp. 266-81. On US policy toward the region and its implications for US-Turkish relations, see Stephen Larrabee, S. (1997), 'US and European Policy Towards Turkey and the Caspian Basin,' in R. Blackwell and M. Sturmer (eds.), *Allies Divided: Transatlantic Policies for the Greater Middle East,* MIT Press, Cambridge, Massachusetts.

20 On Greek-Turkish relations during the post-Cold War period, see Bahcheli, T., 'Turkish Policy Towards Greece,' in Makovsky and Sayari (eds.), *Turkey's New World*, pp. 131-152. See also Wilkinson, J., 'The US, Turkey, and Greece–Three's a Crowd' in Abramowitz (ed.), *Turkey's Transformation and American Policy,* pp. 185-18.

21 See Sayarı, S. (2000), 'Turkey, Caspian Energy and Regional Security', in R. Ebel and R. Menon (eds.), *Energy and Ethnic Conflict in Central Asia and the Caucasus,* Rowman and Littlefield, pp. 225-46; and Sasley, B., 'Turkey's Energy Politics' in Rubin and Kirişci (eds.), *Turkey in World Politics*, pp. 217-33.

22 See Kuniholm, B. (2001, Spring), 'Turkey's Accession to the European Union: Differences in European and US Attitudes and Challenges for Turkey,' *Turkish Studies*, pp. 25-53.

23 On the Kurdish issue, see Kirişçi, K. and Winrow, G.M. (1997), *The Kurdish Question in Turkey*, Frank Cass, London.

24 See Diehl, J. (2001, October 1), 'Pendulum Shifts in Foreign Affairs,' *Washington Post*.

Chapter 3

Turkey and the European Union: A Troubled Relationship or a Historic Partnership?[1]

Ozay Mehmet

Introduction

Arguably the single most important decision of the Helsinki Summit of European Union (EU) leaders in December 1999 was the declaration recognizing Turkey as an official candidate state for full membership in the EU, on equal terms with all other candidate countries. Representing an essential step toward the long-cherished Turkish goal of Westernization,[2] full membership in the EU would at last fulfill Atatürk's dream of attaining a place within European civilization. In the words of the Turkish Foreign Minister İsmail Cem, full EU membership would allow Turkey to join 'the (European) family' and, as such, it would be an event of truly historic significance.[3] However, membership may compromise Kemalist concept of national sovereignty,[4] for example, if the powerful military felt that Turkish national security requirements were being compromised in the case of the European Security and Defense Identity (ESDI), on Cyprus or other cases of national interest. The September 11 attack on the USA in 2001 by Islamic terrorists has, besides giving NATO a new lease of life relative to ESDI, greatly enhanced Turkey's strategic importance in the war against Islamic terrorism.[5]

No date or timetable for Turkish accession was fixed at Helsinki. As will be discussed below, any prospective date, even for the start of the screening stage would involve a considerable degree of uncertainty, not the least of which is the severe financial crisis which occurred in Turkey in February 2001. Nevertheless, the prospect is unique in several respects, not the least of which was the courting of Turkey by 'Mr. Solana, the [European] Union's Mr. Fixit',[6] who flew to Ankara at the eleventh hour of the Helsinki Summit to sell the EU's terms to a less-than-enthusiastic Turkish cabinet. Turkey poses special challenges as a candidate country, because of its large population and character as a Muslim country. As such, Turkish accession would be a truly historic event, replacing a Huntingtonian 'clash of civilization'[7] along a cultural fault-line dividing the Muslim and Christian worlds. Incorporation of Turkey within the EU would, once and for all, get rid of the image of the Union as a 'Christian Club'. Furthermore, in the aftermath of the

September 11 atrocity, the Turkish secular model for the whole of the Muslim world, has assumed a unique importance, which the EU views as an historic opportunity. In the shorter-term, full Turkish membership in the EU is capable of eliminating competing ethno-nationalism in the Aegean and the Eastern Mediterranean and replacing it with peace and friendship amongst Greeks and Turks within the wider context of a united and enlarged Europe. However, it is evident that the road towards Turkish accession is almost certain to be bumpy and difficult, with many irritations and headaches. How long this road to full membership will be, or even whether it will result in a successful outcome, depends on whether one is an optimist or a pessimist about the pace of EU enlargement, and even more significantly, about how the EU politicians handle Greek-Turkish relations. Alternative scenarios will be considered at the concluding part of this chapter.

Optimists in Ankara aspire to full membership in the next round of enlargement scheduled for 2003/4, or, at the latest in the second round planned before the end of the first decade of the 21st century. However, given the large number of challenges to be overcome, prior to the commencement of accession negotiations, some observers argue that Turkish membership is one or two decades away. In any event, much goodwill will be required on the part of the EU, while in Ankara a new and progressive mindset is essential to maintain Turkish foreign policy in a steadfastly European mode, especially with regard to Turkey's relations across the Aegean, in Cyprus and in the Middle East.

The early 2000 appointment of Mesut Yılmaz, a key partner in the Ecevit coalition, as the Minister in charge of EU relations, was seen as an important step forward, and was expected to increase the pace of reforms in Ankara. Thus far Yılmaz has played a key role in two important reform measures: first, in the preparation and approval of the National Program, representing government's response to the EU Accession Partnership Document; second, in the landmark decision by Parliament in early October 2001 to amend, by an overwhelming 474-16 vote, to amend and democratize the constitution in line with EU standards. These amendments, while falling short of meeting all of EU expectations, are nevertheless vital in that they guarantee key human rights and remove the death penalty, except in cases of terrorism and treason. Despite these positive developments, irritations and tensions remain between Brussels and Ankara on several critical issues, such as the Cyprus dispute, Greek-Turkish relations over the Aegean, as well as actual progress on the advancement of human rights inside Turkey. Furthermore, the agenda of Turkish relations have been greatly influenced as a result of the February 2001 economic crisis, and, most recently, by the war in Afghanistan and the larger question of international terrorism which is fluid and evolving as the Bush administration has yet to outline a clear anti-terror initiative.

This chapter seeks to provide an account of the attitudes hampering Turkish accession from both the Turkish as well as the European perspectives and is organized into four sections. Following the introduction, the second part focuses on the road to full Turkish membership, utilizing the Copenhagen Criteria (CC) to summarize and highlight the potential obstacles and irritations for both sides. The third part is devoted to a discussion and evaluation of the benefits of an 'historic partnership' between Turkey and the EU, and finally the last part highlights the principal conclusions of the chapter.

The Road-map to Full Membership: Copenhagen Criteria, Potential Obstacles and Irritations

The Copenhagen Criteria (CC), originally drafted for the benefit of former communist countries in Eastern Europe in an effort to facilitate their transition to liberal democracy and eventual accession to the EU, have now become the principal guidelines for all potential candidates seeking accession to the EU. However, the CC is not cast in stone and does not represent a fixed set of pre-conditions. Rather, given the fact that the EU institutional reforms are 'deepening',[8] and decision-making procedures are themselves still evolving, the CC are no more than an ever evolving set of general guidelines intended to prepare candidate countries for full membership. Furthermore, EU decision-making has its own pace and thus, the EU Commission, acting on behalf of the Union, published in November 2000 a Pre-Accession Document (APD) that fell short of Ankara's expectations.[9] Similarly, Turkey's National Program (NP), finalized in March 2001, appears to have had a similar response in EU circles.[10]

In general terms, the CC reform package can be divided into three areas: (1) Economic, (2) Political, and (3) Institutional Preparedness. In each area there are serious challenges and irritations for both sides that will involve time-consuming and delicate negotiations. Indeed, given the range and complexity of these issues, a successful outcome is far from certain. On the positive side, the Turkish government, specifically Foreign Minister Cem, views the CC as:

> Human values are universal. The Copenhagen Criteria are values that are not particular to the EU; they are values millions share, both inside and outside Europe. They are values we share and that we have developed and will continue to develop.[11]

The implication of these remarks is that Turkey is strongly committed to the implementation of the CC, not so much for satisfying EU conditionalities, but rather because the Turkish government and society wholeheartedly endorse these values. Yet, despite these positive sentiments, the path to full Turkish membership is burdened with contrasts and difficulties. What are the potential irritations and headaches for Turkey and the EU? We shall explore these in each of these three fields covered by the CC.

Economic Difficulties: Market Reforms and Fiscal and Monetary Policy

In the economic field, Turkey has, even despite the February 2001 crisis, 'achieved most of the hallmarks of a market economy'.[12] Unlike many other candidate countries, it already has a Customs Union (CU) agreement with the EU, and the Turkish industry has proved itself to be relatively competitive. Prior to Helsinki, however, the CU had delivered to Turkey few of the promised financial benefits, owing chiefly to the Greek veto in the EU. Greece, utilizing its privileged position in as a member of the EU, repeatedly exercised its veto to block EU financial assistance that had been intended to help Turkish industry adjust to the CU. Following the CU there was a significant deterioration in the Turkish trade balance, with imports from the EU rising rapidly relative to exports.[13] In 1999, the bilateral trade deficit was $7.1bn (as opposed to $2.4bn in 1992).[14] At the same time, there has been a loss of some $2.5bn in customs revenue collected from the EU trade. Further, it appears that Turkish export markets in the Middle East may be adversely affected by trade diversion under such programs as the Euro-Mediterranean Partnership[15] that seeks new markets for EU trade and investment. On the other hand, in the private sector, the much-feared dislocation and plant closures expected to accompany the increased competition from European imports failed to materialize.[16] In terms of economic benefits, the EU is the largest source of foreign investment in Turkey, accounting for over 60 per cent of the total. There has also been an increasing flow of financial aid under several EU Financial Protocols, although, until recently, these also have been subject to a Greek veto.

Turkey's domestic economic difficulties, which exploded with a massive devaluation in February 2001, are primarily in the macro-management field, stemming from structural and policy inefficiencies.[17] Turkish inflation, budget deficits, and interest rates are excessively high for any reasonable definition of CC. In the course of 1999/2000, however, the Turkish authorities agreed to follow the dictates of the IMF, and introduced an economic reform package. Central in the IMF austerity package was a pegged exchange rate based on a targeted 2.5 per cent maximum monthly devaluation over a two year time-frame, which aspired to reduce inflation to less than 10 per cent p.a, along with a gradual decline in interest rates as the government budget deficit was expected to fall. In the first year, indicators behaved according to plan: interest rates sharply fell from over 100 per cent to 30 per cent and inflation, in both consumer and wholesale prices, declined for the first time in years to below 49 per cent on an annual basis. However, unforeseen disaster occurred when external shocks hit the economy including the devastating earthquake of August 1999, a second quake in November 1999 and financial crises in Asia, Russia and Mexico all clouded the Turkish devaluation plan. The government inflation target in 2000 was 25 per cent, though it had to be abandoned due to the unplanned costs of reconstruction and emergency spending. In addition, sudden increases in oil prices in 2000 worsened the Turkish trade imbalance. Most significantly, imports from the EU surged while export earnings stagnated. The Turkish Lira (TL) gradually became an over-valued currency and speculators, both domestic and foreign, began to hedge against the Turkish currency. One celebrated speculator, George Soros, the man who had brought the British Central Bank down virtually single-handedly in an earlier round of currency trading targeted against the British pound, is believed to have made millions selling TL for US$ in the days just prior to the floating of the TL on 21 February 2001.

The effect of the 2001 currency crisis is that the Turkish economic performance is even more drastically above the acceptable standards outlined in Maastricht for economic and monetary union with the EU. Turkey immediately started major reforms in the monetary and fiscal policy fields, but the task is huge and the reform is beset with institutional and political obstacles. A major institutional problem that remains is the fact that the Central Bank of the Republic of Turkey has been far from an independent monetary authority for effective macro-economic management. The Ecevit coalition government, risking confrontation with Turkish organized labor unions, has adopted a fairly disciplined monetary as well as fiscal policy. However, it cannot altogether abandon concern for social cohesion and stability in a period of rising unemployment and economic hardship. Conforming to EU standards in macroeconomic management will now be even more difficult than before February 2001.

The formal declaration of Turkish candidacy in Helsinki has provided both greater coherence as well as a sense of urgency to the goal of economic stabilization. In the first quarter of 2000, there were encouraging signs that inflation and interest rates were declining and that greater monetary and fiscal discipline had been achieved. In addition, the capture of PKK terrorist chief Abdullah Öcalan has markedly reduced military spending in the Southeast which was estimated to be $8 bn. a year.

One area in which the Turkish government desperately needs significant success is in privatization. In 2001, after years of delay and political maneuverings,[18] the Turkish authorities passed enabling legislation for major privatization in such key economic sectors as telecommunications, petrochemicals and energy as well as in agriculture, banking and finance. These reforms became new 'conditionalities' of a $15.7 billion rescue package from the IMF under the management of the new Minister of the Economy, Kemal Derviş, a former VP of the World Bank. Unfortunately, however, the global recession slowed Turkey's privatization program, while also effectively postponing the potential benefits in terms of foreign investment and technology transfer that are badly needed to further modernize and increase the global competitiveness of the Turkish economy. In the meantime, at the end of the summer of 2001 Turkey had experienced a successful tourism season, and the Turkish trade balance began to show a healthy improvement, primarily owing to a sharp decline in imports, with exports continuing to lag.

Clearly essential economic policy reforms in accordance with EU norms will remain a major stumbling block between Ankara and the EU. Thus, at the Nice Summit of EU leaders at the end of 2001, Turkey was not even mentioned along with the 12 Candidate Countries in the Enlargement program extending to 2010. This caused much irritation in Ankara, giving the impression that Turkey had no realistic hope of becoming a full member till well after 2010. As well, there are further potential irritations for the EU, which must be overcome with realism as well as urgency in Ankara. Turkey, unlike many other candidate countries, is a large country and the costs of integrating Turkey into the EU, under existing EU rules, will be a major drain on the EU budget. This is especially true in the case of agriculture, as subsidy levels to Turkish farmers are extremely high, even when compared with the EU's own highly protective Common Agricultural Policy. Both the EU and Turkey would be obliged, in any future accession negotiations, to agree to major reforms to harmonize their respective agricultural policies. In the meantime, trade difficulties with regard to agricultural products, such as beef imports to Turkey, may prove problematic.[19] Similar concerns would apply for regional development funds from the European Union budget. This has potentially significant implications given the massive regional development financing that would be required in Turkey's Southeast region. To date, Turkey has received limited financial benefits from the EU commensurate with European concerns for Kurdish human rights. However, it should be noted that lack of funding in this area is as much due to the poverty of suitable project proposals submitted by the Turkish side.

Labor and migration issues are especially troublesome subjects in EU-Turkish relations. There are, currently, over 2 million Turkish citizens living and working in the EU, mainly in Germany. The citizenship status and the identity politics of these Turks, in particular the second generation of children born in Europe, have become a domestic concern within many EU countries. Likewise, the future flow of Turkish workers as job seekers in the EU would be a major headache for EU countries, especially in the light of the high unemployment levels currently prevailing in Western Europe.[20] As a result of these concerns, it is almost certain that a mutually acceptable management of mobility rights for Turkish citizens will have to be negotiated as part of accession negotiations between Ankara and the EU.

An equally important concern for the EU is the transit or illegal immigration from Asia of migrants and refugees passing through Turkey destined for EU member states.[21] This migration is increasingly being linked to international terrorism[22] and Turkey has lost some 30,000 lives in the last 16 years to PKK sponsored terror. In future, and as part of international cooperation to fight global terrorism, the Turkish police and security intelligence organizations will need financial and technical assistance for more effective border control, once the borders of the EU are extended to coincide with Turkey's eastern frontier in the rugged and conflict-prone Southeast region. Indeed, given the high EU concern for the Kurdish question, it is only natural to expect increasing EU funding and development assistance in this heavily Kurdish populated region as it is transformed from a zone of conflict and terrorism to one of economic development.

Political Obstacles: Democratization, Human Rights and the Kurdish Question

Turning from economic to political irritations, three sub-heads dominate this category: viz. Democratization, Human Rights and Kurdish/PKK issues. Regarding the Kurdish/PKK issue, as far as Ankara is concerned there is no Kurdish problem in Turkey, only PKK terrorism. The Turkish elite[23] view is that all Turkish citizens are equal under the law and constitutionally enjoy the same legal, social and political rights with the recognition that there are regional differences in economic and social standards. In the Southeast for example, income levels and social standards are considerably lower than the national average. The provision of such basic services as education and health has been hampered by years of PKK terrorism. With the arrest, trial and conviction of PKK leader Abdullah Öcalan, under Turkish justice with extensive international and EU monitoring, the Ecevit coalition government now needs to address regional inequalities in the Southeast.

In this regard the constitutional amendments of October 2001 is a significant step forward, but hopefully this first step will be followed up with greater democratization.

The Turkish private sector, in particular, must invest in this region to expand income and employment opportunities. Now that the large-scale South Anatolian Project is providing expanded opportunities for irrigated farming in the region, there is a huge potential for private sector led industrialization in such subsectors as food processing and garment and textile manufacturing. The important point is that these industries tend to be relatively labor-intensive, precisely what is needed to promote employment growth and commensurate regional socio-economic development. Regional development would be the most effective way of arresting the high volume of migration from the region to the already overcrowded cities in the western part of the country, while also bringing rising prosperity to the heavily Kurdish population of the region.

Perhaps the most significant encouragement to regional development in the Southeast would come from the normalization of economic (and political) ties between Ankara and Baghdad to restore the volume of cross-border trade to its historical pre-1990 levels. Such a restoration would also greatly benefit the economic prosperity of the Kurdish population in the region. The pace of social and political reforms must be accelerated in Ankara, in order to provide expanded educational and cultural opportunities for the Kurds in this long-neglected region. These social and cultural reforms are good investments in themselves, and they would also go a long way in satisfying European criticisms that Ankara has not done enough for its Kurdish population. Nevertheless, the role that the EU plays in promoting Kurdish rights must be balanced. Offending Ankara would hardly be helpful, especially given the Ecevit government's decision to postpone the fate of Öcalan until after the European Court of Justice delivers a judgment on the case. In September 2001, the Ecevit coalition recalled the Parliament from recess, specifically for the purpose of adopting a 37-clause constitutional reform package, including the abolition of the death penalty except treason and terrorism, in an effort to meet EU standards. Although the discussion still continues in the country about the total removal of the death penalty and allowing languages other than Turkish to be taught in schools, Ankara hopes that the October 2001 constitutional reform package, will result in a positive report on Turkey by the EU Commission, removing another significant roadblock to EU membership.

Many other thorny issues on the human rights agenda remain. However, cooperation, rather than confrontation, between Ankara and the EU is, of course, the desirable option. The Turkish parliament has already updated hundreds of pieces of legislation in the human rights field (including prison reform and measures to prevent torture), but much work yet remains to be done in government and societal institutions in the execution of the new legislation. The EU has to realize that the pace of human rights reform, and the o democratization of politics, must be commensurate with the institutional and financial capacity of the state to implement these reforms, while also taking into account the mood of Turkish public opinion. The EU, however well meaning, are expected to show sensitivity, especially in taking pains to avoid any appearance of lending support, covertly or overtly, to any separatist movement or propaganda on the PKK or equally sensitive Armenian questions.

From the perspective of the EU, the Turkish state still manifests 'certain anomalies in the functioning of the public authorities, persistent human rights violations and major shortcomings in the treatment of minorities'.[24] Thus, the Kurds are viewed as a 'minority' and the EU takes the high moral ground declaring, without outlining any specific program or offering any incentives, that: 'A civil, non-military solution must be found to the situation in southeastern Turkey, particularly since many of the violations of civil and political rights observed in the country are connected in one way or another with this issue'. Similarly, the special role of the armed forces in Turkish politics comes in for strong criticism from EU circles. 'The lack of civilian control of the army gives cause for concern. This is reflected by the major role played by the army in political life through the National Security Council'.

This is a major source of irritation for policymakers in Ankara. The Turkish elite's perception is that Europeans exaggerate the role of the army in Turkey's politics stemming from an inadequate understanding of the special role played by the army in the creation and preservation of a secular Turkish Republic. In fact, the majority of Turkish citizens has greater confidence and trust in the Turkish military than in Turkish politicians.[25] In much the same fashion, Turkish citizens tend to underestimate the deep European mistrust of allowing for military involvement in politics and, the significance of the principle of civilian supremacy in matters of national defense. In the Turkish state tradition, the boundary between the military and civilian politics has been largely non-existent. How these contrasting views in Turkish-EU relations will be resolved will depend, largely, on the elements of the entire package of terms and conditions for accession. In the end, if the principle of civilian supremacy were to emerge as the sole sticking point, it is conceivable that the Turkish military command, always sensitive to what it perceives to be 'the national interest', would opt for such reforms, or even the abolition of the National Security Council (NSC), as a necessary compromise for Turkey's accession to the EU.

Institutional Preparedness

The portion of the guidelines in CC about 'institutional preparedness' is a minefield of competing values and norms between Turkey and the EU, and trouble always lurks just beneath the surface. Harmonizing Turkish values and state traditions with the CC may prove the most challenging and time-consuming single category of harmonization in readying the Turkish state for full EU membership. Another major root cause of divergence in institutional preparedness stems from the centralist Ottoman state tradition in comparison to that of European liberalism. Turkey is still governed through a highly centralized state in a top-down hierarchical system controlled from Ankara. Kemalist ideology has strong populist foundations,[26] but reformism did not outlive Atatürk, and much of the urgently required decentralization in institutions remains pending. Indeed, such decentralization in both political and economic decision-making, facilitating in particular the eventual solution of the PKK/Kurdish problem, is expected to be one of the major benefits of EU membership.

Similarly, implementation of constitutional and legal reforms in line with the European Union's *acqui communaitaire* may lead to significant improvements in the rule of law and respect for individual human rights. The Turkish legal profession itself will have to be modernized and encouraged to adopt an increasingly European and internationalist orientation. In addition, law schools in Turkish universities will need to expand their curricula in European and international legal practices and take measures to increase the supply of lawyers able to communicate in several European languages.[27]

As part of a concerted program of democratization, Turkey needs to ban the death penalty and enshrine such basic human rights as the freedom of thought, including the freedom of religious belief in the Turkish Constitution. The Turkish President, Ahmet Necdet Sezer, who is dedicated to the rule of law, has given positive signals in this healthy direction and in October 2001 Parliament started enacting these reforms. As a result of these long-overdue reforms, coupled with the shocking attack on the USA on 11 September 2001 by Islamic terrorists, EU circles and the Turkish elite may be growing closer. In particular, European governments, parliamentarians and human rights organizations may adopt a more realistic understanding of PKK terrorism in general, and more particularly in such cases as Öcalan, Leyla Zena and action of political parties. Europeans will have to proceed with sensitivity in this field to overcome historical mistrust, still widespread amongst the Turkish population, as a result of their collective experience when a hostile Europe exploited 'reforms' to benefit Christian minorities while at the same time promoting the partition of the Ottoman Empire. Fears of the ill-conceived *Treaty of Sèvres,* providing for the creation of an independent Armenia and Kurdistan in Eastern Anatolia, still linger in the minds of many in Turkey.

The most difficult test of Turkish-EU relations will be Turkish bilateral relations with Greece. Thanks to the Helsinki decisions, the EU has now emerged as a self-appointed referee of all disputes between Athens and Ankara. Consequently, how these bilateral relations evolve in the near and medium term will depend, to a significant extent, on their management by the EU. Even-handedness and creative diplomacy on the part of the Commission and the Council of the EU is essential, as clearly evidenced in Helsinki. In future, it will be even more essential as the 'tough nuts' in Greek-Turkish relations are placed on the negotiating table. The 'tough nuts' include the Aegean dispute, in particular the definition of the territorial sea and the continental shelf on the basis of equitable sharing as well as sovereignty over airspace.[28] Greece has declared its intention of extending its maritime sovereignty to a distance of 12 miles, which effectively would make the Aegean a Greek Sea. In response Turkey has announced that this action would amount to a declaration of war, a situation to which the two countries have, on several occasions, come close.

Negotiating this complex issue prior to 2004, when the EU is expected to revisit the subject in accordance with the Helsinki declaration, will test even the most skilled diplomats. To date, the Simitis government in Athens has steadfastly refused to enter into any dialogue with Ankara on the Aegean question, preferring to refer the dispute to the European Court. However, even doing this would require preparatory dialogue to determine the substance and terminology of any legal reference. Instead, Athens has tried to utilize its privileged position inside the EU to wrest concessions from Ankara prior to any formulation of Turkish full membership.[29] Almost certainly only well-timed incentives, coupled with even-handedness from the EU, carefully crafted with skillful and objective diplomacy, will prove to be the most effective way to break the logjam in bilateral disputes between Greece and Turkey. In addition to these obstacles, the key to Greek-Turkish relations is clearly the long-standing problem of Cyprus. Since the unilateral application for accession by the Vasiliu government in Southern Cyprus in 1990, the EU has parachuted itself into the Cyprus imbroglio,[30] and, to date, it has done so in a highly pro-Greek fashion promising Greek Cypriot accession to the EU, apparently ahead of Turkey.[31] As far as the formal EU position goes, there is only one 'Cyprus' (i.e. the Greek-Cypriot controlled, Southern Cyprus). Indeed, Southern Cyprus has been declared to be eligible for membership, and included in the next round of EU enlargement, along with Malta, Hungary, Poland, Estonia, the Czech Republic and Slovenia. At Helsinki, it was announced that the absence of a political settlement of the Cyprus dispute would not preclude the admission of (Southern) 'Cyprus' to full EU membership. Gunter Verheugen, the EU Commissioner for Enlargement, has repeatedly stated that 'Cyprus' is like a train ready to depart from the station, and that it is up to the Turkish Cypriots to get on board (i.e. submit to the Greek Cypriots and get on the train) or they will miss a wonderful opportunity to join this most exclusive club. This is an astonishing view that reflects a total lack of sensitivity to Turkish Cypriot rights and grievances. Verheugen was, of course, reflecting the official pre-Helsinki position of the EU on Cyprus. In the post-Helsinki context Turkish sensitivities need to be accommodated. In this new environment threatening terminology or pro-Greek conditions on Turkey's accession should be avoided, particularly in the Accession Partnership Document, and in all later discussion along the road to full membership. Key European Union members will need to have sufficient tools to resist and overcome attempts by Athens, which sees Greek-Turkish relations, quite irrationally, in *zero-sum terms.*

As far as the European Union's position vis-à-vis the Turkish Republic of North Cyprus (TRNC) goes, a more evenhanded position must be developed in Brussels. In the past, the EU has officially adopted an essentially Greek Cypriot perspective, refusing to recognize the TRNC as representative of all Turkish Cypriots. This has resulted in an asymmetrical position between the UN and the EU. The former recognized Turkish Cypriots and Greek Cypriots as equal parties to the Cyprus problem, and indeed, accepted the 'political equality' of the two communities. The EU, however, has often taken decisions, badly timed and inspired by Athens, that effectively sabotaged UN-sponsored negotiations towards a political settlement. Not surprisingly, from a TRNC perspective, the EU has been seen as pro-Greek, with no prospect of acting as a 'catalyst' or 'honest broker' in efforts to find a negotiated settlement, so long as the European Union non-recognition of Turkish Cypriots persists. A starting point for enhancing EU-TRNC relations, would be the acknowledgment, by the European Union, of the UNSC

Resolution terminology that the two Cypriot communities are indeed 'on equal political footing'. How this acknowledgement may evolve in the future can be discussed in terms of scenario analysis.

One scenario is that the implications of a divided Cyprus in the EU must be considered. On a balance of probabilities, it seems unlikely that the Greek Cypriot portion of Cyprus would be accepted *as if* it controlled the land of the TRNC with its large Turkish military presence. In this eventuality, it would be up to European leaders to determine the legal implications of, for example, the validity of such international agreements as the Treaty of Guarantee, under which the Turkish troops are currently stationed in TRNC, and which is, of course, an integral part of Cypriot independence negotiated in 1960. Another related question is how to reconcile a large military presence from a non-EU country (i.e. Turkey) inside an EU member (i.e. 'Cyprus'). However, perhaps the most serious consequence of the ascension of solely the Greek portion of the Island would concern the on-going UN-sponsored negotiations to seek a solution in Cyprus. It is unlikely that these negotiations would survive a successful Greek Cypriot succession. Such an accession would, clearly, remove any incentive for the Greek Cypriot side to remain in these negotiations, as a result it is almost certain that Greek Cypriot success at winning accession to EU membership, ahead of Turkey, would result in the permanent partition of the island.

Alternative scenarios are, of course, a postponement of any Cypriot accession to the EU until after a political settlement has been achieved regarding the island. Several key EU countries including France, Holland and Italy have, in fact, raised objections to the Greek Cypriot application, risking a showdown with Greece, which has threatened to veto the entire enlargement process involving Central and Eastern Europe if Southern Cyprus is excluded. Therefore, if Greek demands prevail and, as intimated at Helsinki, Greek Cypriots are rewarded by full membership in the next round of EU enlargement ahead of Turkey, this would be a severe blow to Turkish aspirations for EU membership. Greek-Cypriot membership in the EU would offer the Greek side a second potential veto against Turkey in the EU, killing any chances of full Turkish membership and effectively placing Ankara-EU relations into cold storage.

With Turkey thereby excluded from the EU, Europe would suffer several significant strategic losses, and in cultural terms, the EU would be seen as a 'Christian Club' signaling to the entire Muslim world that inter-faith cooperation is undesirable to Christian governments. The terrible cost of such a negative image has been tragically demonstrated in the attack by Muslim terrorists on the USA on 11 September 2001. Ankara has repeatedly pleaded in the past for European support in the fight against terrorism, and it is now imperative that Turkey, the only Muslim country in NATO as well as other European institutions, should also be included in the EU precisely because it is a Muslim country. Its inclusion is essential not only in the fight against terrorism, but in promoting a Christian-Muslim partnership and dialogue for greater democratization within the Muslim world. In trade relations, a Turkish failure to gain full membership may also place the Customs Union in question, in view of its lopsided trade benefits, which have to date predominantly been in the EU's favor. In addition, the EU's Mediterranean policy would receive a major blow, and its access to, and dependence upon, energy resources from the Middle East and the Caucasus would become more vulnerable. Similarly, in a post-NATO scenario with a Turkey excluded from EU membership, European security would appear vulnerable.

Although in 1999 there was a warming in Greek-Turkish relations, largely as a result of 'earthquake' or 'seismic' diplomacy,[32] it is doubtful that there will be a smooth ride in the future. In fact, trouble may be on the horizon. The Cem-Papandreou personal relationship, the major factor behind this breakthrough in relations, will be increasingly challenged by the inclusion in the new Simitis government of Mr. Pangalos, a hard-talking critic of Ankara who may be expected to offset the earlier positive influence of Papandreou. This possibility became evident in October 2000 when Greece withdrew from NATO military exercises to protest at the entry of Turkish jets into what Greece considered its national airspace. Nevertheless, by far the greatest potential threat to bilateral Greek-Turkish relations lies in the EU's own priorities. If, for example, the Greek Cypriot side is indeed included in the next round of enlargement ahead of Turkey, then, as previously stated, it is virtually certain that EU-Turkish relations will be frozen once again, recalling the aftermath of the disastrous decisions in Luxembourg in December 1997.

The Benefits of a Historic Partnership

There is, however, a ray of hope that the catastrophic scenario outlined above, may be avoided, though it will take great tact and foresight on the part of the architects and decision-makers of the EU in their management of Greek-Turkish relations. Creative diplomacy is required to restore the historic balance in the Eastern Mediterranean, broken by the accession of Greece in January 1981, when it became the tenth member of the EU. Since then, Greece has successfully utilized this privileged membership to promote its bilateral objectives at the expense of Turkey's national interests.

Thanks to the Helsinki decisions, the EU has a historic opportunity to build a post-modern Europe including Turkey, undoubtedly the most secular, democratic Muslim country. This would be a new Europe, peaceful and prosperous, stretching from the Scottish highlands to Caucasia; a multi-ethnic and multi-religious community, on a higher plane of civilization, transcending the competing nationalism of the 'Nation-State'.

It remains to be seen if the EU can play a constructive role in promoting an end to competing ethno-nationalism in the Eastern Mediterranean. Hopefully the EU may prove successful in operating as a catalyst in promoting friendship and cooperation between Greece and Turkey in the region, across the Aegean and on the Island of Cyprus. Tozun Bahcheli has postulated two possible scenarios that are discussed in the following section.[33]

An Optimistic Scenario for 2004

This first scenario operates on the assumption that all outstanding Greek-Turkish disputes would be well on their way to settlement by 2004, and that a just and lasting solution on Cyprus could be achieved which would be acceptable to Greek- and Turkish-Cypriots alike. As a result, under this scenario, Turkey and the new State of Cyprus would both be included in the next round of EU enlargement.

This optimistic outcome, however, would require a recasting of the EU's Cyprus policy bringing it more in line with the UN's position of 'two politically equal communities' on the Island. In practical terms this would necessitate a significant upgrading of EU-Turkish Cypriot relations, possibly including direct EU financial aid to Northern Cyprus. Given such an evenhanded EU stance, it would then follow, that the EU would opt for a simultaneous accession of both Turkey and the new State of Cyprus in the EU enlargement process. The Greek and Greek-Cypriot side would probably not be very enthusiastic about this approach, which of necessity would imply that they would have to abandon the myth of Cyprus being a 'Greek island'. However, in view of the significant advantages for all sides that such a situation would generate, may nevertheless be the most sensible course of action for the EU to take.

This scenario, of a simultaneous accession by both a unified Cyprus and Turkey in the first round of EU enlargement, is seen as 'optimistic' given the relatively short time frame for settling all of the complex Greek-Turkish disputes, and the great challenges which must be overcome to prepare accession, not only in the case of Turkey, but as regards North and South Cyprus as well. However, in view of this time constraint, a more realistic alternative may have to be considered.

A More Realistic Scenario 2007/10

This second scenario may be termed more realistic in that it would allow more time to prepare for the accession in Turkey and Cyprus, with membership coinciding with the second EU enlargement in 2007/10. This option would almost certainly meet some resistance from Greek-Cypriots who are eager to join the EU even if UN negotiations fail to lead to a mutually acceptable political settlement. Nevertheless, while doing so may satisfy some Greek and Greek-Cypriot nationalists, it will be seen in Ankara and North Cyprus as hostile, and result in heavy costs. There would, for example, be a permanent division of Cyprus, potential conflict in the Aegean, along with a wider cultural divide between an all-Christian EU and Muslim Turkey, which possesses a large population, growing market and a strategic location along Europe's energy lifeline.

Clearly the more rational win-win scenario is to opt for Turkish accession. The *sine qua non*, the precondition in both scenarios outlined above, is the *simultaneous accession* of both Turkey and a Cyprus that has successfully negotiated, thanks to creative EU diplomacy support, rather than undermining UN negotiations toward a just and lasting settlement between its Turkish and Greek communities. A continuation of the one-sided and pro-Greek policy in the EU represents an almost certain prescription for further conflict in the Eastern Mediterranean.

Conclusion

The principal conclusion of this review is that the prospect of Turkish accession to the EU represents a historic opportunity for a comprehensive European peace, further prosperity and a security zone in the Balkans and the Middle East. Without stabilizing these regions around Western Europe, it is futile to view the ESDI as an instrument of peace and security in the Balkans and the Eastern Mediterranean. Including Greece and Greek Cypriots, but excluding Turkey, in fact, would destabilize the Balkans and the Middle East. Turkey is an essential part of both the Balkans and the Middle East, and, its cooperation and contribution are vital in stabilizing these regions. Greek-Turkish cooperation and friendship, therefore, hold the key to regional peace and stability. The EU can make or break Greek-Turkish relations, or put differently, it can stabilize or destabilize the Aegean.

The Osama bin Laden-inspired terrorism attack on the USA on 11 September 2001 puts Turkish-EU relations in a new perspective. Secular Turkey has suddenly re-emerged as a critical Western ally in the fight against international terrorism. Accordingly, Turkish membership in the EU should henceforth be assessed constructively precisely because Turkey is a Muslim country. The Turkish secular state is the most realistic model of development for the entire Muslim world. Thus, the expected payoff from an eventual Turkish full membership in the EU is greatly heightened, and can lead to the following *positive-sum* outcomes:

- First, inclusion of Turkey in the EU would contribute to European security, especially in relation to the escalating problem of international terrorism. In economic and trade terms, it would also create the world's largest and most prosperous single market comprising some 500 million inhabitants living in a huge territory extending from the Scottish highlands to the borders of Caucasia. Europe, then, would become an increasingly multi-ethnic, multi-religious union; it will be a richer, post-modern European civilization with an identity that would signal the end of 'a Crusade Millennium', for, by incorporating Turkey in it's midst, Europe would transform itself into a cultural bridge between the Christian and Muslim worlds and show the way to harmonious governance within the Global Village, ridding it of such global public 'evils' as terrorism, religious intolerance, racism and xenophobia.
- Second, a new post-modern Europe, inclusive of Greeks and Turks, would at last halt competing ethno-nationalisms in this region. Through constructive and evenhanded diplomacy, the EU could play a valuable role as a 'catalyst' in promoting friendship and cooperation between Turkey and Greece. The Aegean can then truly become a sea of peace and cooperation, in the spirit of the Atatürk-Venizelos grand reconciliation.[34]
- Third, there would be significant benefits from Turkish accession to the European Union for both Cypriot communities on terms of political equality. As far as Greek Cypriots are concerned, they would immediately benefit in terms of attaining their 'three freedoms' (mobility, residence and ownership) within an enlarged EU, ideals to which the EU is dedicated, but which can

> only be realized with Turkish Cypriots included as equal partners. Given this, the Turkish Cypriots would achieve their security safeguards as a result of full Turkish membership in the European Union. In the larger context of Greek-Turkish relations, Turkey's accession would help cement peace and cooperation between Ankara and Athens, creating major spillover benefits to the Cypriot population in economic,[35] as well as in political terms. However, Europe can become a legitimate midwife to this socio-political birth if, and only if, it succeeds in promoting a balanced settlement of all outstanding Greek-Turkish disputes in Cyprus and across the Aegean. This will require an evenhanded approach and not, as has happened in the past, through pro-Greek policies, that offer accession to the EU for the Greek portion of Cyprus.

Both of these scenarios require, as a necessary pre-condition, the simultaneous accession of both Turkey and the new Cyprus into the EU. Further, both scenarios involve political risk. The implementation of Turkish reforms in fulfillment of the Copenhagen Criteria is, of course, in the mutual interest of both Turkey and the EU and there are increasing signs of Ankara's genuine commitment to undertake these changes.

It is hoped that the EU will advance with goodwill and incentives, evenhandedly promoting Greek-Turkish friendship. It will be necessary to abandon its pre-Helsinki counter-productive pro-Greek bias, and move closer to the UN position on Cyprus by acknowledging the existence of politically equal ethnic communities on the Island. If this is done, either of the scenarios outlined above might offer a happy prospect, a ray of hope for peace and cooperation in the Eastern Mediterranean and across the Aegean. A Greco-Turkish friendship within the EU would also contribute toward a stabilizing of the Balkans and Eastern Europe, and would be a major step toward a stronger, enlarged and safer Europe in the 21st century.

Notes

---

1 An earlier version of this paper was presented at the 3rd International Conference, organized by the International Center for Contemporary Middle Eastern Studies located at the Eastern Mediterranean University, Gazimagosa, North Cyprus on 28 April 2000.

2 Westernization, the great legacy of Mustafa Kemal Atatürk, in fact predates Atatürk. For the Turkish policy-makers, EU membership for Turkey would be confirmation that Atatürk's Republic has finally reached the highest level of 'contemporary civilization' built on secular and modern foundations, largely imported from Europe. See Atasoy, S. (1999), 'Globalization and Turkey: From Capitulations to Contemporary Civilization' in S.T. Ismail (ed.), *Globalization: Policies, Challenges and Responses*, Detselig Enterprises Ltd, Calgary, Alberta, Canada.

3 Cem, İ. (2000, June-August), 'Turkey and Europe: Looking to the Future from a Historical Perspective', *Perceptions, Journal of International Affairs*, 5, 2, p. 10.

4 'Is it adieu to Atatürk?' *Economist*, 18 December 1999, p. 26.

5 The USA is aware of this, but the row between Ankara and the EU over ESDI was still unresolved at the time of writing (in January 2002).

6 *The Economist*, 'The European Union decides it might one day talk Turkey' 18 December 1999, p. 25

7 Huntington, S. (1993, Summer), 'The Clash of Civilizations?' *Foreign Affairs*. See also, Huntington, S. (1996), *The Clash of Civilizations and the Remaking of the World Order*, Simon and Schuster, New York.

8 Eralp, A. (1998), 'Turkey and the European Union', in Aydın, M. (ed.), *Turkey at the Threshold of the 21st Century*, International Relations Foundation, Ankara, p. 142.

9 In particular, APD's conditionalities on Cyprus and Aegean disputes, essentially demanding concessions from Ankara, generated considerable anger amongst Turkish observers.

10 Predictably, the NP appears to have disappointed those EU circles who expected binding Turkish commitments on Kurdish (i.e. minority) rights, abolition of death penalty, and civilian control of the armed forces. So far as the EU reaction to constitutional amendments of October 2001 is concerned, this was still awaited as this paper was being finalized.

11 Cem, *Turkey and Europe*, p. 10

12 *1999 Regular Report from the Commission on Turkey's Progress towards Accession*, 13 November 1999, p. 17.

13 Ibid., *Statistical Annex*, p. 54

14 These figures are from *İşbank Review of Economic Conditions*, at http://www.isbank.com.tr.

15 Villaverde, J. N. (1998), 'Turkey-European Relations in the Framework of the Euro-Mediterranean Partnership' in Aydın, *Turkey at the Threshold of the 21st Century*.

16 Uzunoglu, S. (1999), 'The Implementation of the Custom Union in Turkey and its Macroeconomic Effect', in *Die Turkei in der EU-Zollunion: Empire-Theori-Perspektiven, Zentrum fur Turkeistudien*, ed., LIT Verlag, Munster, pp. 69-70.

17 For a comprehensive examination of past macro policies, see Öniş, Z. (1998), *State and Markets, the Political Economy of Turkey in Comparative Perspective*, Boğaziçi University Press, İstanbul.

18 Thus, as part of these political maneuverings a number of Ministers, including for Energy, Transport and Tobacco Monopoly, were obliged to resign, in some cases their names being linked to corruption.

19 *1999 Regular Report*, p. 32.

20 Martin, P.L. (ed.), (1991), *The Unfinished Story: Turkish Labour Migration to Western Europe*, International Labour Office, Geneva; Koray, S. (1993, March), *Developing Cooperation on Migration between Turkey and the European Union*, ZfT Aktuel No. 17, Essen.

21 *1999 Regular Report*, p. 36.

22 Finally in 11 September 2001 international terrorism struck with horror at the financial and military heartland of the USA. For years, Turkey has been attempting to bring the subject to the international arena, but while having some success with the USA government, the EU circles have preferred to show active sympathy (on grounds of human rights) to PKK sponsored terror.

23 For a recent empirical study of this elite, see McLaren, L.M. (2000, March), 'Turkey's Eventual Membership of the EU', *Journal of Common Market Studies*, vol.38, no.1.

24 This and the following quotes in this section are from *1999 Regular Report*, p. 8.

25 This is repeatedly evidenced in the public polls frequently published in the Turkish news media. Thus, it was reported, in the aftermath of the economic crisis in 2001 that, political corruption is so extensive in all parties represented in Parliament that, in the event of a snap election, none of the parties would pass the 10 per cent threshold required for qualification hold seats in Parliament.

26 For an extended discussion of this point, see Mehmet, O. (1983), 'Turkey in Crisis: Some Contradictions in the Kemalist Development Strategy', *International Journal of Middle East Studies,* vol.15, no.1. This article has recently been reprinted in T. Niblock and R. Wilson, *The Political Economy of the Middle East, vol. 5,* An Elgar Reference Collection, Cheltenham, UK, pp. 264-83.

27 For example, the Law Faculty of the Eastern Mediterranean University, an English instruction institution, can develop a 'niche' by offering these courses in English.

28 See Bahcheli, T. (1990), *Greek-Turkish Relations since 1955,* Westview Press, Boulder,Colorado esp. ch. 5.

29 Thus, in Fall 2000, during the final drafting of the APD, the Simitis government was successful in inserting pro-Greek paragraphs into the text much to the annoyance of Ankara. In September 2001, the EU Parliament adopted a highly pro- Greek report on Cyprus, penned by the former Foreign Minister of Luxembourg Poos, who stated categorically that Turkey 'can forget about EU membership' if Ankara were to retaliate against EU decision to admit Cyprus before first solving the Cyprus problem. These are clear signs that the long road to Turkish membership will be extremely difficult, to say the least.

30 Dodd, C. (1998), *The Cyprus Imbroglio,* Eothen Press, London.

31 Thus, in the Commission's *1999 Regular Report on Cyprus' Progress Toward Accession,* there is the astounding general evaluation that 'Cyprus fulfils the Copenhagen political criteria.' (p. 15) even though the next sentence notes that there has been 'little progress' toward a settlement on the island.

32 See the recent draft paper by Tozun Bahceli, 'Turkish Policy Toward Greece' (mimeo.), King's College, London, Canada, no date

33 For other scenarios on this theme, see N. Nugent (2000, March), 'EU and the Cyprus Problem', *Journal of Common Market Studies,* vol.38, no.1.

34 These two protagonists of Greco-Turkish relations in modern times achieved a historic reconciliation in 1930. They both had some remarkable similarities and common memories. Venizelos was born an Ottoman citizen in Crete, while Atatürk was born and brought up in Salonika, then a town in Ottoman Turkey. 'They were leaders of two nations which had fought a life-and-death struggle in the early 1920's. Less than ten years later they managed to unite their nations in friendship.' Vali, F.A. (1971), *Bridge Across the Bosphorus, the Foreign Policy of Turkey,* Johns Hopkins University Press, Baltimore and London, p. 270.

35 For example, there is a real potential of sharing Turkish excess waters in the region. For an extended discussion, see D.B. Brooks and O. Mehmet (eds.), (2000), *Water Balances in the Eastern Mediterranean,* IRDC, Ottawa.

Chapter 4

The New European Security Architecture and Turkey

A. Seda Serdar

Introduction

The European Security and Defense Policy (ESDP) in place since the end of the Cold War, has become one of the major issues discussed among the members of the European Union. The ESDP, among other policies of the European Union, plays a considerable role in this supranational institution. Despite the transfer of certain rights of the nation-states to the EU, most of the member countries still fear a total shift of sovereignty and the security issue is one of the most delicate matters. Even though there is a general unanimity on security matters, there are certain differences among the leading EU countries.

Moreover, ESDP and its counterpart in NATO, the European Security and Defense Identity (ESDI), have caused considerable discussion within NATO between the EU members and the US on the one hand, and between Turkey and the EU on the other. So much so that the issue has become a test case for Turkey's European credentials; the stand taken by non-EU members of NATO with regard to allowing the EU to use NATO military assets, showed how strong the Turkish objections to this issue were. This article, therefore, will examine Turkish arguments in light of German, French and British perceptions, which obviously differ from Turkish views. The American perspective will be touched upon as well, since the discussion on ESDP is closely related to NATO policies, which makes it impossible to ignore US views.

Turkish-EU relations have had a troubling history, each decade since the 1964 Ankara Agreement has witnessed a series of seemingly 'unsolvable' problematic issues. The latest thorny topic, which will be examined in this article, is the ESDP which, with its repercussions within NATO as well as on Turkish-US relations, has come to dominate the Turkish-EU security agenda since the conclusion of the Cold War. The European desire to create an independent European security system in the face of a diminished Soviet threat following 1991 has left Turkey and the EU in a 'no way out' situation, as Turkish demands do not coincide with the EU proposals. In other words, Turkish desires to be included in any new security arrangements in Europe and along with an unwillingness to allow the EU to use NATO assets without Turkey's participation on the one hand, and the EU's reluctance to allow Turkey to have any direct say in any envisaged European security system, before Turkey becomes a full EU-member on the other, have added to an already problematic EU-Turkish agenda. Moreover, the conflict between the EU and Turkey over the new European security system cannot be isolated just within Europe, as it affects the future of the Western Alliance system as a whole. The direct involvement of NATO in this discussion necessarily implies US involvement and therefore, a more complex transatlantic dimension. Consequently, the ongoing discussion is inevitably constructed within a NATO framework.

Since the end of World War II, Turkey has been a reliable ally of both the US and Europe in facing the Soviet threat. Until the collapse of communism, NATO remained the sole institution concerning European security issues, while the attempt to create the Western European Union (WEU) produced only an ineffective security structure. However, today, Europe is aiming to create a so-called 'independent force' by relying on NATO assets, while at the same time excluding its most loyal non-Western ally, Turkey, from taking an effective part in any envisioned structure. To understand the problem that this European attempt has created for Turkey, it is necessary to briefly review the history of Turkish-EU relations, as well as Turkish objections to, and rifts within, Europe about the proposed structure. This will show that the disagreements on the security issue involve rather substantial objections from Turkey, bordering on a perception of the survival of the country in its present form, and that it would be overly optimistic to believe that this problem will be easily solved within a short period of time.

Turkey and Europe during the Cold War

The defeat of Nazi Germany at the end of the Second World War marked the beginning of a new era in international relations. France and the United Kingdom, while satisfied by the victory they had won with the help of the United States, now faced a new threat in the 'backyard' of Europe. The threat was similar for Turkey as the USSR, an emerging superpower at the time and northern neighbor to Turkey, was perceived as a growing threat to the security and stability of both Turkey and Europe. The division of Germany among the Allies was a clear step towards the Cold War that would only end with the fall of the USSR at the beginning of the 1990s.

After Europe had experienced two world wars, and the Soviet Union had expanded into central and eastern Europe, the immediate reconstruction of the destroyed continent seemed necessary in the eyes of both American and European leaders. In such an environment, the idea of a 'unified Europe', aiming to create an anti-communist and anti-fascist continental block, was attractive to the US. Turkey, facing similar threats, was also attracted to the formation of such a security alliance. The idea of a 'unified Europe', which had long ago been imagined against the Muslim Turks and Orthodox Russians (Europe's 'others'), re-emerged during the Second World War in a different context as the Ventotene Manifesto, which was drafted by Altiero Spinelli and Ernesto Rossine, and published in late 1941.[1] It emphasized the need for Europe to be united against internal divisions and external threats, and asserted that if such a unity were not created, 'national jealousies would again develop, and [each] state would again express its satisfaction on its own existence in its armed strength'.[2] This idea and the thoughts of other 'Europeans', such as Jean Monnet, Winston Churchill and Charles de Gaulle, led to the emergence of cooperation among the European countries, the main theme of which was the creation of a control mechanism through interdependence. The long lasting German-French conflict was to be taken under control via the establishment of the European Coal and Steel Community (ECSC), which aimed to create a mechanism that gathered the authority of six European countries under one roof concerning the two most used natural resources in war efforts at the time (i.e., coal and steel).

While these discussions were taking place in Europe, Turkey was left isolated at the end of the Second World War and not involved in the ongoing international developments among the victorious allies because of its less than reliable policies during the War. Although Turkey had managed to stay out of the war until the very end with a policy of 'active neutrality', Turkey had alienated the USSR and disappointed the US and the UK as a consequence of its policy. Thus , Turkey was not in a very desirable position when the war came to an end with the German surrender in 1945. Furthermore, being a founding member of the United Nations, thanks in large part to its last minute declaration of war on Germany, did not prove helpful to Turkey with regard to threats to its security. Thus, as a result of this isolation, Turkey wished to promote closer relations with the western states, both as a continuation of its long standing policy of westernization begun over a century earlier, and as a result of its need for allies in the face of the 'perceived' Soviet threat.

Indeed, since the foundation of the Turkish Republic in 1923, 'westernization' has been one of the most fundamental aspects of the Turkish state, and it has pursued this policy successfully while jealously guarding its independence. However, the end of the Second World War led to a new balance of power where the leading players were the United States and the USSR and countries like Turkey felt the need to ally with one or the other. Moreover, Turkey, in this new game, felt more insecure than most other developing states due to its Soviet northern neighbor and, to provide for its security and prosperity, wanted to take part in Western organizations that were being created in the post-war era. On the other side of the Atlantic, the US believed for a time that after the war the USSR would be a partner in keeping a global balance, this approach ended when the USSR showed expansionist intentions towards central and eastern Europe. From that point onwards, the emerging Soviet 'threat' become one of the cornerstones of Turkish-US-European relations. On the European side of the Atlantic, countries such as the UK, France, Belgium, Holland and the Netherlands felt obliged to form a new security alliance and therefore signed the Brussels Treaty (17 March 1948), in which it was stated that if any of the allied countries were attacked, the other signatory states would join forces to defend the country under attack.

However, since the US had not participated in this alliance, it seemed unlikely that these countries would be able to defend themselves, if and when they were attacked. As a result, the North Atlantic Treaty Organization (NATO) was created on 4 April 1949 with US leadership. A month later, the Council of Europe was formed on 5 May 1949 by the same countries that had signed the Brussels Treaty along with other European countries, namely Denmark, Ireland, Italy, Norway and Sweden. Turkey was not among the signatories of either NATO or the Council of Europe. This exclusion, felt bitterly in Turkey, initiated intensive Turkish efforts to become a member state and came to a successful resolution two months later when Turkey, Greece and Iceland were invited to join the Council of Europe in Strasbourg.

This invitation, though bringing Turkey a step closer to the West, did not change the fact that it has been excluded from NATO, the main security apparatus of the then emerging Western Alliance system. Due to the security concerns discussed above, Turkey applied for NATO membership in May 1950 and argued that the security of the Mediterranean region would be incomplete without the inclusion of both Turkey and Greece. This argument, though substantial, was not the main instrument that carried Turkey to NATO membership. Rather, the participation of Turkey in the Korean War alongside western forces persuaded both the Europeans and, more importantly, the US to open the doors to Turkey's NATO membership, which then became the cornerstone of Turkey's security and foreign policies, as well as its connection to Europe.

However, NATO membership, though important, was not the sole Turkish connection with 'western civilization'. During the Cold War, close ties with the US were created while at the same time, membership in the European Community appeared as an extremely reasonable option for Turkey. As a result, Turkey signed the Ankara Agreement with the then European Economic Community in 1964, becoming an associate member and beginning a long process expected to lead to full membership. Even though almost nothing went according to plan, Turkey filed its application to the European Commission in April 1987 for full European Community membership. However, due to a range of issues, the Turkish application was rejected two years later, in 1989.[3]

Turkey and Europe in the Post Cold War Era

With the collapse of the Soviet Union, a new era emerged in international affairs, which affected Turkey as much as, if not more, than it has affected the European Union and the US. It has been argued, 'perhaps no other country outside the former Soviet block has seen its strategic position more radically transformed by the end of the Cold War than Turkey'.[4] The disintegration of the Communist Bloc, among other consequences, added a new dimension to the relations between Turkey and the EU. At the same time, the existence of NATO, the anchor of Turkey's western vocation, was also being questioned as a result of the end of the Cold War, which brought such a security organization into the limelight as a cumbersome institution and a no longer needed anachronism.

Until 1990, Turkish foreign policy and the country's relations with Europe were highly influenced by the ups and downs of its domestic politics. The frequent coups d'état caused tension between the EU and Turkey but did not lead to serious damage to the established relations. The realization of the Customs Union was, however, delayed due to domestic factors. The frequent changes between weak coalition governments and European reactions to frequent military interventions, together with a weak economy, have caused delays in realizing the necessary customs reductions. However, even during the periods of domestic turmoil, Turkey did not loosen its ties with the EU, showing a clear preference for a larger relationship with Europe that carried into the post Cold War era.

After the retreat of communism in central and eastern Europe, the EU gave increasing importance to this region while Turkey was relegated to a second-class position. Thus, Turkey had to adjust its foreign policy *vis-à-vis* the European Union, as this new status left Turkey in a political limbo while continuing instability beyond its immediate borders caused further concern, as Europe, increasingly feeling more secure, started to question the validity of NATO. Even though EU members wanted to control the former eastern block countries and bring them under the single European domain, these former eastern European states needed to be restructured both economically and socially, as they had been under communist rule since 1947. As a result, in order to facilitate this transformation and the further integration of these countries into west European structures, a democratization program was adopted in 1992, which came to be known as the Copenhagen Criteria.[5]

The European Union believed that the implementation of the Copenhagen Criteria would also be necessary for Turkey, as Turkey had experienced three coups d'tat since 1960 and therefore needed particularly to be included in the democratization process. This inclusion, in turn, resulted in disappointment on the Turkish side since relations with the EU had long predated the creation of the Copenhagen Criteria. Furthermore, Turkey found it degrading to be perceived on the same level with the former Eastern Bloc countries that had long been under communist rule, whereas Turkey had been experiencing democracy since 1923. Nonetheless, Turkey eventually was forced to accept the new criteria for EU membership. Accordingly, it formulated a new policy aiming to fulfill the criteria in order to become a full member of the EU within a reasonable time period. Turkey was initially convinced that the fulfillment of these criteria would have brought full membership and this played a significant role in the somewhat hasty acceptance of the Copenhagen Criteria by the government in Ankara.

However, the Luxembourg Summit of December 1997 led to a major alteration in Turkish policy towards the European Union. During the Summit, Turkey was excluded from the list of countries that were announced as official candidates, which would join the EU within a clearly set timetable, prompting Turkey to question the sincerity of the EU as to whether it would be allowed to become a full member, even if it fully complied with the Copenhagen Criteria. The dominant feeling in Turkey was that it would not be allowed into the EU, and that the EU would create further obstacles should Turkey successfully implement all the conditions, based on some elusive reasons, mainly under the rubric of so-called 'cultural differences'.

In other words, 'Turkey's rejection by the EU [in the Luxembourg Summit] raised the question of whether Europe, despite its frequent reassurances, saw Muslim Turkey as truly European and, if not, whether Turks could consider themselves as such'.[6] Although the border between who is European and who is not is difficult to determine, and makes little difference when socio-political and economic development or the security system is concerned, in European perceptions, it goes deeper.

> What is involved here is more than just the name and the commitment in the EC's founding treaty to 'an ever closer union among the peoples of Europe'. Article O of the Maastricht Treaty specifies that it is 'European' states that may become members of the Union. (...) With Turkey, things are more complicated because its claim of belonging to Europe cannot so easily be dismissed due to history, geographical position, prior international agreements and the way these are conceptualized in the public debate. (...) One way out of this dilemma is to promote the model of Turkey – like Russia, Japan and Israel – as a 'Westernic' state which can never be purely Western or European by definition.[7]

Perceived as such by the Europeans, this exclusion led to huge disappointment in Turkey, whose progressive elite has prided itself as being 'European' for years. As a result, the Turkish government took the December 14 decisions, just after the termination of the Luxembourg Summit, that the economic relations with EU members were to be maintained, but political relations were brought to a standstill. In fact, the former Prime Minister and the then State Minister responsible for European Affairs, Mesut Yılmaz, made it clear that although Turkey would continue to move towards full membership in the EU, it would not accept the conditions laid down at the time by the EU. Thus, 'political dialogue will be vastly reduced. Turkey will not discuss matters like human rights, Cyprus and relations with Greece with the EU as a whole, but only on a one-to-one basis with other EU member countries should the situation arise. In line with this decision, the Customs Agreement to boost bilateral trade between Turkey and the EU will not be developed to [its] previously planned potential levels'.[8]

The Luxembourg Summit was a major loss of prestige for the EU in the eyes of the Turkish public, politicians and intelligentsia as almost all scholars perceived the EU as the road to westernization and thus such a disappointment weakened their belief in the sincerity of the EU. Despite strong longstanding relations with the EU, the search for emerging alternatives was obvious within the Turkish academic world.[9]

The anti-EU perception during this period came to focus on the negative results of the Customs Union, and affected the views of Turkish politicians. Moreover, the emergence of the lack of trust towards the EU was also the result of the popular realization that because the negotiations with the EU had not gravitated towards any kind of improvement, (once again) Turkey had become the last country to be taken into consideration on the list. The Turkish people, for their part, perceive relations with the EU on a more superficial basis and are manipulated easily by the media and the level of tension that is reflected in daily publications. Furthermore, the Turkish intelligentsia, which traditionally chose to focus on both the positive and negative aspects of EU membership, lost its homogeneous pro-EU attitude. •

Two years after the Luxembourg Summit a surprising alteration occurred in Turkish-EU relations, even though nothing had changed either in Turkey or its position *vis-à-vis* membership. In 1999, the Helsinki Summit officially announced the recognition of Turkish candidacy for EU membership. This put Turkey on an equal footing with other candidate countries and in the short term, dissolved the tension with the EU. However, the Helsinki Presidency Conclusions were still not in complete agreement with Turkish views, especially with regards to the Cyprus issue.[10] A 2004 deadline was stated in the Conclusions to solve the Cyprus problem, before the island was to be admitted to the Union. The candidacy also resurrected the Copenhagen Criteria, making them more prominent as now Turkey had taken a step closer to the Union.

Almost a year later, on 8 November 2000, the 'Accession Partnership' document for Turkey was published by the European Commission, spelling out in detail the necessary improvements in political and economic criteria, including compliance with EU law.[11] Even though the Accession Partnerships are not legally binding, candidate countries are required to fulfill these conditions by placing them in their 'National Programs', which are open to the EU's evaluation. Though its preparation caused controversy within the country in regards to regarding thorny issues such as national sovereignty and minority rights, Turkey published its 'National Program' on 19 March 2001, including the aspects stated in the 'Accession Partnership', thereby putting Turkey once again on the road to EU membership.[12]

Creation of the ESDP and Turkey

While the establishment of the European Security and Defense Policy (ESDP) does not date back to the founding treaty of the European Union (Treaty of Rome), it is the result of the EU members' desire, following the Cold War, to be a global power and move beyond the limits of economic influence, hence the necessity to have common foreign and security policies. The first step taken in this direction was the Single European Act in 1987, followed by the Maastricht Treaty in 1992. Another meeting in the same year, held in Petersberg, Bonn, brought the 'Petersberg Tasks' to the agenda.[13] The next major step was taken at the NATO Summit of January 1994, where NATO gave 'its full support for the development of the European Security and Defense Identity' and expressed the member countries readiness and willingness to make Alliance assets and capabilities available for Western European Union (WEU) operations.[14] Turkey consented to these announcements as an associate member of the WEU, but could not have foreseen what was to follow.

The EU Amsterdam Agreement, signed in 1997, confirmed that the Petersberg tasks were incorporated into the EU Treaty and that the integration of the WEU into the EU was a possibility. One year later, in 1998, as a conclusion of the Anglo-French Summit in St. Malo, the decision was taken to create a capacity to act 'autonomously' with a military power to support this mobility. The crises in both Bosnia and Kosovo accelerated the discussions on the need for a European defense capability. Following the St. Malo Summit, a decision to integrate the

WEU into the EU was taken in 1999 at the Köln Summit, bringing Turkey into the limelight as it was the only non-EU member of the now defunct WEU.

Another significant EU summit took place in December of the same year, in Helsinki, which considered the creation of a Rapid Reaction Force (RRF). According to the 'Headline Goal' adopted during the Summit, Europe should develop the ability to deploy a corps-size ground force of 60,000 men within 60 days and should be able to sustain it for one year.[15] Following the Summit, the Nice Agreement was signed, in 2000, relating to decisions concerning the non-EU European countries such as Turkey. Consequently, the Nice Summit became a watershed for entrenching and the enlargement of the European Union. During this Summit, decisions were taken concerning the institutional structure of the Union and how it would function after the enlargement. Although all member countries favored the creation of the ESDP, they also differed over the details primarily according to their diverse historical backgrounds and perceptions of international relations.

Diverging Views on the ESDP

Among EU members, Germany has been at the forefront of articulating the need for a fully integrated, supranational security system, though earlier, during the initial post-Cold War era, France had championed the idea of a more vigorous European security policy. While France continues to desire the creation of the ESDP, independent from NATO, the enthusiasm of Germany in wanting to create a supranational European security system is not shared by the French government. Accordingly, Germany comprehends further integration as an ultimate necessity for the future of the European Union, while France still chooses to preserve certain areas under the control of the nation state, among which the European security system would hold an important place. Britain, on the other hand, a close ally of the US, is skeptical about both the ESDP and the ability of European states to sustain their security without US participation. It perceives security cooperation within Europe as necessary, but opposes sidelining NATO and has been reluctant towards full integration into the EU.

On the other side of the Atlantic, the formation of NATO after the Second World War signaled US dominance in Western Europe and overall in western security issues. The role of NATO remained clear until the dissolution of the Warsaw Pact and the fall of the Soviet Union in 1991, but became confused, following the removal of the threat against which it had been established. The US, however, has continued to emphasize the necessity of NATO even after the Cold War, and this has led to the enlargement of the organization, through its embrace of former communist central European countries. At the same time, the US believes that EU should establish a parallel security system, which would be capable of dealing with conflicts closer to its borders. This approach has led to calls for burden sharing by the US' allies while not surrendering its domination in Europe.[16]

However, the picture is different when seen from the European perspective. Even though many European states wish to establish their own military force, they also favor a strong reduction in defense expenditures,[17] although at present, Europe lacks significant military equipment, such as troop transport planes and ships. Furthermore, there is an increased need for intelligence gathering services, which the EU plans to dovetail with similar NATO operations and capabilities for the benefit of the RRF, which is planned to be operational by 2003. The contradicting situation inherent in the desire to create an RRF while simultaneously reducing military expenditures, can be explained by the different approaches within the EU. The above picture justifies US concerns about military expenditures and demonstrates clearly the reasoning of the US intention to help create a European security system. However, this does not imply that the US approves of a completely independent ESDP. America believes that European security should be built, within and under the control of NATO, and at this point, the American and Turkish approaches coincide.

Turkish Views on ESDP

Turkey's relations with the EU, as outlined above, have always been complicated and filled with obstacles. However, the problems surrounding ESDP have proven particularly intractable in recent years as, in the eyes of Turkish public and decision makers, it threatens Turkey's connection with the western alliance system without creating a satisfactory alternative, thus fundamentally jeopardizing its national security. Generally stated, the dilemma arises from earlier settlements in the area of European security, which date back to Turkey's relations with the WEU and NATO. More specifically, the bottom line of the problem between the EU and Turkey lies in the decision-making process. Turkey, as a member of NATO and an EU candidate country, desires to take part as well in the decision making process within the ESDP framework from which it has thus far be excluded by the EU. To fully understand the demands of both parties, it is first necessary to comprehend how the new security system will function.

Institutional Framework

As stated earlier, the EU decided during the Helsinki Summit to achieve the 'headline goal' of an RRF by 2003. As Turkey was accepted as a candidate country at the same summit, there was no open criticism of this decision within Turkey. However, the Feira and Nice Summits, which both took place in the following year, made considerable steps towards the institutionalization of the European security system, and have altered the initial acquiescence of Turkey.

The Feira Summit of June 2000 saw discussions about the situation of the non-EU members of NATO (Turkey, Czech Republic, Hungary, Poland, Norway and Iceland – also known as 'the six'), in the proposed security system. Among them, Turkey, with its constant opposition to and blockage of the use of NATO assets by the EU, stood out and created an uncomfortable atmosphere among the EU members wishing to advance the RRF. During the Summit, it was decided that both NATO's non-EU members, and the non-NATO EU candidate countries should be placed within the European security structure, so that they could participate in the necessary dialogue. Besides the inclusion of possible actors, the type of military operations and their procedures were discussed during the Summit, according to which, military operations could be conducted in Europe in three ways: 1) as a NATO-led operation, 2) by European powers using NATO assets, and 3) as an EU-only operation.[18] The first kind of operation presented itself throughout the Bosnia-Herzegovina and Kosovo crises, during which Europe lost prestige for not being able to intervene effectively in crises situations. The second operational type is the thorniest and caused the main rift between Turkish and European representatives, due to a Turkish veto. Finally, the third option is possible when NATO chooses not to be engaged. The way that an EU-only operation would be conducted in the third option is set in six stages, with an 'autonomous capacity to decide' for the EU. First, if a potential crisis situation arises, political consultations with all partners involved will be stepped up and they (15+6) will be engaged in 'deep consultations'. Second, in a crisis situation, the Political and Security Committee (PSC) would ask the EU Military Committee (MC) to issue an Initiating Directive to the Director General of the EU Military Staff (EUMS) to draw up and present strategic military options. Third, the EU MC would evaluate the strategic military options developed by the EUMS and forward them to the PSC together with its evaluation and military advice. Fourth, with a view to launching an operation, the PSC sends the Council a recommendation based on the opinions of the MC in accordance with the usual Council preparation procedures. On that basis, the Council decides on the preferred strategic option and decides to launch the operation within the framework of a joint action ('the autonomous capacity to decide'). Fifth, on the basis of the military option selected by the Council, the EUMC authorizes an Initial Planning Directive for the Operation Commander. Finally, the Operation Commander prepares the Concept of Operations and drafts an Operation Plan. These are evaluated by the MS, then sent on to the EUMC, which provides advice and recommendations to the PSC.[19]

It is this six-stage approach that has created the most tension between Turkey and the EU due to the clear separation of the decision-making and decision-shaping stages. In other words, the stages of Turkish inclusion and exclusion are predetermined under the EU-only operation option. This has brought about Turkish criticism and opposition. The first three stages are considered as 'decision-shaping' phases; the fourth as the decision-making phase, which is also the essential part of the framework for Turkey, while the last two phases explain the planning of the actual operation.

Turkey has raised two main objections: the first is that Turkey does not want to loose the rights acquired due to its membership to the now defunct WEU, (which will be discussed below in detail); the second objection is linked closely to the 1999 NATO Washington Summit. During this Summit, an important thesis was put forward for the smooth functioning of the proposed European security structure. The concept of 'separable but not separate NATO assets and capabilities' for the WEU-led operations was formulated during this Summit, and the non-EU countries were assured of timely involvement in decision making.

The situation has changed, however, since the integration of the WEU into the EU structure. Although earlier decisions concerning the rules of engagement for the WEU operations were taken in consultation with, and agreed upon by, NATO, including the non-EU member countries. The dilemma now arises whenever the EU wants to use NATO assets in the framework of the ESDP independently from non-EU NATO countries with its 'autonomous capacity to decide'. The WEU, while it existed as a separate organization, formed 'a bridge between NATO and the EU', which helped them to 'get around the different memberships of NATO and the EU. Its flexible nature allowed for a creative mix of *full members*, *associate members* – such as Turkey – and *observers*. This allowed [these countries] to make real progress on many thorny issues'.[20] However, this bridge was removed with the WEU integration into the EU, forcing the 'thorny issues' to emerge in their full capacity to destroy both Turkish-EU understanding and also one of the fundamental bases of Turkey's western connection.

It was stated earlier that the ESDP would be built on the existing mechanisms. Consequently, Turkey has argued that the rights granted during its WEU associate membership and the decisions taken at the Washington 1999 NATO Summit cannot be terminated by the creation of a new system. Thus, Turkey has expressed a desire to be a part of the decision-making process within the ESDP. The EU, however, has so far not agreed to this interpretation, arguing that the decision making system within the EU does not allow non-EU countries to participate in the process, though non-EU countries (meaning Turkey) can participate and have an impact during the various stages of the decision-making process and through extensive consultation mechanisms. Obviously, these mechanisms do not imply an automatic impact on, or blockage of, any unfavorable decision from the viewpoint of a non-EU member state, such as Turkey, such that could prevent the implementation of the decisions taken by the EU.

Turkey from the WEU to the ESDP

The WEU was established in 1954 by the six founding members of the EC, along with the UK. Later the number of members rose to ten when Portugal (1990), Spain (1990) and Greece (1995) joined the WEU.[21] In 1992, Turkey joined as an associate member, along with Norway, Poland, the Czech Republic, Hungary, and Iceland. The Associate Membership of Turkey in the WEU differed highly from its Associate Membership to the EU. In contrast to the EU, the WEU had granted various rights to all its associate members.

According to the minutes agreed in connection with the document on Associate Membership, signed on 20 November 1992, it was stated that:

> (...) associate members will take part on the same basis as full members in WEU military operations to which they commit forces. The reference to commitment of forces may cover the provision of logistical and other facilities of a significant nature. If associate members participate in WEU military operations deriving from decisions taken by member States, the arrangements for the conduct of these operations will be established on a case-by-case basis by the participating States.[22]

There are six points explaining what the 1992 statement implies in practice:

> First, both observers and associate members could participate in Council meetings unless a majority of the full members decided otherwise. Second, associate members could participate in all working groups apart from the Security Committee. Third, associate members Turkey and Norway and Denmark as an observer could participate in Working Groups resulting from the transfer of former EUROGROUP activities of 13 European allies. Fourth, associate members could appoint officers to the Planning Cell. Fifth, associate members could participate on the same basis as full members in WEU operations. Finally, associate members had full rights and responsibilities in WEU armament activities.[23]

Having enjoyed the opportunities of the WEU, Turkey found itself in a different position with the integration of the WEU into the EU, where these abilities were limited in three ways. First, Turkey would be able to participate in just three Council meetings per Presidency, only one being at the Ministerial level in the framework of the ESDP. Second, Turkey would have to wait for an invitation, without assurance, to take part in all committees and discussions. Again, an invitation would be necessary to participate in the operations organized under the ESDP. Finally, the decision-making structures vary greatly between the WEU and the ESDP. The new framework requires unanimity in taking a decision. This troubles Turkey since it is likely that certain countries, such as Greece, would block Turkish interests.

The EU, on the other hand, perceives this matter from a different standpoint. During the Nice Summit in 2000, Turkey was not excluded from the European defense system according to the EU, as Europe offered Turkey to be part of the *decision-shaping* stage instead of being an actor in the *decision-making* process. However, from the Turkish perspective, this was not viewed as an inclusion since it was excluded from the decision-making stages, and prompted accusations that the EU was not being loyal to the already accepted international criteria.

In the case of Turkey and other non-EU NATO allies, 'the guiding principle of inclusiveness was put aside by the EU and the decisions adopted [during the Cologne, Feira, Helsinki and Nice Summits] fell well short of properly addressing this vital question'.[24] The reason for Turkey's exclusion from the decision-making process was stated clearly: Turkey was not an EU member and decisions within the EU could only be taken by full members of the Union. However, this explanation did not satisfy Turkey since the location of most of the likely crisis spots where the EU would take action, surrounded Turkey. Thus, an ability to influence the decision-making process in the new European security structure is of crucial importance for Turkey. This perceived difference between the approach of the EU and that of Turkey led to a deadlock in Turkish-EU relations. After having been excluded from the decision-making stage, Turkey saw the European desire to use NATO assets for the RRF as a major trump card. In reaction to being barred from the developing ESDP, Turkey commenced blocking the road for the development of a European security system.

The determined reaction of Turkey both surprised and angered those in the European Union calling for the ESDP. Despite the strong objections of the EU, however, Turkey believes that the European Union wishes to build its own security structure based on the current European capabilities of the Atlantic Alliance and thereby gradually replace NATO. Accordingly, it has clearly stated that 'the accession model cannot be accepted by Turkey before it takes [its] place in the decision-making mechanism. The EU wishes to attain more powers beyond those achieved by the Western European Union without making any sacrifices', and thus is not acceptable to Turkey.[25]

The reaction of the Turkish government is understandable when one glances briefly at the former experiences of Turkey with the European Union. The road to full EU membership seems to have been blocked from the beginning, and Turkey has paid a high price for the setbacks and delays. A striking example is the Customs Union in which Turkey is not a part of the decision-making process. Unlike other candidate countries, Turkey has participated in the Customs Union without becoming a full member, thus leaving the decision-making authority with the EU, a situation that has resulted in extensive losses of revenue for the country. Turkey, having learned from former mistakes, appears no longer willing to be party to structure in which decisions are taken without its influence.

Although the question of the 'satisfaction' of other non-EU European NATO members could be raised, at the moment, only Turkey among 'the six' seems to be disturbed by the WEU turnover to the EU. This difference emerges from the unique military and political position of Turkey *vis-à-vis* Europe. Poland, the Czech Republic and Hungary joined NATO in 1998 and will most likely join the EU in 2004. For this reason, they already feel a part of the ESDP since their compliance with the necessary criteria is underway. As for Norway, the situation is slightly different, though similar to Iceland. Strategically, neither Norway nor Iceland is faced with a considerable threat, consequently, being a NATO member and taking place only in the *decision-shaping* stages seem presently sufficient for both countries. At the same time, after twice rejecting full EU membership, the Norwegian people have signaled marginal support for the EU they envisage.

On the other hand, the picture is totally different for Turkey. The strategic position of Turkey is almost enough to explain why Turkey is insistent on taking place in the *decision-making* procedure. In fact, 13 of the 16 major spots that NATO has listed as likely crises areas in the post-Cold War era, are within the immediate vicinity of Turkey. Besides this, Turkey is also not happy with the fact that the EU and its new members from eastern Europe, who did not contribute to the build up of NATO assets, would use these NATO abilities and assets, while Turkey sacrificed to develop these assets during the Cold War. Thus, Turkey continues to oppose the denial of Turkish involvement in the emerging European security structure, which would almost certainly place Turkey in an insecure environment.

Concluding Remarks: Turkey During The Belgian Presidency

The ESDP was a highly discussed issue during the Presidency of France between June-December 2000, which led to the Nice Agreement where the partial take over of the WEU was formalized. Over the following six months, under the Swedish Presidency, the European Security system was also discussed and the 'Presidency Report on European Security and Defense Policy' was published, underlining the necessity for cooperation with non-EU European NATO member countries.[26] The EU Presidency was handed over to Belgium on 1 July 2001, when Belgium stated that security issues would be dealt with on the same level as during the Swedish Presidency.[27] This was interpreted to mean that the enhancement of civilian conflict prevention capacities of the EU would remain a priority. However, this approach soon had a new dimension with the importance that Belgium accorded to European security issues. Even before taking up the Presidency, the Belgian Foreign Minister stated that crisis management should also be an aspect of ESDP that needs to be dealt with during the term of the Belgian Presidency.[28]

Belgium, being in favor of further integration within the EU, believes in deeper cooperation among the member countries for the establishment of a stronger and more integrated European security architecture. This determination naturally had led to tension between Turkey and the EU. The Belgian Foreign Minister Louis Michel, has clearly stated; 'We cannot accept the Turkish veto. A country, that is not a member of the European Union, should not prevent European Union member states from proceeding within this area'.[29] This understanding demonstrates the approach of both Belgium and the European Union, since Belgium holds the Presidency until the end of 2001. Turkey, however, does not seem willing to terminate the right to use the veto just because the EU is not fond of it. One hopes that there will be a realistic solution, satisfactory for both sides that will end this impasse.

The Turkish veto in NATO, on the other hand, causes turmoil in other aspects of Turkey-EU relations, as well as within the transatlantic connection. The situation cannot simply be isolated within the EU-Turkish dimension as it also affects US-Turkish and US-EU relations, as well as the cohesion of the entire Western Alliance. The US, as stated earlier, aims at the development of a European security system under the control of NATO. America, while criticizing the Turkish use of its veto to a certain extent, has also tried to convince the EU to make an acceptable offer to Turkey. An acceptable offer for Turkey at the moment, on the other hand, would only be an offer to take part in the *decision-making* process, and this is not acceptable for the EU. An optimistic solution would, perhaps, be to provide a partial *decision-making* right that would include the crises points around Turkey. However, even for these spots, the EU is only willing to offer participation in the *decision-shaping* and *consultation* stages, not in *decision-making*. This is a position that will only lead to further deadlock.

The EU, with its existing military capacity, is not capable of forming either a European army which could compete with NATO, or an RRF that has the ability to function on its own. The lack of military capacity in terms of intelligence and military units causes the creation of an RRF to be unrealistic in the near future, most assuredly the 2003 projection. Under the Belgian Presidency, however, the aim is to formally declare the RRF as operational at the December 2001 Laeken Summit. This implies the construction of an institutional framework that lacks a military structure. At this point, cooperation with Turkey in military terms would enable the EU to be stronger and less dependent on NATO, while conducting conflict prevention and crisis management operations with relative ease. Furthermore, the feeling of exclusion from the EU felt by Turkey would also weaken if a strong cooperation in the area of security were realized. Closer relations with Turkey on security issues could also hold the key to Turkish admission to the EU as a full member in the near future, and would enhance the developments needed to comply with the EU standards in all areas. However, neither seems likely in the current impasse.

Notes

1 Nelson, B.F. and Stubb, A.C-G. (eds.), (1998), *The European Union*, 2nd Edn, Lynne Rienner Publishers, London, p. 3.

2 Ibid., p. 4.

3 The various reasons were the result of both domestic and international politics. Turkish internal instability and the fall of the Berlin Wall created the main obstacles for Turkish membership. Additionally, a weak economy, high inflation rates and the deficit in democracy led to the Turkish rejection. Moreover, the EC, after the collapse of the Soviet Union, has showed a certain preference to return its 'long lost cousins' in Eastern Europe to the European family over accepting a former 'other', (i.e., Turkey with is 'different' culture).

4 Mortimer, E. (1993), 'Active in a New World Rule', in *Turkey, Europe's Rising Star: The Opportunities in Anglo-Turkish Relations*, published for the Turkish Embassy, by Lowe Bell, London, p. 44.

5 The Copenhagen Criteria is composed of three titles; political criteria, economic criteria and *acquis communautaire*. The political criteria is briefly consist of democratization and respect to human rights. The economic criterion is based on creating a functioning economy that is able to compete with the liberal market economy. Finally, the *acquis communautaire* implies the necessity of compliance with the European law in all areas, i.e. agriculture, energy, free movement of labor, environment etc.

6 'Turkey: If Neither West Nor East, Then What?' (1999), *Strategic Survey 1997/98*, Oxford University Press for IISS, London, p. 133.

7 Buzan B. and Diaz T. (1999, Spring), 'The European Union and Turkey', *Survival*, vol. 41, no. 1, p. 49.

8 For Yılmaz's statement, see Web Page of the General Directorate of Press and Information, http://www.byegm.gov.tr/yayinlarimiz/chr/ing97/12/97X12X15.htm, 15 December 1997.

9 The works of Erol Manisalı and Suat İlhan can be regarded as examples of rising non-EU thought within the country.

10 See Helsinki European Council, 10-11 December 1999, *Presidency Conclusions*, Article 12 at http://europa.eu.int/council/off/conclu/dec99/dec99_en.htm.

11 For the full text of the Accession partnership document look at http://europa.eu.int/comm/enlargement/dwn/ap_11_00/ap_turk_en.doc.

12 The most controversial issue in the Accession Partnership was the articles about the right to use a language other than Turkish in the education system. Turkey, in the National Program, stated that the official language was Turkish and that other languages could be used on daily basis provided that they did not harm the democracy and the unity of the nation-state. For the full text of the Turkish National Program, see: http://www.abgs.gov.tr.

13 The Petersberg Tasks can be classified as follows: humanitarian and rescue tasks; peacekeeping tasks; and tasks of combat forces in crisis management, including peacemaking.

14 The WEU was created in 1954, as a successor to the Brussels Treaty, signed after the Second World War in order to create a common defence system to protect Europe from possible Soviet attack. However, since the United States was not involved in the system, it lacked credibility. The WEU was formed as an international organization, composed by the countries of the Brussels Treaty powers (The Benelux countries, and the UK) and of Germany and Italy. Turkey joined in 1992 as an Associate Member.

15 See 'ESDP: From St. Malo to Nice', *Euro-Forum*, vol. 2, no. 9, Center for Strategic and International Studies, Washington, USA, December 18, 2000; at http://www.csis.org/europe/euroforum/v2n9.htm.

16 There are two main reasons for calls to burden sharing with the Europeans. The first is based on financial concerns: The US believes that the cost of overseas defense is high and Europe should participate in military expenditures; the second reason is the complexity that the US faces in its domestic politics. The US government has difficulty in explaining to its own public, the reasons why American soldiers have to fight overseas. For further analysis of the issue, see Hulsman, J.S. (2000, June/July), 'The Guns of Brussels', *Policy Review*, no. 101, pp. 35-50; Serfaty, S., 'The US-European Relationship: Opportunities and Challanges', *Congressional Testimony*, April 25, 2001 at http://www.csis.org/hill/ts010425serfarty.htm; and text of the speech by Donald H. Rumsfeld at *Munich Conference on European Security Policy*, Munich, Germany, 3 February 2001, at http://www.defenselink.mil/speeches/2001/ s20010203-secdef.html.

17 According to a research carried out by the International Institute of Strategic Studies (IISS), European defense spending has been falling 5 per cent a year. See http://www.euobserver.com/index.phtml?selected_topic=9&action=view&article_id=2346.

18 For the conclusions of the Summit, see:http://www.euractiv.com/cgi-bin/eurb/cgint.exe/58742-973?1100=1&204&OIDN=250058&-home=search.

19 See:http://www.euractiv.com/cgi-bin/eurb/cgint.exe/58742-973?1100=1&204&OIDN=250058&-home=search.

20 Robertson, Lord G. (2001, January/March), 'Turkey and the European Security and Defence Identity', *Insight Turkey*, vol. 3 (1), p. 45.

21 In 1992, Ireland, Finland and Denmark joined the WEU as observers and were followed by Sweden and Austria in 1995. In 1994, Bulgaria, Estonia, Latvia, Lithuania, Romania and Slovakia joined the WEU as associate partners and were followed by Slovenia in 1996.

22 For the full text of the Minutes, see http://www.weu.int/eng/comm/92-rome-a.htm.

23 http://www.euractiv.com/cgi-bin/eurb/cgint.exe/58742-973?1100=1&204&OIDN=250058&-home=search.

24 Öymen, O. (2001, January/March), 'Turkey and Its Role in European Security and Defence', *Insight Turkey*, vol. 3 (1), p. 55.

25 For the statement of the Head of the Turkish General Staff on the emerging ESDP see http://www.byegm.gov.tr/yayinlarimiz/chr/ing2001/08/01x08x13.HTM#1, 13 August 2001.

26 Riggle, S. (2000, December 18), 'EU Officially Adopts Military Tasks: A Summary of the Nice Conclusions', *Briefing Paper*, Center for European Security and Disarmament (CESD).

27 See *Priorities Note*, The Belgian Presidency of the European Union, 1 July–31 December 2001 at the Web Page of the Belgian Foreign Ministry.

28 Cited in Pauwels, N. (2001, April), 'Belgian Presidency Risks Sidelining Conflict Prevention', *European Security Review*, no. 5, Centre for European Security and Disarmament (CESD) and International Security Information Service (ISIS), Brussels.

29 See:http://www.euobserver.com/index.phtml?selected_topic=none&action=view&article_id=3159, 15 August 2001.

Chapter 5

Perceptions and Images in Turkish (Ottoman)-European Relations

Nuri Yurdusev

Of all the issues in Turco-European relations from the disputes between Turkey and Greece, through the Turkish guest workers and migrants mainly scattered in Germany, France, Netherlands, Belgium and Austria to disagreements on European security and defense policies, the identity question is perhaps the most perplexing and deep-rooted one. This was so for the Muslim Ottoman Empire and Christian Europe, and it is still the case between a secular Turkey and post-Christian Europe. It is generally and widely assumed, though not explicitly stated in official circles, that Turkey and European countries have not only different but also irreconcilable identities, that between Turkey and Europe, there is an incompatibility of values. Turks and the Europeans do not share a common culture or civilization, and thus, Turkey is not a European country. It is therefore concluded that this is the reason why it was difficult for imperial Turkey to enter into the European states system in the past, and for republican Turkey to become a member of the European Union at present.

This chapter slightly disagrees with these commonplace arguments. First, it takes the view that the gap between European identity and Turkish identity, however it is understood, is not as wide as it is commonly assumed. Second, the question of identity is not the only determinant in Turco-European relations. Regarding the identity question, what is significant is not the difference of identity, but mutual positioning and the understanding of identities. As to the determinants of Turco-European relations, *raison d'état* has been as ready affirmation but is rather a policy of managing the other. Europeans and Turks have historically tried to manage each other. Among others, one reason for this policy of management is the fact that Turkey has been one of the most influential 'others' in the European identity formation, a fact that may, from time to time, lead to negation or hate of Turkey by the Europeans or vice versa, but never to indifference. Europeans and Turks cannot simply ignore each other. This chapter deals mainly with the European perception of the Turks as the other, the role of Turkey in the making of the modern European identity and the policy of managing the other.[1]

In Europe but not of Europe

Thomas Naff observed that 'for half a millennium, from the 14th century until the 19th, the Ottoman Empire occupied, controlled, and administered one-quarter to one-third of the European continent. ... The logical conclusion ought to be that the Ottoman Empire was, empirically, a European state. The paradox is that it was not. Even though a significant portion of the Empire was based in Europe, it cannot be said to have been of Europe'.[2] This paradox, 'being in Europe but not of Europe', may be taken as the characteristic feature of Turco-European relations from the very beginning to the present day. In the 1790s the question is said to have been raised in the British parliament as to whether Turkey was within the European balance of power system or outside it. In some respects, she was considered to be within the balance-system because of her traditional alliance with France.[3]

More recently, on 4 March 1997 to be precise, six center-right leaders (of Belgium, Germany, Ireland, Italy, Luxembourg and Spain), at the meeting of European Union of Christian Democrats in Brussels, were reported to have agreed to intensify the efforts to create a special relationship with Turkey built around the existing Customs Union. However, they agreed unanimously that Turkey's human rights record, its size, and implicitly, the Islamic strain in its society made it impossible for the European Union to contemplate admitting the country into the European Union. Mr. Wim van Welzen, President of the European Union of Christian Democrats, said that the EU had cultural, humanitarian and Christian values different from Turkey's.[4] While the European Christian Democrats approve the place of Turkey in Europe under the framework of the existing Customs Union agreement, they cannot even contemplate Turkey entering into the European Union and so becoming part of Europe. The reason why Turkey cannot be a European country can, for the Christian Democrats, be found in different cultural values of which religion constitutes an essential part. In sum, they (the Europeans and the Turks) have irreconcilable identities. Perhaps, the Christian Democrats simply publicly declared what many Europeans implicitly or explicitly believe.

In fact, another official spokesman had earlier raised such questions and doubts. On 15 January 1997, Hans van Mierlo, the then Dutch Minister for Foreign Affairs, delivered a speech to the European Parliament on behalf of the Dutch presidency of the EU. In his speech, Mr. van Mierlo said that he understood Turkey's frustration over the issue of the full membership. Then he stated that it was 'time to be honest' and admit that the problem was also one of admitting a large Muslim country into the European Union. 'Do we wish this to happen?', van Mierlo asked, adding that no one had posed this problem officially before.[5] In contrast to the Christian Democrats and Mr. van Mierlo, the EU contemplated admitting Turkey, 'the large Muslim country', into the European Union confirming her candidate status at the EU leaders' Helsinki Summit of 10-11 December 1999. The European Council in Helsinki declared that 'Turkey is a candidate State destined to join the Union on the basis of the same criteria [Copenhagen Criteria] as applied to the other candidate States'.[6] Yet we shall have to wait and see how this confirmation will influence the case of being in Europe but not of Europe.

Naff's observation with regard to the Ottoman Empire was shared in the debates at the British Parliament in the 1790s. The Ottoman Empire was considered within the European balance system in some respects. In other words, Turkey was not fully part of the European balance. With the Paris Peace Treaty of 1856, the Ottoman Empire was admitted into the Concert of Europe, the then European Union. Nevertheless, both the provisions of this Treaty and the legitimacy of the Ottoman entry into the Concert of Europe and thus her Europeanness, have frequently been subject to discussion.[7] Republican Turkey, officially negating the imperial past had adopted a clear Western orientation and introduced swift secular reforms. For the Turkish elite and policy-makers achieving the integration with the West (Europe) has been a long-standing goal. Despite this, the questions and doubts about the European character of Turkey are still raised in many European quarters as seen from the above statements of the Christian Democrats. Although Turkey's full membership of the EU appears to have been accepted by the EU leaders with the Helsinki European Council, it cannot be said that the debates about the Europeanness of Turkey have come to an end.

The state of being in Europe, but not of Europe, may be seen both from the European and Turkish sides. On the one side, the Europeans do not deny the place or significance of Turkey in/for Europe, even if they do not usually consider her as European. First and foremost, Turkey has been in Europe from the very beginning. The Europeans now and then have always found themselves together with the Turks. Indeed, Turkey has been in Europe in terms of physical occupation as observed by Naff. Turkey was and is in Europe, not just by its physical presence but also as a result of its human presence. Turkey was, and is, in Europe as an actor and element that had/has to be taken into consideration when Europe-wide policies need(ed) to be designed. Turkey is again in Europe at present, as her economy is largely integrated into Europe and her membership of various political organizations of European origin such as NATO, the Council of Europe, the OESC, Association Agreement and Customs Union with the EC/EU. Turkey today is in Europe with the Turkish community living in various European countries as guest workers or migrants numbering now about 3.5 millions, larger than the total population of some countries in Europe. The cultural differences may hinder it for Turkey to be accepted as European, but they, however, cannot prevent her from being in Europe.

On the other hand, Turkey does not just want to be in Europe, but of Europe as well. She claims to be a European country and aspires for the full EU membership. This desire and aspiration have been expressed on every occasion for the last hundred and fifty years. On 19 April 1855, Ali Pasha, the then Foreign Minister expressed this aspiration, to enter into the Concert of Europe, in a drafted treaty article for a possible peace treaty to end the Crimean War as follows: 'The Contracting Powers, wishing to demonstrate the importance they attach to assuring that the Ottoman Empire participate in the advantages of the concert established by public law among the different European States, declare that they henceforth consider that empire as an integral part of the concert and engage themselves to respect its territorial integrity and its independence as an essential condition of the general balance of power'.[8] Davidson rightly detects four basic aspects of Ottoman policy that Ali Pasha put in this statement: a) specification of the importance of Ottoman independence and integrity; b) an observance by the contracting (great) powers of those rights; c) acknowledgment that the Empire was a member of the Concert of Europe; and d) acknowledgment that the Empire was essential to the European balance of power. The Treaty of Paris of 1856 comprised three of those proposals except the last.[9]

What is striking about these proposals is that Ali Pasha explicitly stated the Ottoman desire for entering into the Concert of Europe, and with the consequent treaty the Empire did, in effect, become a member of the Concert system. One may argue that the Ottoman Empire had something of a European character long before she became a member of the Concert of Europe, despite the official rhetoric of being an Islamic state. From Mohammed II onwards, the Ottoman Sultans considered themselves as *Sultan-ı İklimi Rum* (Emperor of Rome). When the German Emperor visited Istanbul in November 1889, Sultan Abdulhamid II met Emperor William not just as Caliph of Islam, but also as a European sovereign.[10]

Just as Ali Pasha had expressed that the Ottoman Turkey shared the public law and system of Europe, the policy makers of Republican Turkey have always declared that Turkey shares the Western (European) ideals, and wants to be a member of the European institutions. In 1989, Turgut Özal, then Prime Minister, boldly said that Turkey's relations with the West could not be reduced to a military alliance and her strategic location. More than this, Turkey shared Western ideals. Similarly, the then Minister for Foreign Affairs, Mesut Yılmaz argued that Turkey should be a member of the European community just as she was a member of the other institutions of the West.[11]

From Ali Pasha to contemporary Turkish statesmen, it has been persistently claimed that Turkey was and is a European state, though she was, and is not, considered as such by the Europeans. On one hand, we have Europeans always recognizing that Turkey is in Europe, but not approving of her as European. On the other hand, we have Turkey publicly declaring itself to be a European state, but not advancing policies to comply with the criteria for being European. The paradox of being in Europe but not of Europe then goes on. This paradox may result from different values as Mr. van Welzem declared; or from the 'two equally formidable bulwarks of religious ideology and culture – one Christian, the other Muslim, both reinforced by ignorance, prejudice, and hostility', as argued by Naff;[12] or from a 'Turkish inadequacy' to comply with European standards, as most Europeans see it; or even from 'European double standards' in dealing with Turkey, as most of the Turks understand it. One reason is the identity formation of Europe and the mutual positioning of Turkey *vis-à-vis* Europe. Turkey and thus, Turkish identity has historically been the perfect 'other' for the Europeans through which the European identity has been affirmed. But first, there needs to be a few remarks on identity and collective identification.

Collective Identity and Identification Process

As a working criterion, I adopt the view that a collective/social identity can be defined, first by common 'objective' elements shared by certain people, such as language, common descent, history, customs, institutions, religion, myths, symbols, style ... etc.; and, secondly, by the 'subjective' self-identification of people concerned, meaning that people are conscious of their commonalities and that they consciously identify themselves with the said collectivity.[13]

A collective social identity begins to appear when the members of the said collectivity internalize the objective elements. The socialization process which a human infant goes through in every society largely carries out the internalization of the elements of a collective identity. The fact that a human infant internalizes many of the values and elements of the society to which s/he is born accounts for the continuity of the said collective identity. This, however, by no means implies that the internalization, and thus the identification process, is confined to the period of human infancy. It is an ongoing and permanent process.

The salient feature of the collective identity in question may be formed according to the emphasis on, or priority of, a particular element. The element of religion, for instance, was emphasized in 'Europe' throughout the medieval period so that Europe and the Europeans were basically regarded as equal to Christendom and Christians. 'Christian' remained as a significant defining epithet for Europeans until well into the late eighteenth century.[14] Nationality and 'civilization' or 'being civilized' in the modern period have replaced the saliency of religion in European identity.[15] Today, the 'Copenhagen criteria' or more properly, the 'Copenhagen political criteria' seem to be the determining element of being European.[16]

Similarly, the salient features of nationality also change according to where the stress is laid. When territory and mutual rights and obligations are prioritized in the account of national identity, we speak of civic nationality and when the common descent and language are prioritized then it is ethnic nationality.[17]

The process of the internalization of the objective elements shared by the members of a collectivity leads us to the subjective elements of a collective identity. To speak of a collective social identity, besides shared characteristics, the members of the collectivity should have some sort of subjective consciousness of belonging to the collectivity. In other words, we need to see if human beings identify themselves with a social entity that we consider as a unit of identity. Apparently, this is an empirical question. However, it must be stated that the distinction between 'objective' elements and 'subjective' identification, put as a working definition, does not mean that the two processes are independent of each other. The very existence of 'objective' common elements indeed reveals that there is a self-identification of human beings with each other, and consequently with all the others sharing the same elements or characteristics. If people have nothing in common, how could they be expected to identify with each other? The question is not only whether there is an identity consciousness, but how cohesive or how strong it is. The question of degree is, in turn, something that depends upon the specific units of identity and historical conditions.

It is a commonplace view that the existence of an external threat is an enhancing factor of identity consciousness. The existence or perception of a common external threat tends to make the members of a collectivity unite, and thus may result in a rise in the awareness of their common identity. It is also natural to expect that the cohesion of a collective identity unit increases if the members of the said collectivity consider it good for themselves. It can then rightly be asserted that, besides the provision of security in the face of external threat, identity consciousness is also evoked if the collectivity in question is beneficent towards (would be) members.[18]

The existence of the 'other', or difference, is not just an ingredient in the formation of the subjective consciousness of identity but it is constitutive of both the objective elements and subjective elements. This is where we come to have a closer look at the role of the 'other'.

Identity Formation and the 'Other'

Years ago, Levi-Strauss stressed that there was a twin relationship between the self and the other. With Derrida, we can now say that every identity exists together with its difference; there can be no collective social identification without its own 'difference' or 'other'.[19] Identity and difference exist in all units of identity. For any unit of identity and identification process, there is a need for the other. This can be shown both logically and historically.

Logically, because to identify something means to differentiate it, and similarly to identify yourself with some group, requires that you to distance yourself from another. However, families with which no identification has been made do exist. If families with which a particular person does not establish identification did not exist, then, there would be no need for identification with one particular family. Similarly, someone who is, for instance, a Turk is also the one who is not English or French or Greek. If all nations other than Turks would disappear then there would be no need for one to identify himself with the Turkish nation. The Turk exists because the English exists. Any identification therefore requires a distinction.

That all forms of identity involve some sort of difference may be expressed the other way round: All difference involves identity and any distinction necessitates some identification. If nothing is identified, then no distinction can be achieved and vice versa. The identity of something depends upon the existence of something else. The need for the other or difference in defining identity thus comes as a logical condition.

Furthermore, the existence of the other/difference in the collective identity formation is not just a logical necessity, but also it appears to be a historical fact. Historically, we see that the identities of all societies have been defined through their difference from other societies. In the identification process, differences from others have sometimes been more defining than the commonly shared characteristics. Thucydides tells us that the Hellenes are identified through their difference from the Persians. According to Thucydides, before the Trojan War there was no identification of being 'Helles' or 'Hellenes' in Greece. Homer did not call them by the name of 'Hellenes'. He did not even use the term barbarian, probably because the Hellenes had not yet been marked off from the rest of the world by one distinctive appellation.[20] Similarly, the English and French mutually determined each other. It has been a generally agreed view that in the formation of the English and French national identities, the Hundred Years War was one of the most significant factors. It was this continuous conflict, Trevelyan wrote, which supplied England with 'strong national self-consciousness; great memories and traditions; a belief in the island qualities'.[21] As will be shown, the Ottoman power in the East had been a prominent factor in the shaping of the modern European identity.[22]

The role of the other in identity formation may be followed through the names of identity units. The units of identity are usually named by others or named upon the encounter with the others. As already seen, this is what happened in the case of the 'Hellenes'. The same goes for the 'English.' The word 'English' is not English, but Latin. The people called 'English' were not named by the English themselves, they were named by the Romans (Latins). Similarly, the root work of the word 'Turk' is not Turkish but comes from Chinese. The Finns were named by the Swedish and the Kurds were named by the Turks. There is no need to extend these examples. The existence of the other seems to be a requirement for the definition of identity. Through the existence of external groups, a group is differentiated and identified, and when external groups are perceived as a threat, it is highly likely that the distinction increases, and the group identification is enhanced.

Consequently, how the other is perceived is rather important in identity formation, and in the relations of different collectivities or groups. The other may be seen solely as a difference, unit of identity or collectivity in question 'familiar'. That is to say, the other may be seen as a 'stranger'. This other may be seen as a threatening force, and this does not make some elements of the identity unit simply familiar, but 'valuable, right and good'. In this case, the other may be regarded as a 'barbarian', and the identity is formed largely in negative terms, and through exclusion. This by no means implies the view that identity is only defined by the other, and in negative terms.

Nevertheless, by treating the other in negative terms, and negating them, one, in fact, makes one's' identity affirmative and positive without ever describing oneself. Moreover, self-definition does not necessarily require the negation of others. It may be done through differentiation or distinction as well. Identification is both an exclusive and inclusive process. In sum, identity is defined in both negative and positive terms. Yet, history and experience provide us with more negative examples. The Turks *vis-à-vis* Europeans presents one such example.

The Turk as the Other of Europe

It has been pointed out that more than any other empire since the early period of Arab conquests and expansion, 'The Ottoman Turks struck terror into the hearts of

Christian Europe, so that the Elizabethan historian of the Turks, Richard Knolles, described them as 'the present terror of the world'. Again, it has been noted that 'of all the negatives known to Europe, the nearest, the most obvious and the most threatening has been the Islamic Near East, represented from the fourteenth century onwards by the menace of the Ottoman Empire'.[23] These quotations rightly tell us that the Ottoman Empire has been the most significant and determining external force in the making of the modern European identity. They may also be taken as an indication that Europe did not derive its identity from itself, and European identity has largely been shaped through its others.

The modern European identity has been formed, argues Delanty, in the encounters with other civilizations, and in a set of global contrasts the terms of which were defined by Europe in the age of imperialism. The culturally and politically shared European characteristics have been far from providing the basis for an enduring European identity[24] Indeed, throughout its history, there have always been different others for Europe such as Islam in the medieval period, the Ottomans, Indians, Russians and Americans in the modern period. We cannot just dismiss the 'objective elements' of European identity such as the Graeco-Roman and Judeo-Christian inheritance, the Barbarian or Germanic invasions, the Medieval past as expressed in the Carolingian unity, Latin language, the Renaissance and the Reformation, secularization and the Enlightenment, emergence of the nation-states and the overseas expansion and so on. However, in the making and shaping of the modern European identity, given the fragmentation into and confrontation and antagonism between the emerging nation states, the existence and construction of others have been functional more than what we would normally assume for the general identification process. As already pointed out, the Turk constituted Europe's most significant other.[25]

It is no wonder that the Turk has been the most influential of all the others for Europe in the modern period. From its emergence as a power in the fourteenth century, the Ottoman Empire expanded at the expense of Europe. It occupied, controlled and administered one-quarter to one-third of the European continent from the fourteenth century to the nineteenth century. The modern European states system is said to have emerged from the fifteenth century onwards and the Ottoman Empire was in Europe when the European system began to come into being.[26] Even though the significant portion of the Empire was based in Europe, as noted by Naff, it was not considered to have been of Europe. In fact, the Turk has not been considered as being of Europe at all for it has rather been the major threat to Europe, or has been perceived as such. The Turk was, to use the present expression, 'otherized', and was described in negative terms so that the European identity could be affirmed. Despite the physical existence of the Empire in Europe, the religious divide has been the basic factor behind the negative perception of the Ottomans. For the Europeans, Islam was an error and Muslims were not trustworthy. While Martin Luther regarded Islam as a 'movement of violence in the service of the anti-Christ' which is 'closed to reason', Voltaire portrayed Mohammed as a 'theocratic tyrant'. Ernest Rennan dismissed Islam as incompatible with science, and Muslims as 'incapable of learning anything, or of opening himself to a new idea'.[27] Such characterizations were extended in the representations of the Turk.

Indeed, the Turk was predominantly portrayed in pejorative terms. Turks were the terror of the world for Richard Knolles, and incapable of feeling friendship for a Christian according to Paul Rycaut.[28] According to Rousseau, Turks were the barbarians who conquered the civilized Arabs.[29] Burke told the House of Commons that the Turks were 'worse than savages' and that 'any Christian Power was to be preferred to these destructive savages.'[30] When classifying the humanity in three categories of the civilized, the barbarian and the savage, James Lorimer defined two groups of the progressive and non-progressive under the savage. Of the Turks, he said that they did not even belong to the progressive races of humanity.[31] In the view of Sir Elliot, the Turks have been a destructive force; they destroyed a great deal and constructed nothing.[32] There is no need to extend the examples.[33] With all these characterizations and representations, the Turks have been used to serve for the affirmation of the Europeans. The Turk then was the 'perfect barbarian' for the Europeans in order to affirm the civilization of Europe. The Turk, thus, has played a significant role in the making of the modern European identity.

The Making of Modern Europe and the Turk

The role of the Turk in the formation of the modern European identity has largely been a means of affirmation through negative representations. Modern European identity was defined as opposed to the Turkish threat. The first appearance of the word 'European' is said to be in the letter written by Pope Pius II to Mohammed II, where the Pope used it interchangeably with Christian.[34] From this date onwards, European unity and European identity were frequently evoked in the face of the Turkish threat.

Yet in the formation of the modern European identity, the conception of the Turk as the negative other, though dominant, does not represent the whole picture. One can speak of the Turkish contribution towards the making of the modern Europe. We may, for example, follow the role of the Ottomans in the making of Europe through specific circumstances and developments. As I have already stated, the Ottomans were, from the beginning, in Europe. They were in Europe, not just in terms of being occupant, but in terms of being a part of the emerging European states system. The Ottoman Empire was functional in the formation and maintenance of the European balance system through which the emerging sovereign states in Europe survived. Centuries before Ali Pasha asked, in 1855, for the recognition of the Empire as essential to the working of the European balance, the Empire was influential both in the formation and continuance of the balance system in Europe.

Even during the first stage of the Italian Wars from 1494 onwards, the Ottoman Empire was an important actor in the Italian system. The Italian courts maintained diplomatic relations with the Ottoman Sultan. When the so-called Second Holy League was signed in 1495 with an almost Europe-wide participation, not just by the Italian states, Mattingly tells us, the Turkish Ambassador was an observer in the signing ceremony. The New League is said to have transformed the Italian system into a European one.[35] The Ottomans later became an active party in the second stage of the Italian Wars and, for a moment, the balance was lost in favor of the Sultan.[36] Just as the Ottoman engagement in the rivalries among the Italian states, in the Italian Wars led to a pan-European gathering with the Second Holy League, it can rightly be said that the struggle between the Ottomans and the Hapsburgs throughout the sixteenth century linked the two European systems, the Southern system centered in Italy and the Northern system that comprised Sweden, Poland-Lithuania and Muscovy.[37]

From the mid-15th century, the Ottoman Empire became an active participant in the European balance of power system. The Sultans pursued a conscious policy of balance, *vis-à-vis* the European powers, so that the rise of nation states was, to a certain degree, facilitated. According to Dehio, the Ottoman Empire became a counter weight to the unifying tendency represented by Charles V. The introduction of Turkey into the European balance of power system, and European diplomacy, played a most significant part in preserving the freedom of the system of states.[38] In 1532, Francis I admitted to the Venetian Ambassador that he saw, in the Ottoman Empire, the only force guaranteeing the continued existence of the states of Europe against Charles V. Indeed, in 1536, we see that this guarantee was, in some sense, given with the attempt for a Franco-Turkish Treaty which is said to have later provided the Europeans with a model in their relations with the Asian empires, in terms of unequal treaties. The role of the Ottoman Empire, in preserving the European balance and thus, nation states, can be seen to continue later in the support and encouragement given to the English and Dutch in the period after 1580 when these nations proved to be the champions of European resistance to the Habsburg's attempts at hegemony. In the sixteenth and seventeenth centuries, support for Protestants and Calvinists was one of the fundamental principles of Ottoman policy in Europe. In fact, the Ottoman pressure on the Hapsburgs was an important factor in the spread of Protestantism in Europe and the Westphalian formulation allowing the co-existence of the multiple sovereign states, became possible through this pressure on the Hapsburgs.[39]

The Ottoman Empire also pursued the balance policy in its trade relations with the Europeans, notably in terms of the Capitulations. In order to prevent the dominance of one state in the Levant trade, they always favored the rival nations. Against Venetian dominance in the fifteenth century, they supported first the Genoese, then the Ragusans, and then the Florentines. In the sixteenth century, the French took the lead and then, in the seventeenth century they supported the English and the Dutch.[40] In short, the Ottoman Empire was a significant force in the European balance of power system from the fifteenth century to well into the end of the seventeenth century, and thus played an important role in the preservation of that balance and consequently, in the rise of nation states.

That the Ottoman Empire was in, and essential to, the European balance system was recognized by both its contemporaries and scholars. As already noted, in the early sixteenth century, Francis I admitted that the Ottoman Empire was the only force to prevent the emerging states of Europe from being transformed into a

Europe-wide empire by Charles V, and in the late sixteenth century, Queen Elizabeth opened relations with the Ottoman Empire. One of the motives of the Queen was certainly the expansion of trade. However, a secondary motive was the idea that the Sultan could balance the Hapsburgs in the East and consequently relieve Spanish pressure on her. Elizabeth I even stressed that Protestantism and Islam were equally hostile to 'idolatry' (Catholicism). In granting Capitulations to the English and the Dutch, the Sultan considered that these nations were champions in the struggle against the idolaters.[41] In the late eighteenth century, as I have already stated, the place of the Ottomans in the European balance of power was acknowledged by the British Parliament. Similarly, it has been reported that Catherine the Great of Russia explicitly recognized this fact,[42] and scholars, too, considered the Ottoman Empire within the European balance system from the Renaissance onwards.[43]

The Ottomans did not only influence the emergence of the modern system of European sovereign states through holding the balance. Somewhat paradoxically, it also gave the Europeans a sense of unity, in the face of the possibility of fragmentation, as a result of dynastic and religious wars. The existence of the Ottoman power is said to have been one of the factors in the continuation of medieval universalism. According to Kohn, the expulsion of the Turks from Central Europe and the extinction of the Spanish Hapsburgs, the last dreamers of a Christian world empire, at the end of the 17th century marked the definite end of medieval universalism.[44] It remains a historical coincidence that the so-called Turkish threat was effectively rebuked with the Treaty of Karlowitz in 1699, and the usage of the term *Respublica Christiana* ceased in the European diplomatic treaties after the Treaties of Utrecht of 1713, just 14 years after the Treaty of Karlowitz. The Ottomans supplied a strong justification for calls for the European unity and indeed, almost all writers on international relations, until the French revolutionary wars, based their claim for European unity on the idea of a common front against the Ottoman Empire.[45]

The role of the Ottoman Empire in the making of the modern Europe can also be found in the European overseas expansion that constitutes one of the major factors in the rise of Europe to a central place in the world. We could say that Europeans were blocked in the East by the Muslims represented in the formidable power of the Ottomans and that the Ottoman stranglehold on the Levant ruined the Venetian trade. Moreover, the Ottoman navy was dominant in the Mediterranean until the second half of the 16th century and that consequently, the principal gateway to the East and its riches was closed. As a result, Europeans were forced to try ocean routes.[46]

To sum up, the Turk, as the most significant other of Europe, has been influential and instrumental in the formation of the modern European identity. I have shown that the Ottoman Empire, being the most significant other of Europe, was the most effective force in the making of modern Europe in various ways. It was not simply a powerful 'external' force, or an unacceptable occupant in Europe against which the Europeans were able to form a sense of unity. The Empire participated from the very beginning in European politics, not just in terms of balances of power, but also in terms of the establishment of alliances and guarantees. And in these, there was the use of the same rhetoric used between the English Queen and the Sultan.

The Sublime Porte exchanged envoys and ambassadors with the European courts, and was, in fact, the only non-European court accepting or having European resident ambassadors by the 19th century. Indeed, it sent temporary envoys to the European courts frequently for long periods until the end of the 18th century when it began to reciprocate resident ambassadors. The Porte and the European states furthermore shared and worked on some common rules and institutions such as diplomacy, conferences, treaties, most notably, the Capitulations. This is by no means a denial of the cultural divide between the Europeans and the Ottomans. As is well known, in its later centuries, the Empire was considered 'the sick man of Europe'. It was not just a 'sick man'; it was 'the sick man of Europe'. We are then justified to assert that the Ottoman Empire may well be considered as being of Europe to a certain degree.

The Turk, as the other of Europe, has been influenced by Europe in the formation of its own identity. As I have already said, the Ottoman sultans considered themselves the Emperors of the Rome. From the 18th century onwards, in response to the decline in military strength, Turkish statesmen embarked upon a policy of modernization and westernization which is, one could rightly say, still going on. From the mid-19th century onwards, they were European sovereigns. In this process, the West, or Europe, was used in defining modern Turkish identity. With the modernization project culminating in the Republican reforms, Turkey defined itself as part of the 'civilized world', the civilized world being represented first and foremost by Europe. Moreover, the majority of the Republican elite rejected the imperial past.

Nevertheless, the past remains as it was and history still hinges on Turkey and Turco-European relations. In some quarters, Turkey is still considered the other of Europe. In the run up to Austrian membership in the EU, the Austrian Foreign Ministry used the argument that they, for centuries, had protected Europe from being overrun by the Turks.[47] Turkey and the Turks also continue to constitute the principal other of the contemporary Greek national identity. Scholars and preachers, from the Archbishop of Canterbury and Richard Knolles in the late 16th and early 17th centuries through Burke, Lorimer and Elliot in the late 18th and 19th centuries, to the present Christian Democrat politicians, have consistently made the case for the Turkish peril. Yet, the 'most Christian King' and the 'Great Queen' in the 16th century, English and Dutch diplomats at the Karlowitz in the late 17th century, the British Parliament in the late 18th century, Anglo-French politicians in the 19th century, and contemporary European statesmen have consistently formed channels of friendly relations with Turkey such as alliances, exchanges, treaties and organizations. This can only be because Turkey is in Europe and to some extent, of Europe. The Europeans cannot and do not, just brush Turkey.aside. They simply cannot consider her not of Europe. Likewise the Turks, no matter how suspicious of Europeans they have been, and are with policies of the Europeans, Turks cannot simply turn their back to the EU and go their own way. No matter how much they doubt the intentions, both sides are so interwoven *vis-à-vis* each other, and their identity formation so historically comprised of a process of mutual otherness, that the result can only be, as already stated, a policy of managing the other.

Legacy of the Past or the Policy of Managing the Other

Ever since the 'Eastern Question' was formulated, from the late 18th century on, the Turks have suspected that Europeans wanted to destroy the unity and integrity of the Turk's state and people. Paradoxically, one remedy for this suspicion has been the Turkish attempt to be part of Europe. Most of the 19th century Europeans did not think that Turkey was a European country. However, due to the principle of *raison d'état,* Turkey was admitted into the Concert of Europe and with this, they managed Turkey for the time being. On the other hand, Turkey, in the face of the Russian threat, introduced reforms, and thus claimed to be a European state, this being the way Turkey managed Europe.

The picture and the strategy have not significantly changed today. Republican Turkey quickly introduced modernization reforms. In Turkish intellectual discourse, during the Republican period, the concepts modernization, secularization, Westernization and Europeanization have been understood interchangeably and used as such. As a complementary policy to its internal reforms, in its external relations, the Republican policy-makers have been very keen on being a member of international organizations in the West or Europe. Despite the ideological negation of the imperial past, this was indeed a continuation of the policy adopted by the late Ottoman statesmen. The only difference is perhaps the fact that it took place at a more accelerated pace. Turkey, as part of this orientation, adopted laws and political institutions based on a European style, and became a member of organizations like NATO, the OECD, the Council of Europe, and the OSCE. In 1963, she signed an Association Agreement with the then European community with a view for future membership, a view that has yet to be realized.

The Europeans, for their part, seemed to have welcomed the European orientation of Turkey and did not hesitate to include Turkey in those European institutions. Of course, the bipolar structure of the international system in the 20th century, and the consequent ideological confrontation of the Cold War years, made European statesmen adopt a policy in line with the principle of *raison d'état* rather than the politics of identity. In spite of Turkey's flirtation with the Soviet Union during the inter-war years, Britain and France guaranteed the integrity of Turkey in 1939, and after World War II, as already stated, Europeans did not exclude Turkey from their international organizations and institutions. The politics of identity did not come on the scene until the late 1970s, or so it seemed during the Cold War years.

Nevertheless, the issue of identity has never faded away. For the Turkish administrative and intellectual elite, all this was a confirmation of Turkey's modern/European identity. It has been an escape from the imperial past, the 'other' of the Republican identity. For Europeans, too, the issue of identity has always been in the background. However, it surfaced in the late 1970s and early 1980s when the Cold War began to lose its grip on international politics. In a newspaper article in April 1990, when Edward Mortimer reviewed contemporary European perceptions of Islam and Turkey, he found them to be echoing the early European writers cited above. 'Educated Turks especially,' noted Mortimer, 'heirs to the militant secularism of Kemal Atatürk, are shocked to find their European identity judged by religious criteria ... for good or ill, the Christian legacy remains a key component of European identity. That is bound to affect the argument over where Europe's border should be drawn, and its relations with Muslim communities, both inside that border and beyond.'[48] The old suspicions between the Europeans and the Turks have re-emerged.

On the one hand, unlike the early homogeneity of the Republican elite, widely heterogeneous elite of the Kemalists, nationalists, leftists, liberals, and pro-Islamists have appeared in Turkey. For the Kemalists and the nationalists from the Right to the Left, the contemporary European policy of 'support' for the Kurdish people is the reminiscence of the Eastern Question and the Sévres Treaty of 1920. For the Islamists, the European's support from the rights of the Kurdish and leftist dissidents, but disregarding the Islamists, is no different from the 19th century Europeans intervening on behalf of the non-Muslim minorities of the Empire. As the homogeneity of the early Republican elite has disappeared, elite opinion on Europe as the cradle of civilization, and the ultimate destination of Turkey is no longer held in a uniform manner. Though the latest opinion polls show that more than two-thirds of the Turkish people are in favor of the EU membership, the established elite seems to have strong reservations.

On the other hand, freed from Cold War necessities, and faced with their natural brethren in Central and East Europe, Europeans have begun to openly question the Europeanness of Turkey, 'a large Muslim country'. Not only the 'Christian legacy', but also the historical legacy of the Turk as the principal other of Europe remains. Europeans are no longer worried about Turkish troops as they are not likely to appear on the outskirts of Vienna but they are quite concerned with the three and a half million Turks living in Europe, and about the 65 million of the Turks in Turkey who have a higher population growth than the European average. Survey after survey of the Eurobarometer shows that the majority of the European public is against Turkey's membership in the EU. Both Europeans and Turks, thus, have mutual suspicions and reservations, yet they cannot simply turn their back on each other due to the logic of culture and the logic of *raison d'état*. Once again, the result is a policy management.

The policy of managing the other is best observed in relations between Turkey and the EC/EU. On 14 April 1987, Turkey presented its application for membership to the European Community. The European Commission put off the decision on the Turkish application until 18 December 1989, more than two and a half years later. The Commission concluded that 'it would not be useful to open accession negotiations with Turkey straight away'. The Commission gave both economic and political reasons, and also noted 'the negative effects' of the disputes between Greece and Turkey and 'the situation in Cyprus'. In its opinion of 1989, the Commission concluded that it would not be useful to open accession negotiations straight away. Some twelve years later, in its 2001 Regular Report on

Turkey's Progress towards Accession published on 13 November 2001, the Commission still concludes that it is not useful to open accession negotiations with Turkey straight away. Furthermore, the reasons are not much different from those give in 1989.

Of course, the EU countries are not to blame for this result as Turkey has not yet fulfilled her commitments and, most notable, the Copenhagen Criteria is said to have not yet been met by Turkey. Yet, it also shows the management policy of the EU as they cannot simply say 'No' to Turkey for well-known reasons. Morocco had applied for membership in the Community a year before Turkey, and the opinion of the Commission, on this application came shortly after. Rabat was simply told that the Community was open only to Europeans. Though both Turkey and Morocco were Muslim countries, the latter was easily turned down because neither the logic of culture and identity nor the logic of *raison d'état* deeply penetrated the relations between modern Europe and Morocco, as is the case between Europeans and the Turks. Europeans cannot be indifferent to Turkey, even though they cannot take her in 'straight away'. They then have to manage it.

In the Luxembourg European Council, December 1997, Turkey was not declared to be a 'candidate country' because of the lack of civilian democracy, and respect for, and protection of, human rights by European standards. Two years later, in December 1999, the Helsinki European Council declared Turkey as a candidate country. What had happened from the Luxembourg Council to Helsinki Council, in terms of those objections advanced at Luxembourg? The Progress Reports of 1998 and 1999,before the Helsinki Council, are full of examples showing how far Turkey is away from satisfying the concerns voiced at the Luxembourg Council. In the 1999 Report, for example, it was clearly expressed that: 'Generally speaking, since the last report, the situation concerning civil and political rights in Turkey has not evolved significantly ... Moreover, certain administrative measures taken in the aftermath of the Öcalan affair show a more restrictive attitude by the Turkish authorities as regards freedom of expression.' Based upon this report, the EU Council in Helsinki extended candidate status to Turkey. In an interview with a Turkish journal, the EU Ambassador to Turkey, Karen Fogg said that no significant improvement had taken place in Turkey in terms of democracy, rule of law and the human rights, except, perhaps, the rather symbolic removal of the judges of military origins from the State Security Courts.[49] In addition, only one-third of European public opinion was in favor of Turkey's EU membership according to results of a Eurobarometer survey in July 1999. Further, from 1997 to 1999 no significant reforms were realized in Turkey, and the majority of the European public was against the accession of Turkey. In the light of this, it could be wondered why the EU designated Turkey as a candidate in Helsinki.

The reason can be found in the EU's policy of managing Turkey. Europeans realized that the Luxembourg formula was not an adequate way to manage Turkey as the formula suspended the political dialogue between the EU and Turkey. A new formula was therefore needed to manage Turkey, and that was the Helsinki formulation. Speaking to the Turkish press, the French Minister for Foreign Affairs, Hubert Vedrine, who is said to have been decisive in the formulating of the Helsinki summit conclusions recognizing Turkey as a candidate, explicitly stated the policy of management. According to Mr. Vedrine, Europeans had two concerns in the Helsinki process: the fact that Turkey was still far away from fulfilling the Copenhagen criteria and secondly, that there was a lack of trust for Turkish policy-makers to make the necessary reforms. However, 'the Europeans finally realized that it would not be possible to find any solution if they remained firm on those two points. It was admitted that a dynamic process would come out by recognizing the candidate status ... Due to those unresolved questions, many countries were against Turkey being a candidate. We told them that those questions could be resolved later. We must start by extending candidate status to Turkey.[50] Indeed, in Helsinki, as expressed by Mr. Vedrine, Turkey was declared to be a candidate country as a result of the search for a new formulation for managing Turkey.

A close look at the Progress Reports of the EU on Turkey since 1998 to 2001 reveals the language and thus the policy of managing Turkey. In those reports, it is repeatedly said that Turkey has not yet met the Copenhagen political criteria. One of the persistent themes of the reports is the lack of effective civilian control over the military, and the latter's frequent intervention in political affairs. The 1998 Report noted that the military was not under civilian control, and that it was too involved in Turkish politics. The Report gave the following examples:

- the significant role played by the Chief of the General Staff in the Prime Minister's Crisis Management Center within the Secretariat General of the National Security Council;
- the fact that the Chief of the General Staff is not normally responsible to the Minister of Defense;
- the fact that the Turkish constitution, via the National Security Council, allows the army to play a civilian role, and to intervene in every area of political life;
- that public criticism of the armed forces may lead to criminal charges being pressed;
- the frequent warnings by the Army to the government in the framework of the National Security Council;
- the upholding of secularism by the Army against certain branches of Islam; and,
- the regular exclusion from the ranks of the Army, persons deemed to be involved in activities incompatible with secularism.

In the 2000 Report, it was again stressed that the military was not under civilian control, and several examples were again given: Contrary to the EU, NATO and the OSCE standards, instead of being answerable to the Defense Minister, the Chief of the General Staff is still accountable to the Prime Minister. The Council of Higher Education and the Higher Education Supervisory Board include one member selected by the Chief of General Staff. The National Security Council continues to strongly influence the political process, and in practice, seriously limits the role played by the Government. There also seems to be too little accountability to Parliament with regard to defense and security matters. Despite all these criticisms, the Accession Partnership Document, adopted by the European Council on 8 March 2001, simply required that the National Security Council be aligned as an advisory body in accordance with EU practice. No details about the civilian control of the Army were given in this document. Unlike previous reports, the Accession Partnership document seems to have been prepared so as not to offend Turkey, revealing the continued strategy of management.

The policy of managing Turkey as regards the issue of the civilian control of the Army is also reflected in the 2001 Regular Report on Turkey, the latest to date. The 2001 Regular Report praises the Constitutional Amendments, adopted by the Turkish Parliament in October 2001. Among them, it cites the 'strengthening of civilian authority' without giving any detail, but alluding to the increase in the number of the civilian members of the National Security Council. The same report later relates that there has been little sign of increased civilian control over the military. Again, the language of the policy of management is reflected.

Considering that Turkey has not yet met the Copenhagen political criteria, one of the contemporary benchmarks of European identity, that it has not been relieved of the historical legacy, clearly Europeans continue to see Turkey in Europe but not of Europe. It is this situation which leads to a policy management by both sides. The adoption of specific documents peculiar to Turkey by the EU can be taken as another example of management. Turkey remains the only country with a Customs Union Agreement with the EU without having become a member. In December 1997, the Luxembourg European Council denied Turkey candidate status, but it drew up 'a European Strategy for Turkey'. Contrary to the Turkish expectation at the start of the 'Screening Process', as with all the other candidate countries, the EU, in its Strategy Paper 2001, suggested a process of 'detailed scrutiny', an instrument never heard of before, and apparently, specifically developed for Turkey.

The policy of management is also seen on the part of Turkey. Since her application for membership in the EC/EU, Turkey has not made progress in terms of the Copenhagen political criteria. She has been criticized for human rights violations, not just in the EU reports but also in the reports of the Amnesty International and the Human Rights Watch Group. In addition, the balance between the Civilian government and the Army has swung in favor of the latter in the 1990s. The military has increasingly infiltrated the domain of the civilian government. After the so-called 'Soft Coup' of 28 February 1997, Heath W. Lowry, who has not been known for his critical views of the official policies of Turkey, observed that the frequent interventions of the military in political life have led in the late 1990s 'to a *de facto* dual-track government, in which many of the nation's real policy objectives are being generated by the NSC … while the duly elected parliamentary government is limited in these areas to implementing decisions generated by the NSC in its monthly meetings. …Real civilian authority in Turkey, in the areas of policy considered crucial by the military, has been curtailed. The TGS via the NSC, not the Turkish Parliament, has become the primary architect of major elements of Turkish foreign and domestic policy, and the elected politicians were to a great extent reduced to the role of apparatchiks who assisted in implementing the decisions generated in the monthly NSC meetings. Between the State (*Devlet*) and the elected government (*Hükümet*), the balance has clearly swung in favor of the *Devlet*'.[51] Despite those criticisms coming from the EU, and the increasing militarization of the civilian political life, the issue of the civilian control of the military has not been addressed in the Turkish National Program for the Adoption of the *Acquis*, adopted by the Government on 19 March 2001. The Accession Partnership has simply spoken of the alignment of the NSC as an advisory body to conform to the European practice. The Turkish National Program does not even refer to it.

The policy of management is also reflected in the National Program. For example, it begins with a strong confirmation of Turkey's European orientation but it does not address the Accession Partnership in detail. The civilian control of military is, as stated, altogether absent from the document. In the Accession Partnership, issues regarding the Cyprus question and Greece are treated under 'Political Criteria'; the National program includes them in the 'Introduction'. Unlike the Accession Partnership, the National Program does not mention the free usage of 'mother tongue' by all Turkish citizens and the right to television broadcasting in their mother tongue. With such lapses and escape clauses, Turkey tries to manage the EU in its National Program for the Adoption of the *Acquis*.

One can observe that in order to manage each other, both the European and the Turkish policy-makers make use of other countries. For years, some European states like Germany made use of persistent Greek objections, as a way of easy management of Turkey. Similarly, Turkish policy-makers have made use of the so-called 'threat of fundamentalist Islam coming to power in Turkey' as a leverage in their argument for Turkey's membership of the EU. The former Prime Minister Mrs. Tansu Çiller told a journalist from *Time* in the run up to the Customs Union Agreement that a failure by the European Parliament to adopt this would allow the Islamicist Welfare Party to come to power. According to Mrs. Çiller, such a development would not only tip Turkey towards the Middle East and away from Europe, but would also allow the Iranian model to gain currency in view of the millions of Turkish speaking peoples of Central Asia.[52] Recently, Mesut Yılmaz has also used the same argument in the German press, saying that the failure by the EU to take Turkey in would only strengthen the two pro-Islamist parties in Turkey. By echoing the historical 'other' of Europe, the Turkish secular politicians actually try to manage the EU.

Conclusion

Europeans and Turks have been in close contact with, and related to, each other throughout the modern period when both of them formed their identities. The modern European identity has been formed on the basis of, among others, a perception of the Turk as one of the most significant others. The 'otherization' of the Turk can be observed on various levels. One can see it, on the European level, from the beginning of the modern period until the 20th century, as shown in those European union proposals from the beginning of the 17th century, and from the writings and debates of the policy-makers. It can also be observed, on the national level, in the case of the Greeks and some contemporary Balkan nations.

The modern Turkish identity has also been formed as a result of the impact of modern Europe. The perception of Europe as some kind of 'other' has affected the process of Turkish identity formation. In the early centuries of the modern period, during the heydays of the Empire, Europe was considered to be the other through which the Turkish/Ottoman identity was differentiated and affirmed. From the late 18th century onwards, the perception of Europe assumed a 'positive' element in the definition of a modern Turkish identity, a process that culminated in Republican Turkey. Nonetheless, the perception of Europe as a 'negative other' has continued in the Turkish psyche. Turks still remember the Eastern Question, defined as the dismantlement of the Ottoman Empire, the Sévres Treaty and the Turkish War of Liberation, fought not just against the Greeks but all the Europeans, and the European 'support' for the Kurdish separatism.

Until the late 18th century, Turks were, to the Europeans, outside the system of Europe because Europe was still defined in terms of religion, and the Turk had a different religion, the error of Islam. In the 19th century, despite the Treaty of Paris, the Turk was again largely considered as not belonging to the European identity, defined on the basis of being 'civilized'. The Turk had not yet achieved the 'standard of civilization'[53] and did not belong to the European club of nations. Contemporary Europeans still think that the Turks have not yet achieved a suitable standard of civilization, and therefore, the EU does not contemplate opening accession negotiations with Turkey straight away. Presently, to be of Europe, one is supposed to meet the Copenhagen criteria. The requirements of the 19th century 'standard of civilization' and the 20th century Copenhagen criteria are more or less the same and Turkey has not yet performed these requirements.

On the other hand, I have shown that Turkey and Europe have been highly engaged with each other historically in their development and identity formation. The history of Turco-European relations has not always been a history of confrontation. A close and careful reading of history reveals that the confrontation between the Turk and Europeans was no more belligerent than those among the European nations. The so-called religious difference, too, reflects a one-sided reading of the texts and history. As is well known, Islam and Christianity do have many theological similarities. Both of them, together with Judaism, are parts of the common Abrahamic monotheistic stream. Historically, conflicts between Muslims and Christians have not been bloodier than internal conflicts within these religious groupings.

As I have shown, there have been alliances between Muslim Ottoman sultans and Christian European kings and queens. Therefore, a comprehensive reading of the history of Turco-European relations will show not just the intensive interactions, but also many commonalities. It is only with such a reading the Europeans can come to accept the 'large Muslim country'. This will enable the EU to define itself as a truly pluralist union. Also, with such a reading of history, Turks can abandon their suspicions *vis-à-vis* Europeans, paradoxically leave behind their imperial past and fulfill the Copenhagen criteria required by the EU. We could then see mutual cooperation and unity, replacing policies of mutual management.

Notes

1 Some of the ideas expressed here have already been discussed elsewhere. See Yurdusev, A.N. (2000, Winter), 'Turkey and Europe: The Other in Identity Formation', *Zeitschrift für Türkeistudien*, 13. Jahrgang, Heft 1, pp. 85-94; and 'Building Europe, Managing Turkey and Escaping from the Burden of History' (in Turkish), *Liberal Thought*, vol.5, no.17, pp. 5-18.

2 Naff, T. (1984), 'The Ottoman Empire and the European States System' in H. Bull and A. Watson. (eds.), *The Expansion of International Society*, Clarendon Press, Oxford, p. 143. Emphases added.

3 Butterfield, H. (1966), 'The Balance of Power' in H. Butterfield and M. Wight (eds), *Diplomatic Investigations: Essays in the Theory of International Politics*, George Allen and Unwin, London, p. 143.

4 *Financial Times*, Wednesday, 5 March 1997.

5 van Mierlo's speech is quoted in I.B. Neumann (1999), *Uses of the Other: 'The East' in European Identity Formation*, Manchester University Press, Manchester, p. 62.

6 Helsinki European Council, 10-11 December 1999, Presidency Conclusions, http:www.europa.eu.int/council/off/conclu/dec99/dec99_en.htm

7 For the text of the Peace Treaty (Paris) of 1856, see Hurewitz, J.C. (ed.), (1975), *The Middle East and North Africa in World Politics: A Documentary Record*, second edition, *vol.1: European Expansion, 1535-1914*, Yale University Press, New Haven and London. For an assessment of the Treaty, see Oaks, A. and Mowat, R.B. (1918), *The Great European Treaties of the Nineteenth Century*, Oxford University Press, Oxford; Temperley, H. (1932), 'The Treaty of Paris of 1856 and Its Execution', *Journal of Modern History*, vol.4, pp. 387-14, 523-543; Wood, M.H. (1943), 'The Treaty of Paris and Turkey's Status in International Law', *American Journal of International Law*, pp. 264-74; and. Yurduse, A.N. and Yurdusev, E. (1999), 'The Question of the Entry of the Ottoman Empire into the European States System and the Paris Conference of 1856' (in Turkish), in İ Soysal (ed.), *The Contemporary Turkish Diplomacy in the Process of 200 Years*, TTK Basımevi, Ankara.

8 Türkegeldi, A.F. (1987), *Mesail-i Muhimme-i Siyasiyye*, second edition, TTK Basımevi, Ankara, vol.1, pp. 60-1. See also Davison, R.H. (1996), 'Ottoman Diplomacy and Its Legacy', in L.C. Brown (ed.), *Imperial Legacy: The Ottoman Imprint on the Balkans and the Middle East*, Columbia University Press, New York, p. 184.

9 Davison, 'Ottoman Diplomacy and Its Legacy', p. 184. Article VII of the Treaty of Paris reads as follows: The contracting powers 'declare the Sublime Porte admitted to participate in the advantages of the public law and system (concert) of Europe. Their Majesties engage, each on his part, to respect the independence and the territorial integrity of the Ottoman Empire; guarantee in common the strict observance of that engagement; and will, in consequence, consider any act tending to its violation as a question of general interest'. For the text of the Treaty, see Hurewitz, *The Middle East and North Africa in World Politics*.

10 Haslip, J. (1973). *The Sultan: The Life of Abdul Hamid II*, Weidenfeld and Nicholson.

11 For Özal's remarks, see Özal, T. (1989), 'Turkey in the Southern Flanks', *Brassey's Defense Yearbook*, p. 6; and for Yılmaz's, M. Yılmaz (1988, September), 'The Political Aspects of the Ankara Agreement and Its Assessment from the Point of our External Relations', *Journal of the Foundation for Economic Development* (İstanbul), no.59, p. 6.

12 Naff, 'The Ottoman Empire and the European States System', p. 143.

13 The understanding of a collective identification in terms of objective and subjective

elements is a practical and functional account that is quite common in the literature. See, for instance, Smith, A.D. (1991), *National Identity,* Penquin Books, Hammondsworth, pp. 14, 20 on nation and ethnié; Kohn, H. (1944), *The Idea of Nationalism: A Study in Its Origins and Background,* The MacMillan Company, New York, pp. 3-24 on nation and nationalism; Huntington, S.P. (1993, Summer), 'The Clash of Civilizations?', *Foreign Affairs,* vol. 72 (3), p. 24 on civilization; Bull, H. (1977), *The Anarchical Society: A Study of Order in World Politics,* Macmillan, London, pp. 13-16 on 'society of states'; and Vincent, R.J. (1982), 'Race in International Relations', *International Affairs,* vol. 58 (4), p. 661 on 'race'.

14 Hay, D. (1968), *Europe: Emergence of an Idea,* second edition, Edinburgh University Press, Edinburgh; and Keens-Soper, M. (1978), 'The Practice of a States System' in M. Donelan, (ed.), *The Reasons of States: A Study in International Political Theory,* Allen and Unwin, London.

15 The best account on civilization being the defining element of Europe remains to be Gong, G.W. (1984), *The Standard of 'Civilization' in International Society,* Clarendon, Oxford.

16 In 1993, at the Copenhagen European Council, the member states of the EU designed the membership criteria which came to be called the Copenhagen criteria according to which membership requirements that the candidate country has achieved: a) stability of institutions guaranteeing democracy, rule of law, human rights and respect for and protection of minorities; b) the existence of a functioning market economy, as well as the capacity to cope with competitive pressure and market forces within the Union; c) the ability to take on the obligations of membership, including adherence to the aims of political, economic and monetary union. In addition, the candidate country is supposed to have created the conditions for its integration through the adjustment of its administrative structures, so that European Community legislation transposed into national legislation implemented effectively through appropriate administrative and judicial structures. The Copenhagen criteria can be seen at http://europa.eu.int/comm/englargement/intro/criteria.htm.

17 This is succinctly described in Smith, *National Identity.*

18 For a similar view, see Bloom, W. (1990), *Personal Identity, National Identity and International Relations,* Cambridge University Press, Cambridge, p. 61.

19 Levi-Strauss, C. (1976), *Structural Anthropology,* Macmillan, London, p. 35; Derrida, J., (1992), *The Other Heading: Reflections on Today's Europe,* trans. P. Brault and M.B. Naas, Indiana University Press, Bloomington, pp. 9-10.

20 Thucydides, (1910), *History of the Peloponnesian Wars,* trans. by R. Crawley, Everyman edition, J.M. Dent and Sons, London, p. 3.

21 Trevelyan, G.M. (1943), *History of England,* Longmans, London, p. 232. Bloom makes a concise analysis of the formation of French and English national identities in the medieval period. See Bloom, *Personal Identity, National Identity and International Relations,* pp. 62-71.

22 Acton, Cf. J. (1950), *Lectures on Modern History,* ed. with an introduction by J.N. Figgis and R.V. Laurence, Macmillan, London, p. 34; 'Modern history begins under stress of the Ottoman conquest.' Coles builds his work upon Lord Acton's statement. Coles, P. (1968), *The Ottoman Impact on Europe,* Thames and Hudson, London.

23 See, respectively, Bosworth, C.E. (1980),'The Historical Background of Islamic Civilization' in R.M. Savony (ed.), *Introduction to Islamic Civilization,* Cambridge University Press, New York, p. 25; and Yapp, M.E. (1992, November), 'Europe in the Turkish Mirror', *Past and Present,* no.137, p. 135.

24 Delanty, G. (1995), *Inventing Europe: Idea, Identity, Reality,* Macmillan, Basingstoke, p. 84.
25 For Europe's others, see Barker, et al. (eds.), (1985), *Europe and its Others,* University of Essex, Colchester; Neumann, I.B. (1991), *Uses of the Other: The East in European Identity Formation*; and Neumann, I.B. and Welsh, J.M. (1991), 'The Other in European Self-Definition: An Addendum to the Literature on International Society', *Review of International Studies,* vol.17, pp. 327-48. For an historical account of the elements of Europe, see, for instance, Fisher, H.A.L. (1935), *A History of Europe*, Edward Arnold, London; and Dawson, C. (1934), *The Making of Europe*, Sheed and Ward, London.
26 For the account of the emergence of the European states system, see Wight, M. (1977), *Systems of States*, ed. with an Introduction by H. Bull, Leicester University Press, Leicester.
27 Hourani, A. (1980), *Europe and the Middle East,* Berkeley: University of California Press, pp. 10-12. See also Daniel, N. (1977), *Islam, Europe and Empire*, The University Press, Edinburgh.
28 Lewis, B. (1968), *The Emergence of Modern Turkey*, Oxford University Press, London, p. 40.
29 Rousseau, J.J. (1913), *The Social Contract and Discourses*, trans. G.D.H. Cole, Everyman edition, J.M. Dent and Sons, London, p. 103.
30 Marshall, P.J. and Williams, G. (1982), *The Great Map of Mankind: British Perceptions of the World in the Age of the Enlightenment,* J.M. Dent, London, p. 165.
31 Lorimer, J. (1983), *Institutes of the Law of Nations*, 2 vols., William Blackwood and Sons, Edinburgh and London, pp. 10-12, 102.
32 Elliot, C. (1965), *Turkey in Europe*, 2nd edn, Frank Cass and Co., London, p. 16.
33 Perhaps it may be better to state here that not all authors demonized the Turks. Bodin praised the degree of religious toleration existing under the rule of the Sultan and Lady Mary envied the degree of the freedom the Turkish women had and appreciated the kindness of the Turkish men. See, respectively, Coles, *The Ottoman Impact on Europe*, p. 151; and Lady Mary, *The Turkish Embassy Letters* (London: 1763) in *The Complete Letters of Lady Mary Wortley Montagu*, vol. I, edited with an Introduction by R. Halsband (1965), Oxford University Press, London.
34 Hay, *Europe: Emergence of an Idea*, pp. 83-7.
35 Mattingly, G. (1955), *Renaissance Diplomacy*, Penguin Books, Harmondsworth, pp. 136-7.
36 İnalcık, H. (1974), 'The Turkish Impact on the Development of Modern Europe', K.H. Karpat (ed.), *The Ottoman State and Its Place in World History,* E.J. Brill, Leiden, pp. 51-2. See also Naff, 'The Ottoman Empire and the European States System', pp. 145-6.
37 Watson, A. (1984), 'European International Society and Its Expansion' in H. Bull and A. Watson (eds.), *The Expansion of International Society*, Clarendon Press, Oxford, pp. 16-17.
38 Dehio, L. (1962), *The Precarious Balance: Four Centuries of the European Power Struggle*, trans. C. Fullman, Vintage Books, New York, pp. 40-41.
39 İnalcık, 'The Turkish Impact on the Development of Modern Europe', pp. 52-3; Mattingly, *Renaissance Diplomacy*, pp. 167-170; Naff, 'The Ottoman Empire and the European States System', pp. 176-8; and Watson, A. (1992), *The Evolution of International Society: A Comparative Historical Analysis*, Routledge, London, pp. 176-8.
40 İnalcık, 'The Turkish Impact on the Development of Modern Europe', pp. 56-7; Inalcik, H. (1994), *The Economic and Social History of the Ottoman Empire*, Cambridge

University Press, Cambridge, pp. 188, 366; İnalcık, H. (1971), 'Imtiyazat', *Encyclopedia of Islam*, second edition, E.J. Brill, Leiden, p. 1179; and Sousa, N. (1933), *The Capitulatory Regime of Turkey: Its History, Origin and Nature*, John Hopkins Press, Baltimore, p. 16.

41 Rodinson, M. (1987), *Europe and the Mystique of Islam*, I.B. Tauris, London, pp. 34-5; and G.R. Berridge, *British Diplomacy in Turkey* (forthcoming). See also the works by Inalcik cited in note 40.

42 Davidson, 'Ottoman Diplomacy and Its Legacy', p. 175.

43 In addition to the works already mentioned such as İnalcık, Mattingly and Dehio, see also Vaughan, D.M. (1954), *Europe and the Turk: A Pattern of Alliances, 1350-1700*, Liverpool University Press, Liverpool; Butterfield, H. (1966), 'The New Diplomacy and Historical Diplomacy' in H. Butterfield and M. Wight (eds.), *Diplomatic Investigations: Essays in the Theory of International Politics*, George Allen and Unwin, London; and Zolberg, A.R. (1981, January), 'Origins of the Modern World System: A Missing Link', *World Politics*, vol. 23 (2), pp. 253-81.

44 Kohn, The Idea of Nationalism, p. 188.

45 Hinsley, F.H. (1963), *Power and the Pursuit of Peace*, Cambridge University Press, Cambridge, p. 34; and, Northedge, F.S. and Grieve, M.J. (1971), *A Hundred Years of International Relations*, Duckworth, London, p. 5.

46 For examples of the works emphasizing the role of the Ottoman stranglehold over the Mediterranean and the Levant, see Barraclough, G. (1956), *History in a Changing World*, Basil Blackwell, Oxford, pp. 132-3; Bowle, J. (1948), *The Unity of European History: A Political and Cultural Survey*, Jonathan Cape, London, p. 175; Coles, *The Ottoman Impact on Europe*, pp. 107-8; Dehio, *The Precarious Balance*, pp. 50-51; Inalcik, 'The Turkish Impact on the Development of Modern Europe', p. 57; and, Toynbee, A.J. (1934), *A Study of History*, Oxford University Press, London, vol. III, p. 199.

47 I have been informed of this by Jörge Monar of Leicester University.

48 Edward Mortimer, 'Is This Our Frontier', *Financial Times*, 3 April 1990.

49 See 'Interview with Karen Fogg on Helsinki Summit', *Liberal Thought*, Vol. 5 (17, Winter 2000, pp. 59-66.

50 *Milliyet*, 15 December 1999.

51 Lowry, H.W. (2000), 'Betwixt and Between: Turkey's Political Structure on the Cusp of the 21st Century' in M. Abromowitz (ed.), *Turkey's Transformation and American Policy*, The Century Foundation Press, New York, pp. 42-4.

52 *Times*, 20 November 1995.

53 The requirements of the standard of civilization as understood by the 19th century European elite and statesmen are well described in Gong, *The Standard of 'Civilization' in International Society*, pp. 14-15. The standard required that a civilized state a) guarantees basic rights (i.e., life, dignity, property, and freedom of travel, commerce and religion); b) exists as an organized political bureaucracy with some efficiency and capacity to run the state machinery; c) adheres to generally accepted international law and maintains a domestic system of courts, codes and published laws to guarantee legal justice for all within its jurisdiction'; d) fulfills the obligations of the international system; and e) conforms to the accepted norms and practices of the 'civilized' international society.

PART III: TURKEY AND ITS NEIGHBORS

Chapter 6

Turkey and the Arab World in the New Millennium

Dan Tschirgi

Introduction

The 21st Century presents multiple and particularly difficult challenges for Turkey's foreign policy toward the Arab World, a situation largely resulting from the sudden terrorist attacks against New York and Washington, D.C. on 11 September 2001. Yet, even prior to that fatal day there were clear signs that the Turkish Republic's approach to the Arab region was undergoing an evolution which promised greater involvement in place of its traditional aloofness from (some would say neglect of) its Arab neighbors. Thus, the 20th Century's final decade saw a series of changes in Turkey's relations with the Arab World.

This chapter first examines the overall pattern of Turkish-Arab relations that prevailed for most of the period following the establishment of the modern Turkish state, then looks at the major alterations that marked the 1990s. Finally, it focuses on the relevance of September 11 and the ensuing US-led War on Terrorism to Turkish foreign policy toward the Arab World, particularly stressing the problems and still-cloudy options that Ankara faced by mid-2002.

The Turkish Republic and the Arab World

'Peace at home, peace in the World' was Atatürk's crisp encapsulation of the Turkish Republic's fundamental goal. The slogan signaled the relationship that the Republic's founder envisaged between domestic and foreign policies: priority was given to the former, and the latter would be developed in light of domestic requirements. It was a logical and necessary orientation, forged under the pressing need to consolidate the new Turkish national state in the wake of the multinational Ottoman Empire's collapse and dismemberment. The clear subordination of foreign policy to domestic concerns also implied that foreign affairs would be pursued in line with the chief hallmarks of an instrumentalist approach – pragmatism and flexibility. Despite the range of profound changes that have affected Turkey since Atatürk's day, these key principles of the Kemalist approach to foreign relations have remained largely unshaken.

With secularization, Westernization and national development constituting the Kemalist state's chief operational objectives, modern Turkey's foreign policy was first primarily oriented toward Europe and then toward the United States. The full independence achieved by states of the Arab World in the years after World War II did not alter this. There is some justification to accusations that Turkey long seemed determined to retain a cool aloofness from its regional neighbors.

On the other hand, and particularly in the decades that followed World War II, economic, political and social ties with the Arab World neither withered nor were placed in abeyance, although they did develop in ways calculated to serve Turkey's concepts of its own interest. On the whole, Turkey had reason to be satisfied with the outcome of its regional approach by the 1980s. This is not to imply that Turco-Arab relations had been entirely free of friction. The Cold War had seen Arab Nationalist currents grow suspicious and resentful of Turkey's role as a pro-Western bastion. More enduring frictions dated back to Turkey's pre-World War II incorporation of the province of Hatay (Alexandretta), to which Syria has yet to become reconciled. Finally, the 1980s witnessed the development of water as a source of tensions between Turkey and the two Arab states on its borders – Syria and Iraq.

Yet, the Arab World's very diversity helped Turkey develop limited, though fruitful, relationships in the area. Turkish contractors and manufactured goods found markets in the Gulf States, North Africa and Egypt. While overall levels of trade remained modest in comparison to the country's economic relations with Europe and other areas, they were not insubstantial. Arab oil producers found a ready market in Turkey, and Ankara worked carefully to foster commercial links with the Gulf States. Turkey's adhesion to the Islamic Conference in the 1970s was more indicative of the value it assigned to economic ties with the Arab World than of any erosion of Kemalist principles within the regime.[1]

In the 1990s, there began to emerge signs that Turkey might adopt a more energetic approach to the Arab World. As Mustafa Aydın has shown, the 1991 Gulf War marked something of a minor watershed in high policymaking circles.[2] Prime Minister Turgut Özal's enthusiasm for a reinvigorated presence in Middle Eastern affairs was a departure from Ankara's earlier determination to retain its distance from the region's tumultuous currents. Although opposition within the foreign policy establishment largely constrained Özal within the more traditional outlook, his reaction to the Gulf War can at least be taken symbolically as initiating the growing Turkish presence in regional affairs that characterized the 1990s.

However, the contention here is that neither Özal nor the Gulf War generated the altered face of Turkish foreign policy. Moreover, evidence appears to indicate that both the nature and degree of Turkey's new regional approach are more accurately seen as modifications of past patterns rather than fundamental changes of policy. From this perspective, Ankara's regional approach in the 1990s was more consistent in adhering to long established principles of Turkish foreign policy than radical in embarking on new departures. It was also explicable as a response to intertwined changes in the global and regional contexts within which Turkey functioned, rather than as the result of any single event or of basic shifts in the outlooks of policymakers.

Thus, when set against the guiding principles of Turkish foreign policy, long-brewing alterations in the international environment explain the chief features of Ankara's policies toward the Arab World in the 1990s. It is perhaps worth recalling at this point what is well known: that Kemalism remains very much alive and well where it counts most in the Turkish political system – in the military. Having long since assumed the role of guardian of the Kemalist legacy, the military has guaranteed that foreign policy serves domestic political objectives, which for practical purposes remain defined in terms of secularism, Westernization and national development.

The impact of Islamism as a regional political force for over two decades has had a direct impact on Turkey's domestic politics, one that has been seen by the country's dominant political forces (and most emphatically by the military) as a threat to be countered through every possible channel, including foreign policy. While Islamism challenges both secularism and Westernization as values underlying the Republic, Turkey's own drive to national development has also generated challenges that have spilled over into the foreign policy arena. On the one hand, the massive South Anatolia Project (GAP), which was launched in 1977, has given Turkey control of vital portions of the water supplies of Syria and Iraq, and a corresponding rise of friction with those countries. On the other hand, Turkish ruling elites' limited view of *national* development has long helped fuel conflict with portions of the country's Kurdish minority, which has inevitably also impacted on foreign policy. In short, the major pillars of the modern Turkish state were increasingly strained long before the onset of the 1990s. However, it was during that decade that the combined influence of major changes at the global and regional levels seriously exacerbated Turkey's problems in this respect.

The most significant global change, of course, was the decline and collapse of the Soviet Union. Disturbing repercussions in several areas of Turkish foreign policy were not long delayed. On the one hand, Ankara's hopes for full acceptance as a European state were badly frustrated as Turkey found itself marginalized from the post-Cold War rush to expand the European Union. This not only constituted a blow to Turkey's Kemalist self-image but also called into question the reliability of Turkey's security ties with the West.

At the same time, the post-Cold War Middle East was undergoing significant changes, many of which Ankara perceived as threatening. In retrospect, the first of these can be seen to have been the Iranian Revolution, which antedated the Soviet Union's dissolution by more than a decade. Although the fall of the Shah had immediately bolstered Islamist tendencies in the Middle East, the Revolution's direct threat to Turkey appeared to become significantly heightened after the long Iran-Iraq war ended in the late 1980s. By the early 1990s, Turkish policy makers had grounds to believe that the now unquestionably entrenched Tehran regime was not only supporting militant Islamist forces in Turkey but also maintaining links to the Kurdish insurrectionary movement, Abdullah Öcalan's Workers' Party of Kurdistan (better known as the PKK).[3]

The 1991 Gulf War marked a second major alteration in Turkey's regional context. Certainly, the conflict drove home a point Turks had long recognized: that the Arab World was unstable and exceedingly volatile. Apart from that, however, the Gulf War raised two more precise and long-term threats. For one thing, the possibility that weapons of mass destruction could be used in the Middle East was no longer an abstract consideration, nor was the prospect that Iraq would be the first Arab country to acquire such weapons. On the other hand, the virtual power vacuum that developed in northern Iraq following the war created a new front for Turkey's ongoing struggle against the PKK.

The third major regional change came in the form of the broadened and accelerated Arab-Israeli peace process that developed after 1991. The Gulf War had highlighted the degree to which the Palestine issue was a destabilizing factor in the Middle East. Turkey could only welcome the prospect that a revitalized peace process might finally lay the issue to rest. Moreover, this very factor provided an impetus for strengthening relations with other regional states who shared the same interest.

In sum, then, the confluence of a variety of global and regional developments, many of which had roots in years long past, created a set of circumstances to which Turkey had to respond in the 1990s. In the process of doing so, the substance as well as the nature of Turkey's relations with the Arab World underwent modification. It is to a closer examination of this process that we now turn.

Turkey and the Arab World in the 1990s[4]

As early as the 1970s, it was possible to identify two major patterns in Turkey's relations with states of the eastern Arab World. For purposes of this discussion, it is convenient to divide the region into 'northern' and 'southern' segments. 'Northern' refers to Turkey's two immediate Arab neighbors, Syria and Iraq. 'southern' refers to Jordan, the Gulf states and Egypt.

Ruling elites of the southern Arab states had little trouble relating positively to Turkey in the decades after World War II, a tendency that was enhanced by the oil boom of the 1970s. While Saudi and other Gulf leaders may have held negative views of Kemalist secularism, they welcomed Turkey's growing oil market, the involvement of Turkish contractors in local infrastructural projects, and the joys of İstanbul as a vacation spot. Turkish manufactured goods also found a growing market in the Gulf. In political terms, Turkey's traditional stance against radicalism, whether Marxist or Islamic, and its subsequent posture during the 1990-91 Gulf crisis were also congenial to Gulf rulers. In short, the ties between Turkey and the Arab Gulf states were marked on both sides by a pragmatic pursuit of practical interests, economic benefits and compatible political goals. Although clearly divided by their respective dominant social values, the two sides related with minimal friction.

The Jordanian Hashemite dynasty's convoluted history of survival in the sometimes dangerous thicket of inter-Arab politics helps explain its overall positive perception of Turkey as a regional actor. When the late King Hussein's throne was threatened by Pan-Arabist sentiments in the 1950s and 1960s, Turkey's pro-Western, anti-radical position discomfited the monarch's Arab rivals. The erratic nature of Jordan's relations with Syria continued to make Amman value warm relations with Turkey. At the same time, the development of Turkey's water resources in the 1980s gave rise to ongoing hopes that some arrangement for a regional water-supply system from which Jordan could benefit might someday be possible.

A little over a generation ago, Egypt – then a Pan-Arabist leader – was at loggerheads with Turkey over the issue of Arab inclusion in a Cold War anti-Soviet alliance. The demise of Pan-Arabism in Cairo has not entirely removed Egyptian suspicions that Turkey is a stalking horse for Western designs against Arab interests.[5] However, the Egyptian government's abandonment of Nasserist values and its ensuing turn to the US have given Cairo a fundamental community of interest with Ankara. Both assign priority to national economic development and are convinced that a stable regional environment is essential for this. Committed to restructuring its economy and looking toward export-led growth, Egypt faces a long and risky process – one that is, in effect, a race against time: Will self-sustained economic growth be achieved before the country's rapidly growing population propels already high rates of unemployment and underemployment to explosive levels?

Cairo therefore has a particular interest in seeing the region's two salient political problems – Iraq's near pariah status and the Arab-Israeli issue – resolved. The post-1991 closure of Iraq's labor market continues to pose a serious problem for Egypt. The re-opening of that market would do much to relieve the growing threat of spiraling unemployment and therefore help buy time for Cairo's economic strategy to prove productive. Resolution of the Arab-Israeli problem, although important in wider ways to Egypt's hopes of economic development, is also desirable for Egypt because of the issue's linkage to Iraq. So long as the Arab-Israeli problem drags on, the current Iraqi regime can be expected to capitalize on the opportunities it offers to foment tensions in the region.

Turkey's actual and potential impact on both problems is therefore of real concern to Cairo. Turkey and Egypt share basically similar goals *vis-à-vis* the Arab-Israeli problem as well as the Iraqi problem. However, differences do exist. Egypt looks askance at Turkish military incursions into northern Iraq, which by the mid-1990s metamorphosed into an enduring, large-scale Turkish military presence in the area. Cairo fears that Turkey's military involvement in Iraq will only further weaken that country and delay its reincorporation into the Arab sub-system. Egypt also takes exception to Turkey's military ties with Israel, fearing that the outcome may reinforce Israeli reluctance to seek an overall settlement that is acceptable to Syria, and therefore to most of the Arab World.

On the other hand, it was clear by the early 1990s that Egypt saw the prospect of a growing regional Turkish presence as possibly a positive development, particularly in economic terms. Plans for large-scale exports to Turkey of Egyptian natural gas figured prominently in discussions between the two states throughout much of the 1990s. Moreover, Egypt's own interest in greater regional economic integration is fully compatible with suggestions that water and hydroelectric power-sharing could become major linkages between Turkey and the Arab World.

From Turkey's perspective, the northern Arab states, Iraq and Syria, have long been – and remain – the most problematical of its neighbors. Baghdad obviously perceives Turkey as linked to its current main antagonists and at times worries that expansionist designs on the Mosul oilfields may be moving Ankara's policies. Moreover, even prior to the Gulf crisis, Iraq viewed Turkey's Southeast Anatolian Project with alarm and reacted negatively to proposed joint water-usage plans. Yet, it should not be forgotten that Turkish-Iraqi relations have on the whole been smooth and mutually beneficial for most of this century, including most of the period during which Iraq has endured the rule of Saddam Hussein. Two factors have been essentially responsible for this.

The first, and most important, is the two states' mutual interest in suppressing Kurdish nationalism. Thus, various security arrangements were adhered to by both parties during the entire period that separated the Turkey and Iraq Treaty of 1926 and Iraq's invasion of Kuwait in 1990.[6] One such understanding is particularly relevant here. Finding its own authority in the northern parts of Iraq waning during the Iraq-Iran War of the 1980s, Baghdad agreed in 1984 to allow Turkish military forces to engage in trans-border operations (in accordance with the doctrine of 'hot pursuit') when fighting PKK guerrillas using the region as a refuge.[7]

Economic ties are the second factor that long underlay smooth relations between Ankara and Baghdad. Trade, including Turkish purchases of Iraqi oil and Iraq's use of the Kirkuk-Yumurtalik pipeline, as well as the export to Iraq of Turkish manufactured goods, was in the interest of each party. As discussed below, Iraq's ostracism from the international community has created both a security and economic burden for Turkey. It is, therefore, understandable why Ankara would welcome Iraq's rehabilitation as an international actor.

Syria remains Turkey's most difficult and long-range problem in the Arab World. Still claiming that Turkey's 1939 absorption of Alexandretta/Iskenderun (Turkey's Hatay Province) was invalid and that the territory remains an integral part of Syria, Damascus sees Turkey as a threatening power. In Syrian eyes, Ankara's participation in Western efforts to enlist the Arab World against the Soviet Union in the 1950s stemmed from Turkey's basically hostile inclinations. The Southeast Anatolian Project's projected damming of the Euphrates in the 1980s only added to this perception. Turkey's 1986 suggestion of a regional joint-usage system was not, and has not since become, attractive to Syria. Syrian support of the PKK guerrillas in the 1990s seemed at least partly designed as a lever that might ultimately be useful in arriving at an agreement with Turkey over water.

How did Turkey's policy toward the Arab World unfold in the 1990s in the light of these developments? The answer offered here is that it did so in keeping with Ankara's long established principles of foreign policy formulation. In other words, Turkish policy toward the Arab World continued to be subordinate to domestic goals, including the protection of secularism and Westernization as well as national development as defined by Turkey's ruling circles. It also continued to be characterized by pragmatism and flexibility. None of this, of course, denies that the 1990s saw an undeniable enhancement of Turkey's presence as a major actor in regional affairs. That, however, was the result of factors to which Turkish policymakers responded, not the consequence of any new vision regarding the role and objectives of Turkish relations with the Arab World.

In operational terms, the 1990s were characterized by an even clearer bifurcation of Turkey's approach to the Arab World, as well as by visible steps to link the two policy wings. On the one hand, efforts were made to cultivate closer ties with the friendly 'southern' Arab states. On the other, the use or threat of military force was injected into relations with the country's problematic 'northern' Arab neighbors. Yet, steps were also taken to merge both approaches by encouraging friendly southern states, particularly Egypt, to help reduce frictions with Syria and Iraq.

Turkey also adopted a more active role in the Arab-Israeli peace process, participating in the post-Madrid Multilateral Track talks (particularly in the working groups dealing with water, arms control and economic development) as well as in an international group whose presence was designed to promote a sense of security among Palestinians in Hebron. At the same time, Turkey moved to forge closer economic and political links with the Palestinians, offering aid for various infrastructural projects.[8]

Finally, in the most significant foreign policy departure of the decade, Turkey placed its overall regional policy within the context of a new military relationship with Israel. Ankara seemed anxious to signal that long-term considerations of national security would henceforth be the bedrock upon which Turkish relations with the Middle East would proceed.

Although trade with Arab states remains subordinate to Turkey's commercial ties with other areas of the world, it is not insignificant. By 1999, 4.9 per cent of Turkey's imports came from Middle Eastern countries.[9] In the same year Algeria, Saudi Arabia, Libya and Syria figured among the top forty sources of Turkish imports. These same countries, minus Libya but including Egypt, were among Turkey's top forty export destinations.[10]

Turkey's energy needs promise to boost Egypt's role in the country's imports. Much of the contact between the two states in the latter half of the 1990s revolved around plans for massive exports of Egyptian liquified natural gas. By the end of 1999, an Egyptian cabinet decision appeared to open the way for a conclusion of a firm, long-term deal.[11] Gulf states, such as Qatar, were also deeply involved in efforts to supply Turkey with natural gas.[12] At the same time, seemingly endless trade delegations traveled between Turkey and the southern Arab states laying plans for increased commercial ties.[13]

Jordan, whose modest trade with Turkey declined in the latter half of the 1990s, was the object of solicitous Turkish efforts. In 1998, Prime Minister Mesut Yılmaz arrived in the Jordanian capital accompanied by eighty businessmen determined to increase 'the trade volume between Turkey and Jordan, as well as [to establish] new patterns of trade'.[14] Turkey was even more interested in involving Jordan in the Turco-Israeli military alignment so as to dampen outcries against the arrangement as an 'anti-Arab alliance.' Ankara was gratified when Jordan sent a high-ranking observer to the first Turkish-Israeli-US joint naval exercise in early 1998. Jordan also joined Turkey in bilateral land training exercises and participated in biannual military review meetings held between Israel and Turkey. By the end of the decade, such contacts – in addition to closer ties between the Jordanian and Turkish intelligence services and the scheduling of Jordanian training flights over

Turkey – led knowledgeable observers to conclude that Jordan had in effect 'quietly joined the Turkish-Israeli alignment...'[15]

In contrast to its dealings with the southern Arab states, Turkey's relations with its northern Arab neighbors during the 1990s were marked by ambivalence, in which bellicosity predominated over, but did not totally eclipse, more peaceful interaction. The elimination of Baghdad's authority from northern Iraq after 1991 created a vacuum of authority in the region that was only partially filled by rival Iraqi political groupings. It also led to an increased presence of Turkey's Kurdish nemesis, the PKK. Under these circumstances, there developed a pattern of increasing, and varied, Turkish involvement in the local intra-Kurdish politics of northern Iraq. Notwithstanding the growth of its presence in the area, Turkey's objective remained clear: the promotion of an environment that would deny operational capability to the PKK. It must also be noted that to date political means have failed to achieve this goal.

The result was that the 1990s saw repeated, massive Turkish military incursions into northern Iraq. Although Turkish forces, claiming to be in hot pursuit of PKK guerrillas, had often penetrated the area during the 1980s (with Baghdad's approval), the operations of the 1990s were on a vastly larger scale. Baghdad regularly protested the violation of its borders and occasionally warned Turkey against developing expansionist ambitions in the region.[16] There is, however, no real evidence that Turkey saw its military involvement in northern Iraq as anything but a necessary expedient to deal with a threatening lack of security in an area that lacked any other effective authority. Ankara's objective has been not only to promote stability along is border with Iraq but, in a longer-term sense, to preserve Iraq's unity.[17]

Inevitably, the overall nature of relations between Ankara and Baghdad during the 1990s underscored their paradoxical connection - one rooted in common economic interests and common opposition to Kurdish nationalism, while at the same time afflicted by military intervention that under normal circumstances would be in total violation of norms governing the interactions of sovereign states. The truth, of course, is that Iraq has not functioned under 'normal circumstances' since the Gulf War. Baghdad has therefore kept a wary eye out for signs of more permanent Turkish ambitions in Iraq's northern regions but has not been unduly averse to Turkish incursions.

It is not surprising that Turkey and Iraq share the hope of an eventual return to their pre-Gulf War relationship. Their common antipathy to Kurdish nationalism provides only part of the rationale. At least equally important is the prospect of reviving their formally large and mutually beneficial economic relationship. Although restricted amounts of Iraqi oil still flow through a pipeline to the Turkish port of Ceyhan under the UN-approved 'Oil for Food' program, and while a substantial illicit overland trade, which includes Iraqi crude oil, continues to take place, Turkey claims to have lost some $30-50 billion in trade with Iraq since the imposition of international sanctions on the country.[18] The loss on Iraq's side would be correspondingly large.

The course of Turkey's relations with Syria in the 1990s does not reveal any such striking congruence of fundamental interests. Divided by their conflicting positions on the Hatay (Iskenderun/Alexandretta) region as well as by tensions over water usage, the two have little common ground, although a fair amount of trade takes place between them. By the mid-1990s, Damascus' support of PKK guerrillas fueled unhidden ire in Ankara. On the other hand, Damascus saw a mysterious spate of terrorist bombings in Syria as the handiwork of Turkish agents. Rising tensions almost led to armed conflict in the fall of 1998, when Turkey threatened military action unless Damascus stopped aiding the PKK and expelled its leader from the country. The crisis was defused when Syria complied. Still, no solid basis for a productive relationship between the two states is yet in sight.

Turkey's 1996 military cooperation agreement with Israel constituted a major regional development. Among other things, the accords provided for joint air and naval exercises and access to port facilities as well as for Israeli training flights over Turkish territory. They also called for cooperation in 'the fight against terrorism'.[19] The new Turkish-Israeli military relationship was perceived in the Arab World as an alliance aimed at ensuring a favorable regional balance of power for its two members. Although Turkey and Israel continued to insist that their military partnership was not aimed against any particular state or group of states, Arab governments – and particularly Syria – saw it differently.

The agreement was negotiated in 1994-95 by Israel's Labor government under Yitzhak Rabin and concluded, after Rabin's assassination, under the auspices of Shimon Peres. Israel had long favored stronger military ties with Turkey. The 1996 agreement was not, therefore, the result of any change in Israel. Instead, as Alain Gresh notes: 'Contrary to the view in the Arab world, and in Damascus in particular, the impetus of the alliance between the two countries did not come from Israel, but from the Turkish generals.'[20]

It is evident that for Turkey as well as Israel the alliance was seen as a long-term measure designed to guard against both foreseeable and unforeseeable dangers. Former Israeli Minister of Defense Moshe Arens succinctly expressed its essential rationale: 'The Middle East will remain an unstable region for decades to come.'[21] That outlook was, and remains, fully shared by Turkey's leaders.

Turkey's alliance with Israel was the one new departure taken by Ankara in the Middle East during the 1990s. Yet, it was 'new' only in terms of Turkish regional policy. In a broader sense, the step was fully in keeping with Turkey's overall approach to foreign policy. Thus, the initiative taken by Ankara to establish military ties with Israel is reminiscent of the sustained campaign that Turkey's government waged to gain entry to NATO in the post-World War II period. Then, as in the Middle East of the 1990s, Turkey's leaders responded to what promised to be a chronically threatening environment by providing the 'impetus' that led to an alliance with a militarily significant power.[22]

Turkey's approach to the Arab World in the 1990s sought to utilize southern Arab friendship as a means of mitigating the disruptive impact of those aspects of its policy that were most likely to offend Arab sensibilities. Egypt's good offices were welcomed and encouraged during the 1998 crisis with Syria, in the obvious hope that Turkish demands could be fully met while allowing Damascus to save as much face as possible. Ankara also let it be known that Egypt's advice was valued in relation to Turkish policy toward Iraq.[23] Turkey's cultivation of relations with

Jordan was similarly pursued largely in order to make the Turkish-Israeli military alignment more palatable to the Arab World.

Accomplishments of the 1990s

On balance, Turkey's policy toward the Arab World in the 1990s achieved Ankara's key objectives. Limited, though significant, military force was regularly applied against PKK forces in northern Iraq without, however, embroiling Turkey in a protracted controversy with Baghdad. Thus, Ankara managed to keep alive the prospect of an eventual return to the fruitful relations with Iraq that prevailed prior to the 1990-91 Gulf crisis. The threat of military force was successfully employed against Syria, triggering a series of events that dealt a severe blow to the PKK, whose leader, Abdullah Öcalan, was subsequently captured in Kenya and returned to face trial in Turkey.

Political, economic and – to the extent possible – military ties were furthered with southern Arab states, particularly with Egypt and Jordan. These relationships were successfully employed to assuage negative Arab reactions to Turkish military muscle-flexing *vis-à-vis* Syria and Iraq as well as Turkey's development of a closer military relationship with Israel.

The Turco-Israeli military cooperation was achieved with little disruption of Turkey's relations with Arab states. Ankara was relieved when the 1996 Arab Summit in Cairo eschewed Syria's demand for strong condemnation (largely because of Jordan's efforts) and only called on Turkey to 'review' its arrangements with Israel. Turkey's foreign minister was able to describe the Arab reaction as 'logical and balanced.'[24]

As a long-term measure, the Turkish-Israeli connection may well provide a protective shield against destabilizing regional forces. If so, it may – as Turkish leaders hope – provide time for Turkey to pursue its own brand of secularist, westernizing national development while the regional environment becomes more settled, predictable, and pacific. Although this proposition remains doubtful – particularly after September 11, 2001 – there were some indications at the end of the 1990s that time might be on Turkey's side. Mohammed Khatami's accession to the presidency of Iran was one such indicator. Reports from Turkey credited the moderate Khatemi administration's desire to normalize Iran's relations with the West as having caused it to provide Turkey with intelligence information that led to the success of major operations against the militant Islamic Turkish Hizballah in January, 2000.[25]

By the end of the 1990s, Turkey was clearly more actively involved in the regional affairs of the Middle East than at any time since the Republic's establishment. However, it was also obvious that Ankara would not be able to avoid dealing politically with challenges in the region by simply sheltering behind a security bulwark, regardless of how strong that might be. The new millennium had hardly begun before the truth of this was driven home in particularly stark terms.

Turkey and the Arab World after September 11

The War on Terrorism declared by Washington following the September 11, 2001 attacks on the World Trade Center and the Pentagon quickly converted abstract worries over the Arab World's potential instability into a series of immediate, difficult and urgent issues that related directly to Turkish security concerns. Within a few short months, Ankara's policymakers were confronted by three interrelated, specific problems: the US military campaign against Afghanistan's Taliban regime; Washington's declared intention to bring about the fall of Saddam Hussein's regime in Iraq; and, the deterioration of the situation in Palestine to a point that by the spring of 2002 it threatened to provoke a wider conflict between Israel and Arab states. Each issue required Ankara to define, and act upon, its position in concrete terms. Each also subjected Turkish policymakers to contradictory pressures emanating from both the internal and international environments. The Turkish response was largely in keeping with Ankara's enduring approach to foreign policy; that is, it was marked by caution as well as a realistic effort to derive as much benefit as possible from the complex international scenario in which it had to act.

Turkey's own lengthy experience fighting terrorism, including Islamist terrorism, predisposed its government to sympathize with hardline US reaction to the September 11 attacks. Indeed, Osama bin Laden's employment of airplanes as weapons undoubtedly had particular significance for Turkey's leaders. Only a few years earlier (in 1998) Turkey's intelligence agencies had foiled a plot, hatched by Turkish Islamist terrorists connected to bin Laden, to crash an airplane into Atatürk's mausoleum during a celebration to mark the Republic's Seventy-Fifth Anniversary that was attended by top government leaders.[26] On the other hand, while this reinforced Ankara's approval of the US military assault on bin Laden's *Al Qaeda* network and its Taliban hosts, pro-Islamist sentiment -both domestic and regional- militated against overenthusiastic involvement in Afghanistan.

Thus, initially strong statements of sympathy for US losses in the September 11 attacks, along with pledges that Turkey 'would do whatever it could' to help its American ally, were paralleled by a marked reserve on matters pertaining to specific forms that Turkish support might take.[27]

The full range of considerations figuring in the Turkish government's efforts to settle upon a response to the US military campaign in Afghanistan became evident as the debate over the question entered the public domain. On the one hand were pressures, and expectations of increased pressure, from Washington and its West European allies, particularly Great Britain, for active Turkish involvement in the Afghan affair. Because of its status as NATO's only predominantly Muslim member, Turkey's active participation was sought by the West as a means of defusing claims that the War on Terrorism was actually a war on Islam. By the same token, however, the widespread condemnation of the US attack on the Taliban that arose in the Arab and Islamic worlds threatened to brand Turkey once again as a mere tool of Western powers. Pleas by leading Turkish spokesmen, such as Chief of Staff General Hüseyin Kıvrıkoğlu, for the US to be especially careful to avoid causing civilian casualties in Afghanistan could not offer an escape from Ankara's dilemma.[28]

Not surprisingly, Ankara quickly found common cause with Washington's closest Arab ally, Egypt – a country that faced a similar dilemma. By late September, Turkish President Ahmet Necdet Sezer was strongly supporting Egyptian President Hosni Mubarak's ultimately futile call for a UN-sponsored international conference on terrorism.[29] Both leaders, of course, hoped that such a conclave could devise a definition of 'terrorism' that might be acceptable to the United States as well as to Muslim opinion.

Sensitivity to Islamic opinion was not the only source of Turkey's hesitancy to commit itself actively to the US venture in Afghanistan. The country's experience under Turgut Özal's leadership during the 1990-91 war against Iraq also engendered caution, for a widespread feeling persisted that Özal's rush to support the US in that conflict had resulted in more burdens than benefits. Indeed, Turkey had been forced to cope with an influx of thousands of Kurdish refugees who, fearful of reprisals from the Baghdad regime, crossed its borders in the wake of the Gulf War. Moreover, by late 2001 Turkish leaders claimed that the decade old post-conflict embargo against Iraq had cost their country approximately fifty billion dollars in lost income.[30]

Other factors militated in favor of an active alignment with the anti-terrorist coalition Washington hoped to forge. Chief among these were considerations related to two longstanding objectives: achieving victory in Turkey's own ongoing struggle with various streams of terrorism (a leftist suicide bomber killed two policemen in İstanbul only a day before the attack on New York and Washington) and, second, strengthening Turkey's alliance with the United States. Turkish policymakers had long been dissatisfied with what they viewed as a lax approach to terrorism on the part of several Western states. They were particularly unhappy with the extent of militant Kurdish nationalist activity permitted by authorities in Germany and Greece. Within three weeks of the terrorist attacks on New York and Washington, General Kıvrıkoğlu publicly warned the EU against adopting double standards on terrorism.[31] Conversely, of course, the Bush Administration's emphatically proclaimed 'zero-tolerance' of any sort of terrorism was welcomed in Ankara. By giving more than just verbal support to the American campaign in Afghanistan, Turkey might hope not only to acquire Washington's influence as an asset in its own effort to eliminate European tolerance of militant Kurdish nationalist groups but also to benefit in other ways -particularly economic- from the gratitude of the world's only superpower. The latter was especially important in light of the particularly dismal 2001 performance of the country's chronically failing economy.[32]

While Turkey was spared the violent anti-American demonstrations that greeted the initiation of the US bombing of Afghanistan in early October 2001 throughout most of the Middle East, Turkish public opinion was strongly (66 percent) opposed to the American campaign and even more strenuously (86 percent) against the suggestion that Turkish troops might be sent to Afghanistan.[33] The government, however, promptly showed that it had overcome its initial inhibitions against close identification with the US effort and was prepared to embark on a policy sharply at variance with the prevailing regional outlook. Permission was granted for US transport planes to utilize air bases in Turkey in support of the Afghanistan campaign, and this was shortly followed by the government's success in winning parliamentary approval for the dispatch of nearly one hundred Special Forces troops to Afghanistan. Although the troops' role was to train anti-Taliban Northern Alliance forces, Foreign Minister İsmail Cem acknowledged that they might also engage in combat.[34] By the spring of 2002, over 250 Turkish soldiers were serving in Afghanistan and Turkey had agreed to assume command of the international security force charged with maintaining order in Kabul once Britain relinquished the role. Plans were announced to increase the Turkish force in Afghanistan to 1600 soldiers.[35]

The development of Turkey's policy toward Afghanistan after September 11 demonstrated that Ankara accorded far higher priority to maintaining and nurturing its relations with the West than to cultivating ties with the Arab World. In doing so, Ankara left no doubt as to its conviction that Turkey's long-range interest lay in strengthening its alignment with the West instead of responding to current opinion, whether domestic or regional, which rested on the belief that a gulf necessarily existed between the Middle East and the West. This calculation appeared to have been borne out within months, as the United States used its influence to secure a $16 billion IMF loan to Turkey. The new loan brought to $31 billion the total IMF help extended to Turkey since 1999, making the country the largest IMF borrower since the Fund extended giant rescue packages to Russia, Indonesia and South Korea in 1997 and 1998.[36] An additional $228 million in aid was extended almost at the same by the US to encourage Turkey's willingness to lead the international security force in Kabul.[37]

The decision to become actively engaged in the American-led Afghan venture did not mean that Turkish leaders had decided to turn their backs on the Arab World and the broader Middle East. In February 2002, they had a major opportunity to promote what they saw as their country's ideal role: that of a bridge between the West and the Muslim world. The occasion was a joint meeting in İstanbul between the Organization of the Islamic Conference (OIC) and the European Union (EU). Attending this unique summit were government ministers from 72 European and OIC countries. Held in the shadow of Washington's War on Terrorism and the ensuing global discussion of a possible 'clash of civilizations,' the encounter led to a final communiqué which, among other points, affirmed that 'terrorism cannot be justified for any reason' and stressed that the Palestine issue should be solved 'in a just and comprehensive manner' linked to a ''two state' solution.' It also proclaimed Turkey's 'readiness to facilitate communication among the participating countries and organizations if the need arises.'[38]

The OIC-EU meeting provided only a brief respite from the pressures under which Turkish policymakers had to function after September 11. Rather than serving as a 'bridge', Turkey's post-September position between the Arab world and the West increasingly more resembled that of a strained link between two objects that were inexorably drifting apart. The dynamic fueling this uncomfortable situation was rooted far more in the uncertainties surrounding the futures of Iraq and Palestine than in the question of Afghanistan.

As the second year of the new millennium began, these two enduring problems pushed the Middle East to the edge of a major crisis that soon raised the possibility of widespread regional war. Washington's overthrow of Afghanistan's Taliban government in mid-November heightened tensions throughout the area as the Bush Administration appeared to target Iraq for the second phase of its War on Terrorism. At the same time, the situation in Palestine – where the 'second *intifadah*' had raged unchecked since late 2000 – threatened to spiral out of control. By late March, the vicious cycle of Palestinian terrorist attacks and Israeli targeted-assassinations and collective punishment culminated in a major Israeli offensive against Yasser Arafat's quasi-government. Under the direction of Israel's hardliner Prime Minister, Ariel Sharon, the military incursion appeared to be directed against the civilian population of the occupied territories as much as at militant Palestinian groups. In Arab eyes, the United States fully shared responsibility with Israel for the Palestinians' plight.

Saddam Hussein's regime was the greatest beneficiary of the grim climate into which the Middle East was plunged by the late spring of 2002. From the start, popular opinion in the Arab World as well as Arab regimes had strongly opposed the extension of the War on Terrorism to Iraq. The crisis in Palestine raised this opposition to unprecedented levels, immeasurably complicating – if not altogether undermining – US hopes of toppling Saddam in the short run.

Turkey was alarmed from the start by the prospect that Iraq would be targeted for military action in the aftermath of the Afghanistan campaign. Ankara feared that war in Iraq would seriously harm its already ailing economy.[39] Even more worrying from the Turkish perspective was the possibility that the demise of Saddam Hussein's regime might lead to the breakup of Iraq and the establishment of a Kurdish state that would adopt the cause of Kurdish separatism in southeastern Turkey. Finally, with tens of thousands of Turkish troops already maintaining order in northern Iraq, Ankara feared that Turkish forces would be dragged into any major war in that country.[40]

On the other hand, Turkey's early opposition to US military action against Iraq was not necessarily immutable. Turkish leaders not only feared Saddam Hussein's drive to acquire weapons of mass destruction but also viewed his regime as a generally destabilizing force in the region.[41] Signs that Ankara might be persuaded to countenance an American offensive against Iraq abounded. In late 2001, for example, the Turkish Ambassador to Washington stated that his country might reconsider its position should evidence of an Iraqi link to terrorism be produced. This position was soon reiterated by the Turkish Defense Minister. Almost simultaneously, Prime Minister Ecevit and Chief of Staff General Kıvrıkoğlu publicly indicated that Turkey would have no objection to a change of regime in Baghdad, provided the country itself did not disintegrate.[42] Following a visit to the United States in early 2002, Ecevit sent a much publicized letter to the Iraqi leader urging him to allow UN arms inspectors to resume their duties. Ecevit warned that both Turkey and Iraq might suffer 'considerable damage' should Iraq not accede to the request.[43]

Palestine has long challenged the skills of Turkish policymakers, who have struggled to promote Turkish interests through productive relations with Israel as well as with the Arab states and Palestinians. The attempt to project a principled stance in favor of a negotiated peace that would provide for Israel's security as well as a viable Palestinian state was inevitably rendered much more difficult by the spiraling tensions that gripped the Middle East after the September 11 attacks on the United States. The escalation of the perennial Palestine crisis that accompanied Ariel Sharon's offensive in the spring of 2002 was particularly embarrassing to the government as public opinion swung strongly in favor of the Palestinians. Massive rallies in İstanbul and other major cities saw Islamists and Leftists join forces to condemn Turkey's military ties with Israel. By April, Ecevit – whose government had managed to avoid any criticism of Israel in the final communiqué of the OIC-EU forum months earlier – was condemning Israeli 'genocide' against the Palestinians while equally blaming 'radical elements within Palestine...for the current situation.'[44] This effort to placate domestic opinion while retaining a balanced posture toward the Palestine conflict was strictly in keeping with Turkey's established approach, though it was increasingly hard to sustain.

By the late spring of 2002, the future of Turkey's relations with the Arab world seemed to be approaching a critical juncture, one that would constitute a defining moment. All too much seemed likely to depend on forces beyond Turkey's control. Were the US to pursue military action against Iraq, Turkey would have to decide whether, and to what degree, it would cast its lot with the West. By the same token, were the Palestine crisis to lead to a wider regional conflict, Turkish leaders would be forced to define the limits of their country's ties with Israel.

If the currently critical Middle East situation is resolved with no major upheaval, Turkey will almost certainly still be unable to avoid becoming increasingly involved with the Arab world. Ankara's own plans for national development will require it to reach some acceptable understanding on water usage with Syria and Iraq. At the same time, the post-September 11 turn of events in Palestine can only reinforce Ankara's conviction that the Arab-Israeli peace process must be settled once and for all, and that Turkey must actively engage the issue at every opportunity with this end in mind.

The coming years therefore promise to see a growing Turkish presence in the Arab world, a process that will determine the extent to which that country can indeed fulfill its promise to be a bridge between East and West.

Notes

1 Tschirgi, D. (1998), 'Turkey's Challenges in the Arab World', in *Atatürk ve Modern Türkiye Uluslararası Konferansı*, Ankara Üniversitesi Siyasal Bilgileri Fakültesi, Ankara, pp. 589-99.

2 Aydın, M. (1998, Spring), Turkish Foreign Policy During the Gulf War of 1990-91, *Cairo Papers in Social Science*, vol.21, no.1, The American University in Cairo.

3 Turkish analysts maintain that in 1993 Öcalan, whose forces were then embroiled in conflict with the militant Islamic Turkish Hizballah, appealed to the Iranian-backed Lebanese Hizballah for help in arranging a cease-fire. He was, however, told to deal directly with Iran. Once Öcalan did so, the PKK and the Turkish Hizballah were able to meet in Teharan and negotiate the desired cease-fire under Iranian auspices. See, Akyol, T., 'Iran ve Hizballah', *Milliyet*, 16 February 2000.
4 Portions of this section have been adapted from Tschirgi, D. (1998), 'Turkey and the Arab World: Regional Partners or Rivals in the 21st Century?,' in M. Aydın (ed.), *Turkey on the Threshold of the 21st Century*, International Relations Foundation, Ankara.
5 This has been made very clear since 1996 by the nature of Egyptian press commentary on the development of Turkish-Israeli relations.
6 Olson, R. (1992, September), 'Turkey and the Middle East: A Review and Commentary,' *Turkish Studies Association Bulletin*, 16:2, pp. 246-47.
7 Robbins, P. (1991), *Turkey and the Middle East*, The Royal Institute of International Affairs, London, pp. 60-1
8 Sayarı, S. (1997, Spring), 'Turkey and the Middle East in the 1990s,' *Journal of Palestine Studies*, vol.XXVI, no.3, p. 50. See also, Turkish Ministry of Foreign Affairs, 'Middle East Peace Process', http://www.mfa.gov.tr/grupa/ai/html.
9 Turkish Government Economic Data: 'Imports By Country Group,' http://gov.tr/ead/english/treconomy/treconomy.htm.
10 Ibid.
11 See Lyon, A. (1999, December 3), 'BP Amoco Welcomes Egyptian Gas Export Decision, ' *The Middle East Times*,; see also 'Egypt Explores Gas Export Potential,' *Business Monthly*, April 2000.
12 'Egypt, Qatar Line Up Gas to Turkey,' *Middle East Times*, 8 June 1997.
13 See, for example, Lyon, A. 'Turks Keen to do Business in Egypt Despite Snags,' *The Middle East Times*, 25 October 1998.
14 See 'Jordan, Turkey Agree on Trade,' *Middle East Times*, 13 September 1998.
15 'Issues in the Middle East Security,' *Jane's Defense Weekly*, vol.31, no.10, 10 March 1999. See also, Dibner, G. (1998-99, Winter), 'My Enemy's Enemy: Turkey, Israel and the Middle Eastern Balance of Power,' *Harvard International Review*, vol. 21, no. 1, pp. 34-41.
16 'Issues in the Middle East Security,' *Jane's Defense Weekly*, vol 31, no. 10 (10 March 1999). See also, Dibner, G. (1998-99, Winter), 'My Enemy's Enemy: Turkey, Israel and the Middle Eastern Balance of Power,' *Harvard International Review*, vol. 21, no. 1, pp. 34-41.
17 Sayarı, 'Turkey and the Middle East'.
18 'Turks Say US Pipeline Strikes Unacceptable,' Reuters, http://www.duth.gr/maillist-archives/thrace/tl52/msg00049.html. See also Biedermann, F. 'Turkey Fears Iraq May Be Next on US Hit List,' *Agence France Presse*, 9 October 2001, at http://web.lexis-nexis.com/universe/docu...zV&_md5=d7cdd4c6b5c112f658bda13914b8cacd.
19 Gresch, A. (1998, Spring), 'Turkish-Israeli-Syrian Relations and Their Impact on the Middle East,' *Middle East Journal*, vol. 52, no. 2, p. 189.
20 Ibid, p. 190.
21 Ibid, p. 189.
22 See Yongaçoğlu, N.T. (1979), 'Laying the Foundations of Turkish Foreign Policy: 1945-1952,' Unpublished Ph. D. dissertation, The University of Toronto.
23 See, for example, 'Demirel, Mubarak Discuss Iraq Situation,' *Middle East Times*, 31 January 1999.

24 'Will It Last?,' *The Economist,*' 29 June 1996, p. 40.

25 'Iran ve Hizballah'.

26 The German-based terrorist group's leader, Metin Kaplan, styled himself the 'Caliph of Cologne.' A delegation from his group reportedly met with Osama bin Laden in Afghanistan a year before the planned attack on Ankara and members of the group were subsequently sent to Afghanistan for training. See Frantz, D., 'A Nation Challenged: A 1998 Crash Plot', *New York Times*, 2 February 2002.

27 On September 12, for example, Prime Minister Bülent Ecevit pledged 'solidarity' with the struggle against terrorism but refused to comment on the prospect that Turkey would allow US use of İncirlik Airbase to launch possible reprisal attacks. *Deutsche Presse-Agentur*, 12 September 2001, http://web.lexis-nexis.com/universe/docu...zV&_md5-298616545c7a143764bb7910c495466.

28 See 'Turkey Debates Its Stance,' *Mideast Mirror*, 10 October 2001.

29 *Agence France Presse*, 'Turkey Backs Egypt's Call for Terrorism, Invites Mubarak,' http://web.Lexis-nexis.com/universe/docu...zV&_md5=8f5369bcd8269dcda698102e0a6ff2a.

30 Biedermann, 'Turkey Fears Iraq May Be Next on US Hit List,' op. cit.

31 'Turkey Debates Its Stance'.

32 Frantz, D. 'Turkey's Leader Visits US to Plead for Urgent Economic Aid,' *New York Times*, 14 January 2002. In 2001 Turkey's economy shrank by 8.5 percent, the Lira lost more than fifty percent of its value, and the year ended with consumer inflation standing at 68.5 percent.

33 Frantz, D. 'Turkey Says Troops to Join US Campaign and Train Anti-Taliban Forces,' *New York Times*, 2 November 2001.

34 Ibid.

35 'Turkey May Delay ISAF Takeover', *United Press International*, April 10, 2002; http://web.lexis-nexis.com/universe/docu...zV&_md5=e0ccd96095276853e6ff30de30d38a6d.

36 Kahn, J. 'IMF Offers Turkey $16 Billion in Loan Aid,' *New York Times*, 5 February 2002.

37 Gordon, M. 'US Offers Aid to Turkey to Lead Kabul Peace Force,' *New York Times*, 20 March 2002.

38 OIC-EU Joint Forum Press Release, 13 February 2002.

39 'Turkey Mulls Over Impact of a War Next Door,' *Turkish Daily News*, 13 February 2002.

40 'United States Turkey Commentary Iraq,' *Middle East News Online*, http://web.lexis-nexis.com/universe/docu...zV&_md=aa4b963009daf781525fac77a7fc7e36a.

41 'Ankara Warming to the Idea of Life Without Saddam,' *Turkish Daily News*, 10 January 2002.

42 Ibid.

43 'Turkish PM Calls on Saddam Hussein to Allow Arms Inspectors Back', *Deutsche Presse-Agentur*, http://web.lexis-nexis.com/universe/docu...zV&_md5=9892563ff109460e632d6f6d3d41ccc.

44 'Turkish Premier Says Israel Carrying Out "Genocide"', *BBC Monitoring International Reports*,4April2002,http://web.lexisnexis.com/universe/docu...zV&_md5=04db25e2763d334b7d08ff4bc8f22e44.

Chapter 7

Turkey and the Russian Federation: Towards a Mutual Understanding?*

Oktay F. Tanrısever

Turkey and the Russian Federation, which play only peripheral roles in European affairs, are the most important regional actors in the Eurasian region. The evident difference between their positions in Europe and Eurasia has shaped their bilateral relations in the post-Cold War era. The relations between these two states had generally been problematic until the end of 1997. In this period, Turkey has sought to become a role model for the post-Soviet Turkic states in Eurasia, while the Russian Federation has been struggling to maintain its great power status in the region. Thus, the Russian Federation saw Turkey as a rival country undermining its political presence in the Eurasian region and its control over the regional energy resources. Surprisingly, Turkey and the Russian Federation have started to promote their bilateral relations in all fields since 1997; they have increasingly become aware of their interdependence on each other in order to foster economic growth and to promote their own security under the unstable conditions of the post-Cold War era. The main objective of this chapter is to examine the emerging patterns in Turkey's relations with the Russian Federation since the collapse of the Soviet Union in 1991. In addition, we will explore the opportunities and the limitations in Turkish-Russian relations.

The chapter hopes to demonstrate that Turkish-Russian relations could be understood better by exploring the changing positions of these states in the international system rather than by focusing on their bilateral interactions. It is the assumption of this chapter that the systemic and structural factors play a much more important role than the actor-level national factors in the deterioration or improvement of bilateral relations. Therefore, the chapter argues that the structural opportunities and limitations in the international system have significantly affected the pre-1997 geopolitical rivalry and the post-1997 rapprochement between these states. Until 1997, both Turkey and the Russian Federation had competed with each other in order to increase their standings *vis-à-vis* the Western powers in the international system. However, the signing in Brussels of accession protocols between NATO and the Czech Republic, Hungary and Poland on 16 December 1997 despite the Russian objections, and the 1997 European Union (EU) Luxembourg Summit decision not to grant 'candidate status' to Turkey consolidated their position *vis-à-vis* the Western powers.

The chapter is organized as follows: To begin with, we will explore the positions of Turkey and the Russian Federation in the aftermath of the Cold War. Then, we will investigate the problematic nature of the post-Soviet reform process in Russia and its impact on Russia's relations with Turkey. Next, we will examine the rapprochement between Turkey and the Russian Federation through analyzing the convergence in the positions of these two states in international system, and their economic and security cooperation in the post-1997 period. The penultimate section will explore the opportunities for a 'strategic partnership' between Turkey and the Russian Federation, and the existing structural limitations in their relations. The article concludes by discussing the emerging trends in Turkish-Russian relations.

Turkey and Russia in the Aftermath of the Cold War: A Fresh Start?

The rise of the Russian Federation out of the ashes of the Soviet Union opened a new chapter in the long history of Turkish-Russian relations, while the 500th anniversary of the establishment of diplomatic relations between the two countries was being commemorated in 1992. In the aftermath of the Soviet collapse, Russia's influence over Turkey was severely weakened as its territorial borders had receded far from Turkey with the emergence of the independent states of Azerbaijan, Armenia and Georgia. Furthermore, there was no Soviet control over the Eastern Europe and the Balkans. Under these conditions, Ankara started to see Russia not as an 'enemy' but a 'normal state' with which it could do business. According to Sezer-Bazoğlu, this was not purely because of Russia's economic and military weakness since 'a great country like Russia is likely to recover in due time', but 'the more meaningful reason is the new image of Russia as a power no longer driven by territorial and ideological expansion, as in former times'.[1] We could note that the collapse of the ideologically defined bipolar international system played a crucial role in the formation of new images of Russia and Turkey.

In fact, it would be easier to question the myth of Russo-Turkish enmity if we study the history of Turkish-Russian relations, which have been greatly affected by the changes in international system. Between the eighteenth and the nineteenth centuries, the rise in the Russian Empire's power and the decline in that of the Ottoman Empire characterized the international system. In this period, the two empires had had a common border in the Caucasus and struggled for domination of the Black Sea. The two imperial dynasties, the Romanovs and the Ottomans, fought several wars and the Russians expanded both geographically and politically at the expense of the Ottomans. In 1877, the armies of the Russian Empire even came close to capturing the capital of the Ottoman Empire. Meanwhile, Russia constantly sought to gain access to the Mediterranean through supporting the Serbian, Greek and Bulgarian national liberation movements in the Balkans.[2]

Following the collapse of both the Russian and the Ottoman Empires by the end of the First World War, the Bolshevik Russia and the modern Republic of Turkey had found themselves in similar positions in the inter-war international system. They both perceived the West as a source of threat for their survival. Thus, the newly formed regimes in the Soviet Union and Turkey were able to develop pragmatic relations in the early 1920s. Although neither of them forgot the limitations of geography and lessons of history, Turkey and the Soviet Union respected each other's interests for nearly twenty years. Ankara consulted Moscow in almost all-major foreign policy decisions, while Moscow tried to be attentive to Turkish concerns. The Friendship and Fraternity treaties of 1921 and 1925 formalized this new approach to Turkish-Russian relations. Nevertheless, these treaties did not stop the Soviet Union from interfering in Turkey's internal affairs.[3]

These 'friendly' relations did not survive the Second World War. On 19 March 1945, Viacheslav Molotov, the Soviet Foreign Minister, informed Selim Sarper, the Turkish Ambassador in Moscow, that Moscow had cancelled the 1925 Friendship and Fraternity Treaty. Moscow was aware of the Turkish isolation from the Western powers at the end of the Second World War due to its war-time neutrality, and used this opportunity to demand the joint control of the Straits as well as the annexation of some of Turkey's Eastern Anatolian provinces on 8 August 1946.[4] The Turkish side interpreted this Soviet move as a hostile attempt to turn Turkey into a Soviet satellite, just like the other East European countries.

The emergence of the bipolar international system in the aftermath of the Second World War enabled Turkey to establish an alliance with the main rival of the Soviet Union, the United States, which was the only power with the ability to check the Soviet ambitions. The Truman Doctrine of 1947 created the basis for Turkish-American alliance against the Soviet expansionism. Despite some tentative attempts at collaboration, the Soviet-Turkish relations followed the East-West divide during the Cold War because the international system was not flexible enough to condone inter-bloc international relations. Turkey, a loyal member of NATO since 1952, became a barrier against the Soviet influence in the Middle East. Under these conditions, diplomatic contacts were rather restricted. Trade, investments and joint projects were seen as instruments of influence by both sides. Turkey tilted towards the Soviet Union during the 1960s and 1970s pragmatically because of the need for the international support to its position on the Cyprus problem.[5]

The collapse of the Soviet Union not only transformed the political regime in Russia but also ended the bipolar international system characterized by the Cold War. The removal of the ideological rivalry as a negative factor in Moscow's relations with Turkey heightened the hopes for a better future. In the post-Cold War era, the westernizing liberals became the dominant political forces in Russia. The pro-western Russian President Boris Yeltsin nominated Andrei Kozyrev, a liberal, as his Minister of Foreign Affairs. Kozyrev saw Russia's membership in the club of developed Western democratic states and the Western international institutions as the main Russian foreign policy objectives. According to Kozyrev, Russia's interest laid in the transformation of Russia into a democratic state, setting up an effective economy, guaranteeing the rights and freedoms of all Russians, and making people's lives materially and spiritually rich.[6]

Since Turkey also shared these values as the basis of its pro-Western foreign policy orientation, it was expected that the relations between these two states would be affected positively from this common ground in their foreign policy orientations. Thus, Turkish Foreign Minister Hikmet Çetin sought to forge a new start in Turkey's relations with the Russian Federation when he visited Moscow on 20-22 January 1992. Russian Foreign Minister Andrei Kozyrev paid a visit to Ankara a month later, in February 1992. An official visit by Turkish Prime Minister Süleyman Demirel to the Russian Federation in 25-26 May of the same year provided the basis for fruitful and comprehensive talks. During the visit, the Turkish-Russian Treaty of Friendship and Co-operation was signed. The Treaty declared that the two countries would base their relations on good neighborliness, co-operation and mutual trust. This treaty, which sets the legal basis and principles of relations between Turkey and the Russian Federation, confirmed the will of both sides to further and to add new dimensions to their relationship.[7] The rosy picture in Turkey's relations with the Russian Federation was maintained when the Russian President Boris Yeltsin visited Istanbul on 25 June 1992 in order to attend the first summit meeting of the Black Sea Economic Cooperation.[8]

This diplomatic climate contributed to the development of economic relations between Turkey and the Russian Federation. Russian Prime Minister Egor Gaidar's economic reform program, which was also known as the 'shock therapy', created many opportunities for foreign investors. To reap the benefits of this reform program through developing and upgrading economic and commercial relations, Turkey and the Russian Federation have formed the Turkish-Russian Joint Economic Commission. Its first meeting was held on 2-6 November 1992 in Ankara. Meanwhile, the Russian economy was in a deep crisis, which made it difficult for Moscow to repay its Soviet-era 600 million dollars export debts to the Turkish Eximbank. In order to restructure these debts, Turkey and Russia signed two major debt-rescheduling agreements on 19 July 1994 and 15 December 1995, the second one being on the basis of the terms and conditions of the 'Paris Club Agreements'.[9]

Problems in Russia's Reform Process and Its Impact on Russian-Turkish Relations

The rosy climate in Turkey's relations with the Russian Federation has been adversely affected by the growing problems in Russia's post-Soviet transition process. The highly pro-Western policies of Yeltsin elicited a growth in the opposition to his policies in the Russian parliament. Yeltsin, who had dissolved the Duma by force in October 1993, chose increasingly to tailor his policies to meet Duma criticism. In this period, it became routine to criticize 'the liberal reformers' for being too naive to shape the foreign policy of the Russian Federation. For example, Sergei Stankevich, the political adviser of Yeltsin, criticized Kozyrev's policy of Atlanticism as 'a policy of self-abnegation'.[10] Moreover, the December 1993 State Duma (the Lower House of the Russian Parliament) elections marked the rise of the pragmatic nationalists. Having received 22.9 per cent of the votes in these elections, the Liberal Democratic Party of Russia (LDPR) strengthened the political outlook of Russian nationalists. Its leader Vladimir Zhirinovskii advocates the restoration of the Russian Empire to its previous borders, even including Alaska. According to him, if Russians fail to revive the Russian Empire, others will revive their own (a reference to the United States, China and Turkey). He developed a special dislike of the Turkey and the Turks, which could be linked to the criticism of Moscow by the Turkic and Muslim minorities in the Middle Volga and the North Caucasus.[11]

Concerning the foreign policy orientation of the Russian Federation, two major political groups emerged within the State Duma by the end of 1993. Apart from the Westernisers, who were united around Yeltsin, there were Eurasianists representing the coalition of the Communists and the Ultra-Nationalists. The Westernisers placed primary emphasis on good ties with the United States and wanted Russia to be part of Western civilization. On the issue of Russian policy toward the 'Near Abroad', they stressed normal diplomatic relations, without Russia seeking to impose its will from a dominant position. The 'Eurasianists', on the other hand, advocated a balanced foreign policy approach for Russia, with equal emphasis on Europe, the Middle East, and the Far East. They also called for the re-establishment of Russian hegemony in the 'Near Abroad'.[12]

The first concrete impact of this pragmatic turn was the adoption of a 'Near Abroad' policy in 1993, when Yeltsin proposed that the United Nations or CSCE should grant Russia a 'security mandate' to preserve order throughout the post-Soviet space.[13] This policy assumed that the former Soviet republics belonged to the Russian sphere of influence. In line with the changing political climate, the Minister of Foreign Affairs, Andrei Kozyrev, began to take a cautious stance towards the West. Nevertheless, this did not prevent his replacement in 1996 by Evgenii Primakov, who advocated Russian pragmatic nationalism. According to Primakov, Russian territorial integrity could not be ensured unless the Russian Federation established itself as a great power in international relations. Primakov's geopolitical perception evolved from security concerns related to the developments in the Near Abroad. This resulted in criticism of the West and a guarded rapprochement towards the East (China, India, Iran, and several Arab States).[14]

Under these conditions, most members of the Russian leadership viewed Turkey as one of the main beneficiaries of the Soviet collapse. In this world-view, new-old divisions were emerging, and Turkey in an alliance with the US and NATO was seen as pitted against Russia. Moreover, Turkish inroads into Central Asia were viewed as 'plots' to encircle Russia by a potentially hostile state. The Russian suspicions peaked when the majority of Central Asian states supported a Turkish idea on creating a custom and tariff union in the summer of 1993. The Russian foreign policy makers viewed this as a vindication of their claim that Turkey and other Western powers sought to isolate Russia from its allies in the Middle East. Although Turkey's policy towards the Central Asian states did not target the removal of Russian influence in the region, the Russian side viewed this as a challenge to its authority.[15] Gökay and Langhorne described Turkey's motivations as follows;

> In the period immediately after the collapse of the Soviet Union, Turkey had great expectations about establishing major influence in many parts of Central Asia and the Caucasus. It was claimed that there existed a very special relationship between Turkey, the Caucasus and Central Asian republics. This was based on the belief that ethnic, linguistic, religious, and cultural affinities would pave the way for closer ties and a major presence.[16]

Another region that increased the concerns of Moscow about the growing Turkish influence in its 'Near Abroad' was the Caucasus. The explosion of separatist conflicts in the Caucasus in the 1990s has given Russia a free hand in manipulating local weaknesses to its advantage. The Nagorno-Karabakh problem is an example of this approach. When the Russian-backed Armenia defeated Azerbaijan militarily in 1992, the then CIS's Military Commander Marshal Evgenii Shaposhnikov warned Turkey of nuclear retaliation if Turkey intervened.[17] This underscored the Russian determination to minimize Turkey's influence in the region. Turkish Prime Minister Suleyman Demirel's May 1992 visit to the Russian Federation, which was discussed above, took place under this atmosphere. Although the Turkish-Russian Treaty of Friendship and Co-operation declared that the two countries would base their relations on good neighborliness, co-operation and mutual trust, the developments in the Caucasus showed that the two states had their suspicions about the motivations of each other.

Moscow controlled Turkey's main gateway to the Turkic states of Central Asia by toppling Azerbaijan's first President Abulfez Elchibey in June 1993. Blaming Elchibey for his failure to stop Armenian aggression in Nagorno-Karabakh, and obtaining the backing of the Russian 104th Airborne Division, Surat Khuseinov, a Colonel in the Azeri Army, instigated an uprising in the province of Gence. Chaos and bloodshed were avoided by Heidar Aliev's intervention and by Elchibey's exile to a small village in Nakhchevan. Aliev's grip on power in the following weeks undermined the Turkish influence not only in Azerbaijan but also in the rest of the region. Aliev, the former Azerbaijan Communist Party First Secretary and First Deputy Chairman of the USSR Council of Ministers, thought that the Nagorno-Karabakh problem could only be solved with the Russian support. Thus, he pursued a pragmatic policy towards both Moscow and Ankara.[18] In December 1993, Azerbaijan transferred 10 per cent of its shares in the exploitation of the Azeri, Chirag and Guneshli oilfields to the Russian Oil Company, Lukoil. Similarly, the oil shares of Turkey, which was initially at 1.75 per cent, later rose to 6.75 percent. Further concessions to these states were made conditional to Moscow and Ankara's ability to convince the Armenians to withdraw from Azeri territory.[19]

As Sezer-Bazoğlu suggests, the clash of Turkish-Russian interests in the Caucasus stems from their differing visions of the regional order in Eurasia. As for Turkey, its Eurasian policy mainly aims to solidify the newly gained independence of those states, which could potentially decrease their dependence on Moscow, and moreover to become a major actor in the region in order to get share of economic and security benefits.[20]

In line with this policy, Turkey proposed to transport 40 to 50 million tons of Caspian crude oil annually (20 million tons of Kazakh and 25 million tons of Azeri oil) through an overland pipeline to be laid from Baku to the Turkish port of Ceyhan on the Mediterranean. Meanwhile, Turkey sought to block the Baku-Novorossisk option by questioning the safety of the oil shipment through the Turkish Straits, because the oil brought to Novorossiisk through the existing pipelines could only reach the oil markets via the Straits. Ankara's argument is that the Bosphorus runs right through the heart of Istanbul, a city of some 12 million people. The channel is a narrow one and there are frequent collisions. Thus, an accident with an oil tanker would be highly dangerous. Arguing that the Bosphorus cannot be 'used as a pipeline', the environmentalists have held protests in the Straits against any more tankers being let through.[21] Taking these considerations into account, the Turkish Parliament adopted a new Straits Regulation on 1 July 1994. The new regulation made the passage of large oil tankers through the Straits expensive. Ships carrying a dangerous load were required to follow special rules, which would mean considerable delay and extra costs.[22]

In response to the Turkey's new Straits Regulation, Moscow challenged the legality of these regulations on the basis of the Montreaux Convention, and brought the case to the International Maritime Organization (IMO) in March 1994. The new rules, the Russians argued, were contrary to Article 2 of the Montreaux Convention, regulating the regime of the Turkish Straits, in addition to several other international treaties. Turkey argued that circumstances had changed since the signing of the Montreaux Convention in 1936. The number of vessels passing through the Straits in both directions had reached almost 50,000 by 1994. This was a development that was not anticipated at Montreaux.[23] According to Mensur Akgün, Moscow's position was weak since it did not want to risk the collapse of the Montreaux Convention. This Convention was essential for Russia's security because it limited the number, type, and weight of non-littoral battleships allowed through the Straits. Submarines and aircraft carriers were also banned from sailing to the Black Sea. For Akgün, any attempt to revise this legally outmoded Convention could easily lead to its collapse and thus put all the rights and privileges of the Russians into jeopardy.[24]

Increasingly disillusioned with its weakness in the Caucasus, which was seen by Moscow as something to the benefit of Turkey, Moscow started to give a special importance to its military control of Chechnya, since it was vital for maintaining its control of Caucasus and Central Asia. Arguably, its loss of the control of Chechnya would greatly encourage the nationalist forces in the Caucasus. In this regard, Russia tried to prevent the interference of other regional actors in the conflict. The Chechen crisis became a flash point in Russian-Turkish relation as Russia claimed that the Chechens were obtaining assistance and volunteers from Turkey. However, Turkey, like the rest of the world, officially recognizes the sovereignty of the Russian Federation over the republic. Although there was sympathy towards the Chechens among the Turkish public opinion, the

Turkish government has refrained from getting involved in this conflict, apart from offering some humanitarian aid to the civilians with the consent of the Russian Federation.[25]

During the first days of 1996, the Chechen question became a very tense issue in Turkish-Russian relations, when nine people with Caucasian origin hijacked a Turkish ferryboat, *Avrasya* on 16 January 1996. The hijackers claimed that they hijacked the ferry in order to support the 'Chechen resistance against Moscow'.[26] During the interview of Aleksandr Nadzharov, a correspondent of *Rossiiskaia gazeta*, with Nikolai Kovalev, director of the Russian Federation Federal Security Service, Kovalev accused Turkey of supporting the Chechens through clandestine activities as follows: 'The Russian FSB made an official protest to the leadership of the Turkish special service in connection with the continuation of its intelligence activities in the North Caucasus region'.[27]

In return, Turkey suspected that Russia was supporting the PKK terrorist organization as a card to increase its influence over Turkey. As Olson argues, the PKK problem in Turkey and Russia's war in Chechnya 'are linked more closely than is generally realized and acknowledged.'[28] Contrary to the Russian Foreign Ministry statement that Russians would not 'open their arms to PKK', Moscow did not prevent the establishment of a 'Kurdish House' with the PKK as its dominant element in the Russian capital. One week after, the Turkish Interior Minister Nahit Menteşe and a group of high-ranking national security officials went to Moscow. After two days of negotiations, Turkey and Russia signed a 'Protocol to Prevent Terrorism' in which two countries agreed to exchange intelligence information to prevent terrorism.[29] Nevertheless, Moscow failed to keep its promises to Turkey when it hosted the Second International Congress of Kurdish Organizations with active PKK participation in 4-8 May 1996. During a visit to Moscow in mid-December 1996, Turkish Foreign Minister Tansu Çiller signed a 'Protocol of Cooperation against Terrorism'. According to Olson, 'Turkey was unable to take advantage of the Russian predicament in Chechnya because of its fight against the PKK'. Thus, it seems that Russia was more effective in limiting Turkish involvement in the Caucasus by playing its PKK card against Turkey.[30]

In Moscow's rivalry with Turkey, it had another leverage over Turkey: the sale of S-300 missiles to Armenia, Syria and Cyprus. In January 1997, the Russian arms firm Rosvooruzhenie agreed to sell a sophisticated surface-to-air missile system, the SAM-300-PMU-1, to the Greek Cypriot government. The 150-km range of the missiles reaches into southern Turkey and, if deployed, would have seriously complicated Turkish air maneuverability over Cyprus. The S-300s were mainly designed to attack any even low target flying objects, so they could have shot down a number of Turkish planes even before they left their bases provided that the range was appropriate. Thus, Turkey took the threat very seriously, and warned that it would not allow the missiles to be deployed, also hinting that it could risk war.[31] The Greek Cypriot President Glafkos Clerides's aim was to attract the international attention and provoke pressure over Turkey to help produce a Cyprus solution. The Turkish side, on the other hand, grew restless as it anticipated that the balance of power in Cyprus was shifting dramatically against it. In any case, after lengthy negotiations between Greece and Cyprus, the Greek Cypriot government gave up its attempt to have Russia's S-300s, and Greece agreed to have them installed on its island of Crete.[32] All these conflicts convinced Turkey that its rivalry with Moscow could get extremely dangerous and even harm Turkey's relations with its NATO allies.

The Rapprochement in Turkish-Russian Relations

By the end of 1997, both Ankara and Moscow recognized that their rivalries were not likely to produce a clear victory to any of the parties. The worse was that the Russian-Turkish rivalry could undermine their national security and their relations with the Western powers. Russia started to recognize that it was not a superpower anymore comparable to the United States. Being increasingly aware of the fact that the Russian Federation was a regional, rather than a global international actor, Moscow's relations with the regional actors in Eurasia, such as Turkey, gained new importance. As to Turkey, it had already recognized that there were structural limitations on its capacity to project power throughout Eurasia. It was the limitations in their capacities that pushed both countries to a more balanced and a generally positive relationship. Furthermore, as Trenin argues, for Turkey and the Russian Federation, 'the nearest pole of attraction has already emerged, and its pull will grow, drawing Ankara and Moscow in the same direction: the European Union'.[33] Nevertheless, the relations of Turkey and the Russian Federation with the European Union, in particular, and the west, in general, have been characterized by ups and downs. In order to increase their positions *vis-à-vis* the Western powers, the leaderships of both countries expressed the need to overcome their differences and to work for mutually beneficial 'strategic partnership'.

Russia's relations with the West had deteriorated since 1993 when the pragmatic nationalists in the Russian Federation started to become very vocal in the formulation of Russian foreign policy.[34] Moreover, NATO has been trying to move forward its enlargement plans since 1994. The Partnership for Peace (PfP) program was the first step in this direction. 26 countries, including the Russian Federation, became partners in the new scheme by signing the Framework Documents. Despite the Russian involvement, Moscow had strong reservations about the unilateral enlargement of the Western alliance. In order to accommodate the Russian politicians, who warned the West that the NATO expansion would be a serious mistake, the 'Founding Act on Mutual Relations, Cooperation and Security between NATO and the Russian Federation' was signed in Paris on 27 May 1997. Nevertheless, this did not prevent the sixteen member NATO first from signing in Brussels of accession protocols with the Czech Republic, Hungary and Poland on 16 December 1997, and later, from integrating three former Warsaw Pact states in Central Europe (Poland, Czech Republic and Hungary) formally into its institutional structure in March 1999.[35]

The expansion of NATO created suspicions within the Russian leadership that Russia's exclusion from NATO also implied its exclusion from the European

Union (EU). Consequently, it was feared that Russia would be completely excluded from the West. In fact, the independence of Ukraine and Belarus had already made Russia less European than it was before. Gradually, pragmatic nationalists called for a non-Western Russia, though that did not necessarily mean an anti-Western Russia.[36]

In order to appease Moscow and to get Moscow's approval to the NATO enlargement, the western powers offered Moscow some modifications in the Conventional Forces in Europe (CFE) Treaty during the CFE Vienna Review Conference in May 1996. This created a 'cold shower' effect on Turkey as its security was compromised by the Western powers in their attempts to create a new security architecture for Europe. This convinced the Turkish security establishment that it was in the interest of Turkey to have good relations with Moscow in order to strengthen its position in the Western security structures.[37]

The suspicions towards the Western powers, on the part of the Turkish elite also reached their climax when Turkey's hopes for future membership in the European Union were dealt a severe blow at the December 12-13 EU Luxembourg Summit. Turkey simply wanted the EU to keep the door open to on the basis of the same objective standards and criteria that are applied to the other applicant states.[38] The EU Luxembourg Summit decision on Turkey's candidature was based on the belief that Turkey's human rights problem and chronic political instability made it a less-than-desirable potential addition to the EU. But alienating Turkey was even a less-satisfactory option, as continuously rebuffed Turkey could become more assertive in its foreign policy. Besides, Turkey could also become more receptive towards Russian overtures particularly in the area of arms acquisitions.[39]

Facing problems related their marginalization in European affairs, both Ankara and Moscow have agreed on a strategy of normalizing their relations through improving their economic relations, because unlike Turkey's problematic diplomatic relations with the Russian Federation, the economic relations between these two states have largely been very good. Bilateral trade relations reached 8-10 billion US Dollars annually in 1997. Official trade accounted for 3.5 billion US Dollars of this figure, with Turkish exports to Russia worth 1.347 billion US Dollars and imports 2.155 billion US Dollars. Including the non-registered trade carried out by visiting tourists, the volume of trade between the two countries was estimated to have reached around 10 billion US Dollars in 1997, putting both countries in the second position in their respective overall (for Russia, non-CIS) foreign trade. Moreover, over 1 million Russians are now visiting Turkey each year, and Turkish contractors continue to consolidate their position in the Russian market attaining over 8.5 billion US Dollars of cumulated business volume by 1997.[40]

Based on this promising base for further economic cooperation, Ankara and Moscow have taken new steps to institutionalize their economic relations. After a period break of three years, the Third Meeting of Turkish-Russian Joint Economic Council was held in Ankara on 4-7 November 1997. This meeting served as a preparatory work for Russian Prime Minister Viktor Chernomyrdin's 16-17 December 1997 visit to Turkey, which was the first official visit in the post-Soviet period by a head of Russia's government. Its main objective was to sign a huge natural gas pipeline project of Blue Stream. The 30 billion US Dollars project envisaged Russia supplying 16 billion cubic meters of natural gas a year to Turkey by the year 2010 through underwater pipelines in the Black Sea. It involves laying a gas pipeline from Izobilnoe (Stavropol territory) through Djubga (coastal town at the Black Sea shoreline of Krasnodar territory) and Samsun (Turkey) to Ankara. The pipeline's total length will be 1,213 kilometers, including 396 kilometers to be laid on the Black Sea floor.[41]

During Chernomyrdin's visit to Turkey, the two countries also agreed to abstain from actions likely to harm the other's economic interests or threaten their territorial integrity.[42] This meant that Russia would not interfere with the construction of the Baku-Ceyhan pipeline if that route were selected as the main export route from Azerbaijan. In return for this deal Turkey promised to hire Russian companies to help build the pipeline to Ceyhan. Shortly after this agreement, the Russian oil company Lukoil expressed its desire to join the Baku-Ceyhan pipeline project.[43]

The backbone of Turkey's rapprochement strategy with Russia through economic relations was dealt a serious blow during the August 1998 financial crisis in Russia. When the Russian government devalued Ruble, which was devalued by 70 percent in black market, foreign investors doing business in Russia, including many Turkish businessmen, lost a significant amount of money. In order to refresh the financial market, the Russian government made a 90-day moratorium in repayment of debts. Foreign investors were also obliged not to make short-term speculative currency exchanges in the financial market.[44] This crisis not only damaged the economic relations between Turkey and Russia, but also created a mini crisis in Turkey. In this, Turkish companies both lost their comparative advantage *vis-à-vis* the local producers in Russia due to the devaluation of the Ruble, and suffered a financial crisis due to their inability collect money from their Russian partners.

Nonetheless, Turkey's relations with Russia gained a new momentum when Prime Minister Bülent Ecevit paid an official visit to Moscow between 4-6 November 1999. During the visit, he met with his Russian counterpart Vladimir Putin, and the two Prime Ministers initialed a Joint Declaration on Cooperation in the Struggle against Terrorism, Agreements on Abolition of Visas for Diplomatic Passports, Cooperation in the Veterinary Field and a Protocol on Cooperation in the Field of Information. The Protocol on Joint Economic Commission was also signed.[45] During the visit, Ecevit conspicuously remained silent about the Russian forces attacking Groznyi in its Second Chechen War, which resumed in September 1999. This gesture was intended to thank the then-President Boris Yeltsin and Prime Minister Evgenii Primakov for their prudence in winter 1998-99, which saved Turkish-Russian relations from diplomatic disaster when Yeltsin refused the Duma decision to grant asylum to the PKK leader Abdullah Öcalan.[46] Vladimir Putin's determination to solve the Chechen problem in accordance with the terms set by Moscow was another reason why Ecevit used a soft language on the issue. In fact, ending Chechen separatism, with the use of brute force if necessary was the single most important domestic priority for Vladimir Putin during his tenure as acting Prime Minister.[47]

Reflecting these improvements in Turkey's relations with the Russian Federation, Prime Minister of the Russian Federation Mikhail Kasianov, accompanied by a large delegation of Ministers, visited Turkey in 23-25 October 2000. During the visit, Joint Economic Commission Protocol, Interstate Co-operation Protocol in Transportation Field and Protocol on the Formation of a Joint Committee on Co-operation in Defense Industry were signed by representatives of the two countries.[48] The three-day visit of Kasianov produced another important agreement on lifting mutual personnel quotas on their respective embassies. During the visit, Moscow intended to show that it wanted to become Turkey's principal energy provider and a respectable arms supplier in Turkey's ambitious defense acquisition scheme. This policy was in tandem with Russia's new foreign policy concept that stipulated a priority to economic factors. Not surprisingly, Moscow avoided talking about the geopolitical rivalry in the Caucasus and Central Asia region but rather focused on increasing bilateral trade and energy deals.[49]

Relying on the newly emerging understanding between the two states, the defense co-operation has also moved up the agenda. It was shared that further progress in this sector would create a basis for expanded trust and economic relations, which was missing in the relations. These concerns have characterized Turkey's attitude during a 4.5 billion US Dollars tender to build 145 attack helicopters. Although Turkey's history of US arms purchases and experience of working with Bell Helicopter Textron in particular were the biggest advantages for the US candidate, the King Cobra AH-1Z, Turkey took the Russian-Israeli bid Kamov's helicopter Ka-50-2 very seriously. Although at the end, Turkey chose Bell Helicopter Textron over Kamov in June 2000, the deal has not been finalized yet.[50] The reason was that the influential US Armenian and Greek lobbies, as well as human rights groups could force the US Congress to block the sale of the King Cobra's because of human rights concerns. The very fact that the Russian Company still maintains its hopes for this tender shows that Russia could even compete with the United States, the key ally of Turkey, in providing military technology to Turkey.[51]

Another recent top-level visit by a Russian was the visit by the Russian Minister of Foreign Affairs Igor Ivanov to Turkey in 7-8 June 2001. This was the first official visit at this level from Russia to Turkey since 1992. During the visit, the sides shared views on developments regarding the Caucasus, Middle East, Iraq and Central Asia and on ways that the two countries may contribute to the efforts for finding solutions to current conflicts in the region.[52] The significance of this visit was that both Turkey and the Russian Federation could extend the level of bilateral cooperation to include their multilateral relations and to coordinate their foreign policies towards a number of regions, where both countries play important roles.

The level of military cooperation between Turkey and the Russian Federation is likely to determine the potency of Turkish-Russian relations. It was one of the issues discussed during Kasianov's visit between 23-25 October 2000, when it was decided that a 'Military Cooperation Commission' be established between Turkey and Russia. The task of the Commission was to provide a proper foundation for greater cooperation, particularly in defense industry. In order to improve the level of military cooperation, General Anatolii Kvashnin, Chief of Staff of the Russian Federation, met his Turkish counterpart General Hüseyin Kıvrıkoğlu in January 2002. They discussed issues relating to bilateral military and military-technical cooperation, Russia-NATO relations, international terrorism, U.S. missile defense plans and European security. The two top generals also signed an agreement for military cooperation and collaboration on military training.[53] The agreement created a strong base for expanded military cooperation.

Turkey and the Russian Federation: Strategic Partners or Strange Bedfellows?

The emerging atmosphere in Turkish-Russian relations could potentially result in greater cooperation in various foreign policy issues of between Turkey and the Russian Federation, though it is far from certain that this cooperation could reach to the level of 'strategic partnership'. The Russian President Vladimir Putin has been very innovative in this respect. For example, his approach to the Commonwealth of Independent States (CIS), which remains a top priority area for Russian foreign and security policy, implies a more subtle and business-like approach. Instead of treating the CIS states as a uniform collectivity whose integration must be tightly gauged by Moscow, he promoted the idea that integration could flexibly proceed at multiple-speeds and levels. This is compatible with Turkey's intention to play a role model for the Turkic states of Central Asia and Azerbaijan. Thus, both states could promote their positions without conflicting with the others. Moscow could benefit from the moderating role of Turkey in Central Asia and Caucasus.

Another area where Turkey and the Russian Federation are likely to deepen their cooperation is the Middle East, in general, and Iraq, in particular. Turkey and the Russian Federation have common interest in maintaining peace and stability in the region, and the territorial integrity of Iraq. Moreover, both Ankara and Moscow seek to lift economic sanctions against Iraq, which weaken their economies.[54]

Nevertheless, despite the fact that Turkey and the Russian Federation have both enlarged and deepened the level of their relations, there are still some structural limitations on the future development of these relations. First, the relations of Turkey and the Russian Federation with the Western powers have been based on conflicting orientations. While Turkey seeks to be a member of the European Union with the help of the United States, the Russian Federation seeks to counter-balance the United States by improving its relations with the European Union. Secondly, both Turkey and the Russian Federation are getting closer towards each other by pragmatic motivations. Since their strategic goal is to improve their relations with the Western powers, either Turkey or the Russian

Federation could opt for improving their relations with the Western powers at the expense of the other party if they consider this in their self-interest.[55]

Clearly, the European Union is much more attractive project for these states than their potential 'strategic partnership'. Although both countries have many problems that make their membership in the European Union a remote possibility, Turkey has a realistic prospect of joining the European Union if it succeeds in fulfilling the Copenhagen criteria and in securing political and economic stability. To make this prospect a reality, Turkey was given a candidate status during the 1999 Helsinki Summit of the European Union.[56] In the case of the Russian Federation, however, Russia's structural political and economic problems as well as its difficulties in the process of federalization make its membership in the foreseeable future very unlikely.

The emerging relationship between Turkey and the Russian Federation could gain a sound and solid basis if this relationship was redefined constructively in coordination with the European Union and the United States. Such an opportunity emerged when Russian President Vlasimir Putin signaled Russia's full support in the fight against terrorism following the terrorist attacks of the September 11 during his meetings with the NATO and the EU leaderships in Brussels on 3 October 2001.

However, it is a mistake to assume that Russia has made a historic choice to become one of America's allies since September 11. Although Putin was sympathetic to the American concerns, he seems to be exploiting America's preoccupation in Central Asia and the Middle East in order to extract specific concessions on such issues as NATO expansion, missile defenses, loan forgiveness, the war in Chechnya. Moscow still strongly rejects the US-centered unipolarity of the post-Cold War world order, insisting on multi-polarity as the cornerstone of international peace and stability. Multi-polarity can be promoted, according to Russian foreign policy-makers, through co-operation with China, India and Europe, since these states share an interest in counterbalancing the power of the United States. Accordingly, the Putin blueprint for Russia's revival as a strong state and as a great power (*derzhava*) is like to cause further tensions between the United States and the Russian Federation, which could have a negative effect on Turkish-Russian relations as well.[57]

Conclusion

Based on our analysis of the Turkish-Russian relations, it could be concluded that apart from the factors intrinsic about Turkey and the Russian Federation, their changing positions in the international system should also be taken into account in analyzing these relations. From this point of view, the relations between Turkey and Russia have taken on a different character before and after 1997. Between 1992-1997, the relations were characterized by a geopolitical rivalry between the two regional powers. Since 1997, however, both parties have moved to normalize their relations as their positions towards the Western institutions also started to converge.

The emerging atmosphere of cooperation between Turkey and the Russian Federation contributes to the adoption of a constructive approach by these states for dealing with the complexities of post-Cold War international system. Since both Turkey and the Russian Federation need to survive under the difficult conditions of the post-Cold War international system, they need each other.[58] For this purpose, economic cooperation is likely to moderate the geopolitical rivalry between the two states. Moreover, their success in fulfilling the Western political norms and in achieving high levels of economic growth could result in improvement in their relations with the Western powers. In any case, it is much better for them to cooperate in forging mutually beneficial economic and political relations, and in understanding each other than being obstructive and locked in a mutually non-beneficial geopolitical rivalry.

Nevertheless, we should admit that there are certain limits to this newly discovered friendship between Turkey and the Russian Federation. Above all, the element of trust, which is vital for any enduring relationship, is missing in their relations. The lack of mutual trust is stems mainly from the fact that these countries have developed their relations without settling their rivalries over the Caucasus and Central Asia, which could re-emerge in the near future. Furthermore, they have different orientations towards the West. While Turkey seeks to be a member of the European Union with the help of the United States, the Russian Federation seeks to counter-balance the United States by improving its relations with the European Union. All in all, we could conclude that despite the success of both countries in getting closer to each other in recent years, their pragmatic rather than strategic concerns establish a natural limitation to the growth of their bilateral relations in the long-term.

Notes

* In the transliteration of non-English words, the rules pertaining to the Library of Congress transliteration system is followed throughout.

1 Sezer-Bazoğlu, D. (2001), 'Turkish-Russian Relations A Decade Later: From Adversity to Managed Competition', *Perceptions*, vol.6, no.1, p. 80.

2 Cutler, R.M. (1991), 'Russian and Soviet Relations with Greece and Turkey: A Systems Perspective', in D. Constas (ed.), *The Greek-Turkish Conflict in the 1990s*, London, Macmillan, pp. 183–206.

3 Bilge, A.S. (1997), 'An Analysis of Turkish-Russian Relations', *Perceptions*, vol.2, no.2, p. 75.

4 See Nizameddin, T. (1999), *Russia and the Middle East: Towards a New Foreign Policy*, London, Hurst & Company, pp. 17-8.

5 Cutler, 'Russian and Soviet Relations with Greece and Turkey', pp. 183–206.

6 Sakwa, R. (1996), *Russian Politics and Society*, 2nd edn, London, Routledge, p. 278.

7 Sezer-Bazoğlu, B. (2000), 'Turkish-Russian Relations: From Adversity to 'Virtual Rapprochement', in A. Makovsky and S. Sayarı, (eds.), *Changing Dynamics of Turkish Foreign Policy*, Washington, DC, Washington Institute for Near East Policy, p. 95.

8 Sayan, S. and Zaim, O. (1998), 'Black Sea Economic Cooperation Project', in L. Rittenberg (ed.) *The Political Economy of Turkey in the Post-Soviet Era: Going West and Looking East?*, Westport, CT., p. 117.

9 For further information on the problems in Turkish-Russian economic relations, see G. Kazgan (1998), 'The Political Economy of Relations between Turkey and Russia', in Rittenberg (ed.) *The Political Economy of Turkey in the Post-Soviet Era*, pp. 137-156.

10 Stankevich, S. (1992, March 28), 'Derzhava v poiskakh sebia', *Nezavisimaia gazeta*.

11 Zhirinovskii, V. (1993), *Poslednii brosok na iug*, Moscow, LDPR, pp. 63-4.

12 Light, M. (1996), 'Foreign Policy Thinking', in N. Malcom, A. Pravda, R. Allison and M. Light, *Internal Factors in Russian Foreign Policy*, Oxford, Oxford University Press, pp. 81-8.

13 Allison, R. (1996), 'Military Factors in Foreign Policy', in Malcolm et. al., *Internal Factors in Russian Foreign Policy*, pp. 271-75.

14 Mlenchik, L. (1999), *Evgenii Primakov. Istoriia odnoi kar'ery*, Moscow, Tsentrpoligraf, pp. 322-29.

15 Tanrısever, O.F. (2001, Summer), 'Russia and the Independent Turkic States: Discovering the Meaning of Independence,' *Eurasian Studies*, no.20, p. 99.

16 Gökay, B. and Langhorne, R. (1996), *Turkey and the New States of the Caucasus and Central Asia*, London, HMSO, p. 32.

17 Trenin, D. (2001), 'Russia's Security Interests and Policies in the Caucasus Region', in B. Coppitiers (ed.), *Contested Borders in the Caucasus*, Brussels: VUB University Press, p. 91.

18 Tanrısever, O.F. (2002), 'Sovyet-Sonrası Dönemde Rusya'nın Kafkasya Politikası', in M. Türkeş and İ Uzgel (eds.), *Türkiye ve Komşuları*, Ankara, İmge, pp. 391-94.

19 Altunışık, M. (1998), 'Turkey and the Changing Oil Market in Eurasia', in Rittenberg (ed.), *The Political Economy of Turkey in the Post-Soviet Era*, pp. 159-162.

20 Sezer-Bazoğlu, D. (2000), 'Turkish-Russian Relations: The Challenges of Reconciling Geopolitical Competition with Economic Partnership', *Turkish Studies*, vol.1, no.1, p. 70.

21 Gorvett, J. (2001), 'Pipelines, Tankers and Economics Attempt to Navigate Turkey's Narrow Straits', *Washington Report on Middle East Affairs*, vol.20, no.4, pp. 28-29.

22 Altunışık, M.B. (2000), 'The Complex Web of Relations in the Caspian Hub', in İ. Soysal (ed.), *Turkish Views of Eurasia*, Istanbul, ISIS Press, p. 169.

23 Güçlü, Y. (2001), 'Regulation of the Passage through the Turkish Straits', *Perceptions*, vol.6, no.1, pp. 125-132.

24 Akgün, M. (1997, Winter), 'Turkey and Russia: Burdened by History and Myopia, *Private View*, no.4.

25 Henze, P.B. (2001), 'Turkey's Caucasian Initiatives', *Orbis: A Journal of World Affairs*, vol.45, no.1, pp. 81-91.

26 Tanrısever, O.F. (2000, Autumn), 'The Battle for Chechnia: Russia Confronts Chechen Secessionism', *METU Studies in Development*, vol.27, nos.3-4, p. 337.

27 Nadzharov, A. (1996, December 20), 'Interv'iu s N. Kovalevom', *Rossiiskaia gazeta*, pp. 4-5.

28 Olson, R. (1998), 'Turkish and Russian Foreign Policies, 1991-1997: The Kurdish and Chechnya Questions', *Journal of Muslim Minority Affairs*, v.18, no.2, p. 209.

29 *Hürriyet*, 25 January 1995.
30 Olson, 'Turkish and Russian Foreign Policies, 1991-1997', pp. 221-223.
31 Kanlı, Y. (1997, January 17), 'Missiles: Provocation or Right of Self Defense?', *Turkish Probe*.
32 Komarov, V. (1999, December 21), 'Russian Defences for NATO Member Greece', *The Russia Journal*.
33 Trenin, D. (1997), 'Russia and Turkey: A Cure from Schizophrenia', *Perceptions*, vol.2, no.2, p. 65.
34 See Pushkov, A.K. (1993-94, Winter), 'Letter from Eurasia: Russia and America: The Honeymoon's Over', *Foreign Policy*, vol.93, no.1, pp. 88-9.
35 Nemeth, Z. (2002), 'Central Europe: Hungarian Perspectives', *Perceptions*, vol.6, no.4, p. 72.
36 Migranian, A. (1997), *Rossiia v poiskakh identichnosti*, Moscow, Mezhdunarodnaia otnosheniia, pp. 399-401.
37 Winrow, G.M. (1998), 'Turkey's Evolving Role in the Post-Soviet World', in Rittenberg (ed.), *The Political Economy of Turkey in the Post-Soviet Era*, p. 104.
38 Eralp, A. (2000), 'Turkey in the Enlargement Process: From Luxembourg to Helsinki', and the European Union in the Aftermath of the Cold War', *Perceptions*, vol.5, no.2, pp. 18-21.
39 Moisi, D. (1999), 'Dreaming of Europe', *Foreign Policy*, no.115, pp. 44-60.
40 Bayar, S. (2000), *Rusya Federasyonu Ülke Raporu*, İstanbul, İhracatı Gelistirme Merkezi, p. 39.
41 *Hürriyet*, 17 December 1997.
42 Sezer-Bazoğlu, D. (2000), 'Turkish-Russian Relations: The Challenges of Reconciling Geopolitical Competition with Economic Partnership', *Turkish Studies*, vol.1, no.1, p. 66.
43 Russia formally gave its approval for its oil companies to invest in the Baku-Ceyhan pipeline project in April 2002. Lelyveld, M. (2002, April 17), 'Russia: Government Approves Investments in Baku-Ceyhan Pipeline Project', *RFE/RL Newsline*.
44 Hanson, P. (1999), 'The Russian Economic Crisis and the Future of Russian Economic Reform', *Europe-Asia Studies*, Vol. 51, No. 7, pp.1154-57.
45 *Cumhuriyet*, 8 November 1999.
46 *Turkish Daily News*, 27 December, 1998.
47 Tanrısever, O.F. (2000, Fall), 'Rusya'daki 2000 Yılı Cumhurbaşkanlığı Seçimlerinin Reform Süreci Açısından Bir Analizi, *Avrasya Dosyası*, p. 281.
48 *Cumhuriyet*, 25 October 2000.
49 Kultigin, K. (2001, January 31), 'Turkey and Russia: A Strategic Partnership?', *Biweekly Briefing*.
50 'Ankara Opts for Bell to Supply Attack Helicopters', *Financial Times*, 22 July 2000.
51 Wright, J. (2000, July 29), 'U.S. Government Pressure Seen in Chopper Contest', *The Russia Journal*.
52 *Cumhuriyet*, 8 June 2001.
53 Fuller, L. (2002, January 17), 'Russian Chief of General Staff Ends Visit to Turkey', *RFE/RL Newsline*.
54 Freedman, R.O. (1998), 'Russia and the Middle East', *Middle East Quarterly*, vol.5, no.18, pp. 8-13.
55 For further information on the sources of Turkish foreign policy, see M. Aydın (2000), 'Determinants of Turkish Foreign Policy-II: Changing Patterns and Conjunctures during

the Cold War', *Middle Eastern Studies*, vol.36, no.1, pp.103-140; and M. Aydın (1999), 'Determinants of Turkish Foreign Policy: Historical Framework and Traditional Inputs', *Middle Eastern Studies*, vol.35, no.4, pp.152-187.

56 Eralp, A. (2000), 'Turkey and the European Union in the Post-Cold War Era', in Makovsky and Sayarı (eds.), *Changing Dynamics of Turkish Foreign Policy*, pp. 184-86.

57 Brzezinski, Z. (2001, November 2), 'A New Age of Solidarity? Don't Count on It', *Washington Post*.

58 Markushin, V. (1997), 'Russia-Turkey: Doomed to Be Eternal Neighbors', *Perceptions*, vol.2, no.1, p. 93.

Chapter 8

Between Euphoria and *Realpolitik*: Turkish Policy toward Central Asia and the Caucasus[1]

Mustafa Aydın

Global Changes and an Enlarged Turkic World?

During the worldwide rapid changes experienced in the late 1980s, a new international system emerged upon the collapse of the USSR and the Eastern Bloc, ending the bipolar world system. Within this new international system, Turkey has found itself at the center of the Eurasian region that has become the focal point of global geopolitics. Further, Turkey has been cited as an important actor because of its strong historical, cultural, ethnic and linguistic bonds with the newly independent states of Central Asia (plus Azerbaijan). Thus, the positive role Turkey might play in this region has been extensively discussed, not only within Turkey but also in the West, whose fear that radical Islam might fill the power vacuum that occurred in the region with the demise of the Soviet Union, led to strong encouragement to the newly independent states to adopt a 'Turkish model' of secular democracy, combined with a liberal economy.

The emergence of eight independent states to Turkey's northeast at the end of the Cold War, arguably enlarged Turkey's role in the world, and made Turkey deeply aware of a vast territory inhabited largely by fellow Muslim, Turkic-speakers. This presented Turkey with a historical opportunity, ending years of introversion, and emphasizing Turkey's common cultural, linguistic, and religious bonds with the Newly Independent States (NIS) of Central Asia and the Caucasus (CA&C).[2]

The truth of the matter is that Turkey in the 1990s faced both tremendous opportunities and potential risks in CA&C, which collectively posed extraordinary and complex challenges. In addition, these challenges presented themselves in a decade when Turkey itself was undergoing vast changes; the 1980s probably brought sharper change to Turkey than perhaps any decade since the 1920s. Thus, this chapter will look at Turkey in its new environment, while concentrating on the CA&C.

Adapting to the New Environment

Having based its post-war foreign and security policies on the strategic importance it played for the West, due to its location *vis-à-vis* the Soviet Union, Turkey, initially, hardly welcomed the end of the Cold War. As the function and relevance of NATO in the post-Cold War world order was opened up to discussion, Turkey suddenly found itself in a 'security limbo' and realized that the end of the 'threat discourse' was fundamentally damaging to its Western security connection, and to the military and the economic benefits derived from it. While the emergence of liberal democracies in Eastern Europe created a buffer zone between Western Europe and Russia, Turkey still felt threatened by the lingering uncertainties regarding its immediate neighborhood and faced, at the same time, the possibility of being abandoned by its Western allies. This shook the very foundation of Turkish security thinking and policy, and the need to reassess its post-Cold War situation *vis-à-vis* potential threats was openly expressed.[3]

At the same time, while it was observed in Turkey that the fundamental paradigms of the bipolar system were radically altered by the fast-changing scene of international politics, it also became clear that Turkey could no longer follow its traditional foreign policy posture based on the relative safety and stability of the Cold War politics. At this juncture, as Turkey was getting increasingly uneasy about its post-Cold War posture regarding its foreign and security policies, the emergence of Turkic states beyond its north-eastern border was a welcome break, as put by the daily *Milliyet*, 'it has been a great thrill for Turks to realize that they are no longer alone in the world.'[4] Nevertheless, Turkey's response to the Soviet Muslims' popular movement during the late 1980s was, perhaps not surprisingly, somewhat cautious, especially at the outset when the status of the new republics was far from clear.

Ever since the establishment of the Turkish nation-state within almost the same boundaries as present day Turkey, its Republican leaders, conscious of the dangers of any kind of pan-Turkist adventures such as had characterized the policies of the last days of the Ottoman Empire, had been quite consistently categorical on their denial to express any interest in so-called 'outside Turks', especially those within the Soviet Union. Thus, when confronted with the opportunity to establish relations with the individual Soviet republics after Gorbachov's *glasnost* and *prestreoika* policies began to open the closed Soviet system, Turkey's main policy was still designed meticulously to avoid any perception of Turkey's seeking to undermine the existing USSR.[5] For example, the then president Turgut Özal was very cautious when asked about Turkey's view of events in Soviet Azerbaijan in 1990. Arguing that Turkey was concerned solely with its own internal problems, and that the Azerbaijan crisis was an internal affair of the Soviet Union, he added that Turkey did not nurture aspirations of a Turkish empire that would encompass the Turkic peoples of the Soviet Union. Rather, it would continue to follow Atatürk's policy of non-entanglement in foreign disputes, and the principle of 'peace at home, peace in the world.'[6]

Since that time, however, Turkish policy toward CA&C has changed dramatically, and after the Soviet Union formally broke up in December 1991, the implementation of a new Turkish policy orientation soon followed.[7] As a result, by the end of 1991, Turkey had completely abandoned its Moscow-centered stance, and embarked full-force on a program of active relations with the Soviet successor states. Indeed, the presidents of Turkic republics were welcomed in Ankara in November and December 1991 in quick succession and given promises of support and assistance.[8]

Although initially cultural, linguistic, and religious affinities were the stimulating factors for forging closer ties, Ankara's new attitude toward CA&C has been based more on pragmatic economic and foreign policy considerations than on simple nationalist rhetoric or sentimental concerns. First of all, as mentioned in chapter two of this volume, 'the international environment has changed and the bloc system is ended. Turkey has to accept, against its will, that it is a regional power.'[9] Thus, it should be admitted that what has happened in Turkish foreign policy in the 1990s was a process of adaptation to the regional and global changes that had fundamentally affected its international setting. In other words, Turkey, 'with its unique culture, geography and history is located at the very centre of this new political and economic conglomerate [i.e. Eurasia]. Therefore, these developments have increased Turkey's regional and international responsibilities,' from which it cannot shy away.[10]

Turkey's responsibilities, as understood by the then prime minister Süleyman Demirel, meant that Turkey could, and indeed should, play a dynamic role in connecting the newly independent Central Asian and Caucasian states to the rest of the world, and help them in their quest for an identity.[11] This role also included efforts towards regional cooperation through such organizations as BSEC and ECO, which, from Turkey's perspective, if worked on the basis of cooperation and mutual benefit, would both help to stabilize the region, eventually contributing to world peace and stability, and also provide an institutional link for these states through which they could connect to the rest of the world.

At another level, Turkey also expected to gain major economic benefits from the development of closer ties with the CA&C republics, which were seen as promising by a growing Turkish industry. In fact, the potential for economic cooperation was quite substantial in the region, and the Turkish private sector, with a heavy backing from the government, had moved extensively to exploit the region's economic potential.[12] At the same time, there was also the expectation that Turkey would become politically more important in regional and global politics because of cultural and ethnic links with the region's large Turkic populations which were undergoing profound political changes. This view was also based on the belief that Turkey's secular and emerging democratic credentials would enhance its importance as a model for future development in the former Soviet republics.[13]

Yet, there were also those in Turkey who objected to pursuing such an 'active' policy in the region, especially when it was coupled with, either pan-Turkic images or with extended aid offers.[14] Objections to such a course were quite substantial, especially when considering Turkey's ability to meet its commitments towards the region without slighting other necessary sectors of the economy. The Turkish economy was, and still is stretched, with a large deficit and high inflation.[15] Accordingly, Turkey found itself unable, after approximately five years, to meet its promises to the regional states, and overcommitted the limits of its capabilities, thus, ending up pleasing no one.

At the time, however, Turkey tried hard to maximize its assets and long-term footholds in the region, by pursuing an active policy. Within the first year of independence alone, over 1170 Turkish delegations had visited the region,[16] and in October 1992 Turkey hosted the presidents of Turkic states in Istanbul for an inaugural Turkic Summit.[17] Direct air connections and a satellite broadcast link have been established, and to facilitate these activities and to co-ordinate the flow of assistance to the area, the Turkish International Cooperation Agency (TICA) was established in Ankara in January 1992.

Aid by TICA (US Dollars)

	1993	**1994**	**1995**	**1996**
Azerbaijan	457,642	783,317	453,192	324,547
Georgia	-	300,407	276,831	166,163
Kazakhstan	1,412,397	5,026,288	4,931,744	1,001,900
Kyrgyzstan	160,705	994,427	1,074,761	524,063
Uzbekistan	130,004	38,205	171,392	384,793
Turkmenistan	134,196	651,993	1,021,286	774,735
Tajikistan	31,073		271,800	212,245
	1997	**1998**	**1999**	
Azerbaijan	243,948	886,606	309,455	
Georgia	87,494	140,038	214,451	
Kazakhstan	2,877,038	1,045,185	3,696,507	
Kyrgyzstan	305,538	4,044,254	566,871	
Uzbekistan	151,373	271,682	356,312	
Turkmenistan	321,780	218,014	324,343	
Tajikistan	147,427	124,803	156,358	

Source: From different country reports of TICA which were published in Ankara in 2000.

At the same time, a greater Turkish role in the region was favoured by the West as a counter-weight against the ambitions of Iran to influence the region. The fear that the vacuum left by the collapse of Soviet Communism could lead to Islamic fundamentalism becoming the politically dominant force among the Muslims of CA&C led to the West's promotion of Turkey as a Muslim, yet secular and democratic model for development.[18] In President Demirel's words, Turkey had proved that 'Islam, democracy, human rights and [a] market economy could go together hand in hand.'[19] Hence, as a result of growing self confidence about its potential and political support in the West, Turkey felt ready to take advantage of the new economic and political opportunities when the new states emerged, one by one, from the former Soviet Union. Thus, following various visits of regional leaders to Ankara, the Turkish Premier toured the area in April 1992 and offered $1.1 billion in import credits and loans.[20] Cultural and economic cooperation protocols were exchanged, and in a direct and unprecedented challenge to Russian interests in the region, the then Turkish prime minister Demirel spoke of the possibility of establishing a 'Union of Turkic States', and suggested that Central Asia might be better off away from the Ruble Zone.[21] Turkey also discussed the possibility of providing military training to the regional countries, actively advocated building gas and oil pipelines through Turkey to market the Caspian energy resources, and encouraged the adoption of the Turkish, that is Latin, alphabet for all the Turkic states. By mid-1992 Turkey had made a bold bid for leadership and influence in the region in the political, financial, cultural, military, and economic areas; the region nevertheless presented important challenges for Turkey.

Disappointments and Facing Reality

Despite all the promising signs, it quickly became clear that Turkey was not alone in its bid to fill the power vacuum emerging in the region following the collapse of the USSR. On the contrary, the competition between the rival countries seeking influence in the rapidly changing CA&C became a 21st century replica of the 'Great Game' that had been played by European imperial powers at the turn of the century.[22] Among the actors envisioned to be key players were the Russian Federation, Turkey, Iran, Saudi Arabia, the US, the EU, Pakistan, China, Japan and Israel, and at least four of them were considered as the 'model' to be emulated by the NIS of CA&C. Each of the countries seeking influence in the region had their specific objectives, and the competition included economic, political, ideological and religious dimensions. Thus, various possibilities for conflict among the regional rivals shortly emerged. From the Turkish perspective, the possibility of military conflict between Turkey on the one hand and either Iran or Russia on the other provided ample concern.

Moreover, the success of Turkey's overtures in the region depended in considerable measure on how the Turkic peoples of the region, who were deeply involved in the painful processes of self-identification and nation-building, would view an alliance of their still emerging position and identity with that of Turkey in the long term. As of 2002, these republics were still being governed by their old Communist party structures and by the same elites that had ruled under the former Soviet system, though now these groups mostly embraced nationalist themes. There is little doubt that, at some stage 'these old leaderships will be … replaced by a new type of leadership' and that 'Islam and nationalism will play an important role in this matter.'[23] However, this development will be the cause of controversy, not only within these states but also between other regional actors and, as the result of this process, will almost certainly determine the future orientations, both domestic and international, of these states. Consequently, these realignments will be discussed as hotly outside these republics as within them, no doubt creating increased tension and suspicion between regional supporters of the various sides within the argument.

Turkey is concerned that Iran will attempt to turn regional states into theocracies in its own image, an apprehension shared by Saudi Arabia, Russia, China, the Gulf States, and the West, generally. On the other hand, Iran is worried that Turkey's active role in the region might create a pan-Turkic hegemony on its northern and western frontiers. Thus, it is likely that the competition between the two opposing models of political development for the Turco-Muslim peoples of the CA&C will continue well into the new century; the secular model of Turkey, with its political pluralism, and the Islamist model supported by Iran. Although it has been pointed out that 'exporting the revolution' has almost ceased in Iran since Khomeini's death, it should not be overlooked that the possibility that 'Iran's competition with Turkey in Central Asia could become more ideological in the future,' especially 'if its relations with Turkey deteriorate elsewhere.'[24] In such a situation 'Islamic politics might be one of the Iranian instruments to be used in its opposition to Turkish or Western influence in the region,' and Turkey in turn would 'undoubtedly view its role in Central Asia as contributing, among other things, to a measured view of Islam in society and politics, and for a secular approach to government,' thus putting itself on a collision course with Iran.[25]

Beyond the regional rivalries and struggles for self-identification within the republics, such a role as Turkey has aspired to play in the region, that of 'linchpin', connecting the Balkans, the Middle East, Central Asia and the Caucasus, also depends, to a large extent, on 'whether Turkey can serve as a viable and acceptable 'model' for the newly independent republics.'[26] Although Turkey, with its modern and secular model, and obvious Western support, seemed briefly to offer the 'central alternative' for regional states to emulate in the post-Cold War world, especially 'in view of their aspirations for organic ties with the West,'[27] it has become clear that it is still too early to argue that the 'Turkish model' has been universally accepted throughout the region without further deliberation.[28] One of the attractions of the Turkish model has been Turkey's relationship with the West, and its application for membership to the EU. While the regional states recognize that Europe is of critical economic importance to them, the question remains that if Turkey itself were denied entry into the EU, how could Turkey facilitate greater ties with Europe and the West?

Furthermore, the chances of NIS's adopting the Turkish model in the region are also hampered by its vagueness, although in general terms, it is secular, democratic, and market-oriented. Its adoption is further hampered by the attitudes of Turkish leaders whose efforts in the region have been motivated by a 'big brother' attitude and by an almost missionary desire to spread the Turkish model for the 'enlightenment of our Turkic brothers' in the region. However, it appears that these republics who have only recently freed themselves from almost a hundred years of Russian domination, are not seeking a new 'big brother' in their search for a model. The CA&C states are looking for cooperation and not a new domination of their newly forged polities. Therefore, while Turkey's policies toward CA&C need to reflect a certain degree of awareness of the needs, constraints, and sensitivities of the local population, it is also important for Turkey to avoid any hint of latter-day domination in either the political or the economic realm.

Moreover, Turkey's moves in the region to forge closer relations have prompted its rivals to question whether Turkey is aiming for regional hegemony and/or a revival of the historical pan-Ottomanist and pan-Turkist unions. Although Turkish leaders have repeatedly expressed that fears of a revival of pan-Turkism as an extension of Turkey's efforts in the region are unfounded, the suspicions of its neighbors have continued to be fuelled by Turkey's prior tendency to refer to all Turkic-speakers simply as Turks, and by talk about the emergence of a belt of Turkish-speaking communities from the Adriatic to China.[29] Further, Turkey's common ethnic, linguistic and cultural unity with the Turkic-speaking people of the CA&C has been extensively emphasized by both Turkey and the West as a part of their promotion of the 'Turkish model' in the region.

Apart from attracting reactive responses from its regional rivals, Turkey's emphasis on commonalties between the people of Turkey and the Turkic-speaking people of the former Soviet CA&C, have also resulted in resentment among those people, since these views appear to contradict with 'the individual and separate self-identity and national awareness formulated by each of these people[s].'[30] It remains clear that most of the peoples in CA&C, despite their common Turkic origin, have a strong sense of their distinctiveness and, at least initially, prefer to assert their own individual identity rather than be submerged once again within a broader cultural and political umbrella.[31]

In addition, there is also the 'Russian factor' to take into account when considering the Turkish policies in the region. Since Russia was, and still is, the only great power in the region, Turkey, understandably does not wish to alienate or alarm Moscow by exerting too much influence within Central Asian states, as the Russians have been acutely sensitive to any pan-Turkic, as well as Islamic, trends in Central Asia. While Russia initially welcomed, Turkish influence in the CA&C as a counterweight against Iranian dominated pan-Islamism, those views have been modified as Turkey has moved to supplant Russian influence in the region.

Thus, Russia, becoming increasingly concerned about Turkish intentions in the region, has become more aggressive in its assertion of its own rights in its 'near abroad'.[32] Russia's policies towards the CA&C appeared to be affected by its fears that the region might become a centre for Islamic fundamentalism or a pan-Turkish aggression that may threaten the security of the Russian Diaspora in the region and increase unrest among Russia's own ethnic Turkic or Muslim minorities in the Northern Caucasus.[33] Hence, after a brief self-isolation, Russia has moved to re-establish its place in the CA&C as a dominant actor. In this Russian maneuver, political, economic and military pressures have been used extensively, with Russian leaders arguing that stability in the Caucasus would be threatened without a Russian presence in Azerbaijan, and implicitly threatening that it could support Armenia in its conflict with Azerbaijan, if the latter did not accept Russian troops and grant oil concessions.[34] In turn Turkey, realizing Russian sensitivities regarding ethnic strife in the Caucasus, has repeatedly reassured Moscow of its opposition to any fragmentation of Russia by Muslim groups, and of its support for the CIS' stability and integrity.[35] On the other hand, Turkey has stood firm in its opposition to Russia's desire to review the Conventional Forces Europe Treaty (CFE) arrangements in the Caucasus. However, in the end, Russia was able to convince the west to modify the treaty and, despite Turkish protests, return many of its military forces previously withdrawn from the Caucasus. Therefore, 'deciding if and when to give priority to Russian concerns in Central Asia [and the Caucasus] over Turkey's interests' has became critical for Ankara.[36] While Turkey, soon after the collapse of the Soviet Union appeared to be gradually shifting its priorities away from Russia in its focus on the new Turkic republics of the former Soviet Union, since 1995 Turkey has become more conscious of the dangers of confrontation with Russia. Now Turkey has adopted a policy stressing that the benefits of co-operation with Russia are still greater than those of the rest of the former Soviet Central Asian republics, and has moved closer to Moscow, at least on the economic front.

In contrast to this activity and rivalry by foreign states to gain a place of influence by appealing to their common national identities, the Central Asian leadership has attempted to avoid highly controversial questions as to the place of religion (Islam) and ethnicity (Turkism) in their identity, and has thereby resisted outside pressure to chose between the various 'models' presented to them on these grounds choosing instead, to focus primarily on the future of their economic relations while keeping all their options open.

In this respect, too, Turkey has been a key object of interest to the Central Asian Turks, and a model of much attraction, economically as well as culturally. However, recognizing the limited capacity of Turkey, the Central Asian Turks have also paid attention to economic ties with the developed states of East Asia, such as Korea and Japan as well as with the Islamic states of Iran, Saudi Arabia and Pakistan in conjunction with ongoing relationships with the Western industrialized nations. As far as the competition between Turkish and Iranian models for Central Asian development is concerned, despite the West's clearly articulated political preferences for Turkey over Iran, the Central Asian Republics realize that they cannot afford to dispense with ties to either of these states. Turkey and Iran's resources are limited and both are crucially important as land routes between Central Asia, the Gulf and Europe.

Moreover the Central Asian republics also realized that although independent, they continued to be influenced by, and dependent on, Moscow, both economically and politically. Further, the continued presence in the region of large Russian minorities who now occupy key leadership positions in many CA&C states, constituted a source of direct and indirect Russian influence and interference. Thus, the NIS have kept all options open, rather than commit themselves exclusively to any one model or patron.

Perhaps resulting from this disappointment, Turkey has subsequently increasingly moved its attention to the Caucasus, a region that may yet prove more promising for partnership than has Central Asia. In addition to geographic proximity, which Turkey can utilize successfully to its benefit, the lures of the Caspian energy reserves and the need to transfer these resources to Western markets, provides an added incentive for closer involvement. Finally, the success of Turkish policies towards the newly independent Turkic states will depend on how Turkey performs with regard to ethnic strife within the CA&C. In this regard, the Caucasus has presented Turkey with a particular challenge, and Turkey's standing in the region will inevitably be determined by its responses to the existing ethnic and nationalist conflicts.

Among others, Turkey's relations with Armenia have been an especially delicate issue because of the legacy of distrust between the two nations. The Turkish-Armenian border may once again become a source of controversy, as Armenia has consistently refused to recognize the 1921 Kars Treaty signed between Turkey and the Soviet Union, which determined a permanent border.[37] In addition, the most imminent and explosive issue remains the Karabakh problem, which holds major implications for the future of Turkish-Armenian relations and, indeed, for the general security of the Caucasus region. From Turkey's point of view, the conflict has presented unacceptable options with dangerous ramifications. Turkish public opinion, stemming from longstanding public sympathy for the Azeris, has strongly encouraged the Turkish government to side with Azerbaijan, even supporting military intervention.[38] The Turkish government, on the other hand, conscious that the intervention might result in a deterioration of the country's relations with both Russia and the US, has refrained from acting on these domestic pressures. Moreover, the conflict has brought to an end tentative moves from both sides of the Turkish-Armenian border to put an end to historic animosities. Although early in the independence process both sides seemed to agree on the need to overcome psychological barriers between the two peoples, moves by the Armenians over Karabakh caused Turkish public opinion to press Ankara to speak out firmly against Armenian actions, and thus halted any process of reconciliation.

However, the Turkish government has been able to steer its way around mounting domestic pressure to intervene militarily and has avoided an escalation of these tensions by trying to mobilize an international response to Armenian attacks in Karabakh. Moreover, Turkey has tried to place the conflict onto the agendas of various international platforms, ranging from the Black Sea Economic Cooperation (BSEC)[39] to the Organization for Security and Co-operation in Europe (OSCE), in order to formulate a process for conflict resolution. Furthermore, Turkey has also displayed its awareness of the importance of the 'Russian factor' to solve the conflict by consistently seeking Russian co-operation, especially after the involvement of the OSCE and the UN.[40] However, when the matter of peace-keeping was discussed following the cease-fire between the warring parties on 12 May 1994, Turkey advocated for the deployment of a multinational force under the OSCE supervision, and against Russian peace keepers as suggested by Moscow. Turkey saw in this, another attempt by Russia to exclude the rest of the world from the Caucasus.[41] Thus, when Western pressure secured Russian consent to an OSCE force, Turkey was eager to establish a logistical support base for it in eastern Turkey.

Turkey has thus far been able to remain clear of any military involvement, and has been included in the peace-making process through the Minsk Group. This conflict firmly underscores the dilemmas that may face Turkey in its future efforts to maintain strict neutrality regarding ethnic conflicts in the former Soviet republics. The Karabakh conflict has clearly demonstrated the manner in which Turkey is likely to behave in the future *vis-à-vis* regional conflicts. So far it has ensured with political measures that the regional ethnic conflicts do not escalate to a level that seriously threatens Turkish security, and thus compel it to intervene militarily. It is far from clear, however, what kind of strategic realignments would be emerging as a result of the volatile nature of Caucasian politics, and thus, whether Turkey will or will not be drawn into some kind of alliance and/or regional conflict. Like the Karabakh issue, there exist various simmering ethnic conflicts within the Caucasus as seen in the Abkhazian secessionist movement in Georgia and in the Chechen struggle for independence from the Russian Federation.

Although the Turkish government has so far chosen to avoid involvement in the quest of the Gagauz for independence in Moldova, [42] and the Abkhazians in Georgia, the Chechen issue, and Turkey's interest in it, have rapidly became a sore point in Turkish-Russian relations. The Chechen crisis has been especially critical for Turkey, not only because Turkish public opinion has shown great sympathy for the Chechen cause, but also because the crisis has similarities to Turkey's own problem with its secessionist Kurdish guerrillas. While, Turkey has criticized Russia for its excessive use of force in Chechnya, it has been quite careful to state that the matter is an internal affair of the Russian Federation.[43] Despite all this maneuvering, however, Turkey's relations with Russia worsened rapidly with Russia's claim that the Chechens were obtaining assistance and volunteers from Turkey.[44] Moreover, it was reported that the Russians were showing signs of supporting the PKK, secessionist Kurdish group in Turkey, in response to the alleged Turkish involvement in Chechnya.[45] However, Turkey, as in the Karabakh conflict, avoided direct involvement. If the past is any indicator, it will, 'seek to avoid any entanglements in the highly localized, passionate, and irreconcilable micro-ethnic conflicts in the Caucasian region,' especially those within Russia itself, as the issue of separatism is a highly sensitive one for Moscow.[46] Additionally, one of the by-products of the conflicts in the North Caucasus – both in Abhazia and in Chechnya – has been a sense of resurgent ethnic identity among the six million strong Turkish citizens of North Caucasian origin, 'the full significance of [this resurgence] is yet to emerge.'[47] Although at the moment they are focused more in the cultural sphere, in future they may become more radical and wish to play a more determining role in the future of the North Caucasus, thus bringing Turkey into conflict with Russian interests in the region.

Moreover, given the volatile nature of Caucasian politics, there may exist situations in which Turkey may be drawn into a conflict in connection with developments beyond its control. One of the more probable and problematic scenarios that Western analysts have paid scant attention, is the existing potential for conflict between Turkey and Iran as a result of the possible spill-over effect of the Azerbaijani independence into Iranian Azerbaijan. While Turkey became the first country to extend recognition to Azerbaijan, Iran did not conceal its concern over the Turkish action, accusing Turkey of pan-Turkism, and the West of instigating such sentiments. Fears were expressed by Iran, that the Turkish recognition would encourage an independent Azerbaijan to lay claim to a 'greater Azerbaijan'. Although, the issue has subsided within Azerbaijan since Heydar Aliyev's ascent to power in Azerbaijan, it is still probable, especially if a nationalist leadership, such as that of Abulfaz Elchibey comes to power in Azerbaijan, that Iranian Azerbaijan with its estimated population of 20 million, might become restless. In such a case, even if Turkey did not seek to provoke the issue, Iran would inevitably view Turkey as the beneficiary 'in these evolving relationships that so directly affect Iran's territorial integrity,'[48] and consequently might involve itself in a high-stakes conflict with Turkey by inciting the Kurds to greater separatism, in its turn.

These factors also complicated Iran's approach to the Karabakh conflict. Although both Turkey and Iran shared similar concerns about the continuation of the Karabakh conflict, there were differences between them about how to solve the problem. While Turkey attempted to have the Karabakh conflict dealt with within the OSCE context, Iran, which also has a large Armenian minority that gives it special relations with Armenia, took a more direct approach by negotiating with, and meditating between, the two Caucasian republics. While Iran's bilateral attempts to solve the problem created concerns in Turkey about a possible increase in Iranian influence in the region, Iran, on the other hand, was concerned about Turkey's cooperation with the US to solve the problem, which was seen as paving the way for 'growing American influence in the region.'[49] Moreover, it seems likely that if Iran ever became suspicious that Azerbaijan was nurturing any separatist sentiment in Iranian Azerbaijan, Iran may choose to support Armenia openly in the Karabakh crisis, thus creating an additional source of friction with Turkey.

Turkey is also concerned that Iran may attempt to turn Muslims in CA&C toward a theocracy: Iran on the other hand is concerned that Turkey's active role in the region is aimed at forging pan-Turkic hegemony on Iran's northern and western frontiers. Thus, competition has ensued between the two opposing sides for the 'hearts and minds' of the Turco-Muslim peoples of the region. In spite of Turkey's and Iran's initial enthusiasm in approaching these republics, it has become increasingly apparent that both states lack the economic resources that would enable either of them to exercise a dominant influence in the region. Moreover, since late 1992 Moscow, which had no coherent policy towards its former colonies on its southern borders following the dissolution of the USSR, began to exhibit a keen interest in the region, redefining it as the 'Near Abroad' so that by 1994, the power vacuum created by the collapse of the USSR had proven to be a temporary phenomenon.[50]

Turkey's Role in the Caspian Basin and the Struggle for Pipelines

One of the peculiar features of the Caspian oil situation is that the regional countries most interested in the early exploration and transportation of oil and natural gas are landlocked and have to rely on the goodwill and co-operation of their neighbors to be able to export their petroleum. As each country has a preference about how the oil and natural gas should be transported to market, and external powers attempt to exert influence to ensure that the selected route best meets their needs, the issue assumes an importance quite independent of production. Indeed, under current geopolitical calculations, Russia is keenly interested in retaining, or recovering, its political influence in the Caspian Basin and in order to acquire this advantage, it has insisted that the northern pipeline from Baku, Azerbaijan, to the Russian Black Sea port of Novorossiysk should be the main transit route for oil from the Caspian region. If Russia is successful, this will ensure Moscow's exclusive and strategic control over the region's resources.

Opposing Russian insistence on the northern route, the United States and Turkey, as well as the Caucasian states of Georgia and Azerbaijan, prefer a western route through Georgia to the Turkish Mediterranean port of Ceyhan. Although there have been various projects developed by the energy-rich states of the Caspian Basin and Western oil companies to move Caspian energy resources to market, the main competition is between the northern and western routes. What is at stake is not only oil and gas transit revenues that both countries can extract from pipelines passing through their respective territories. More importantly, the pipeline network is one of the key factors in securing and maintaining influence throughout the CA&C.[51] Quite clearly, usage of the western route would give Turkey a greater influence than Russia, which, on the other hand, would benefit greatly from the northern route.

US support for the western route is firmly embedded in its wider Eurasian and Middle Eastern strategic priorities, one of which is to strengthen the newly independent states of Central Asia and the Caucasus against the influence of Russia.[52] To be able to achieve this, the United States initially supported Turkey's overtures toward the region. However, as it became increasingly clear that Turkey's financial resources and political weight would not be enough to counter Russia's neo-hegemonic resurgence in its 'near abroad', and given that American oil interests are substantial in the region, the US has moved with more determination to undermine, and even replace, Russian influence directly.[53]

A further strategic goal of the US is the exclusion of 'Iran from participation in the production of Caspian oil and gas', and the prevention of 'the development of transportation routes or pipelines that would lead from the Caspian region to either the Persian Gulf or the Indian Ocean via Iran.' This objective is, on the one hand, closely intertwined with the dual containment policy of the United States against Iran and Iraq, and, on the other, 'connected with the fundamental US strategy in the Middle East of not permitting the emergence of any dominant regional power capable of influencing the oil market in the Gulf.'[54] Although the shortest route for a pipeline from Azerbaijan to the Mediterranean is through

Armenia and eastern Turkey, the unresolved Nagorno-Karabakh conflict makes this route difficult to realize. This coupled with US opposition to passing the pipeline through Iran makes the Georgia route the only possible one for the western line. However, Georgia, too, is struggling with a number of internal conflicts, a situation that obviously is in Russia's interest.

In the late 1990s as the rivalry heightened between the northern and the western routes, the leaders of Turkey and Azerbaijan made several announcements that they believed would propel the Turkish route to the forefront for oil transportation. On 29 October 1998, the presidents of Turkey, Azerbaijan, Georgia and Kazakhstan 'strongly confirmed the accomplishment of their determination in realizing the Caspian-Mediterranean (Baku-Tbilisi-Ceyhan) Project as the main export pipeline project.'[55] On the other hand, President Niyazov of Turkmenistan, who did not wish to put his signature to the Ankara Declaration, signed a similar bilateral document with Turkey, endorsing plans for a gas pipeline under the Caspian Sea and on to Turkey via Azerbaijan and Georgia.[56] Later, the presidents of these states reaffirmed their commitment to the transportation of Caspian energy resources by the proposed Baku-Ceyhan route by signing the İstanbul Declaration during the OSCE's İstanbul Summit on 19 November 1999, with United States President Clinton adding his signature as an observer.

The US government openly put its weight behind the Turkish option, both before and after the Ankara Declaration. As recently as October 1998, when it became clear that the oil companies in the Azerbaijan International Operating Company (AIOC) were unwilling to recommend the Baku-Ceyhan route, US government officials issued a number of statements within days insisting that the Baku-Ceyhan line was the best choice and would 'provide [a] commercially viable way of carrying Caspian oil to the Mediterranean', despite the pipeline's cost.[57] Moreover, in an unprecedented effort, the United States Trade and Development Agency announced a grant of $823,000 to BOTAŞ, the Turkish Pipeline Corporation, to allow it 'to gain access to United States expertise on technical, financial, environmental and legal matters associated with negotiation of the Baku-Ceyhan oil pipeline and the trans-Caspian gas pipeline.'[58] The United States favors the Baku-Ceyhan route because it passes through pro-Western countries and would bind them closer to each other and to Western interests. Moreover, it would also secure Turkey's role as a major player in the Caspian region, which, in turn, 'would boost the status of a loyal NATO ally whose secular, moderate government could', after all, 'serve as a model for post-Soviet states such as Georgia, Azerbaijan, and Turkmenistan' and could check the influences of Iran and Russia in the region.[59]

A final twist in this competition came immediately after the announcement of Russia's new nuclear doctrine in January 2000. Earlier, when it became clear that Russia's war against the rebellious republic of Chechnya might spread to the neighboring Caucasus republics, Georgia became hesitant about the Baku-Ceyhan pipeline deal. In response to this Georgian wavering under pressure from Russia, which claimed that the Chechen rebels had bases and medical facilities in Georgia, the US quickly announced more than $120 million in aid to Georgia to bolster Georgia's staunch policy of opposing Russia.[60] Later, following President Aliyev's visit to Ankara on 9-10 January and President Süleyman Demirel's visit to Tbilisi on 14 January to discuss Georgia's last-minute demands regarding 'land expropriation, environmental standards, security of the pipeline, and transit fees' and growing instability in the Caucasus, a quickly organized mini-summit of Turkish, Georgian and Azerbaijani leaders on 16 January 2000 ended with Turkey calling for a security pact for the Caucasus modeled on a similar European initiative in the Balkans, the Southeast Europe Stability Pact.[61]

Following these developments, the presidents of Azerbaijan, Georgia and Turkey met again in Ankara on 21 January 2000 to finalize details of the Baku-Ceyhan oil pipeline. As a result, the 'Intergovernmental Agreement', 'Host Country Agreement', Turkish guarantee to buy petroleum, and 'Turn-Key Construction Agreement', signed between Azerbaijan, Turkey and Georgia during the OSCE Istanbul Summit on 18 November 1999, was approved by the Azeri and Georgian Parliaments in May 2000, and the Turkish Parliament on 22 June 2000. Later, with the signature of an agreement on 3 October 2000 by the interested parties – countries as well as international oil companies – to establish a sponsor group that would finance the construction of the Baku-Ceyhan Pipeline, the necessary legalities were concluded. Although bickering and negotiations over the pipeline continued with daily ups and downs throughout the 2001, towards the end of the year, Turkey had started the 'detailed engineering' phase, thus signaling both its intention to move ahead with the project and also the running of the project according to schedule.[62]

If the Baku-Ceyhan pipeline is built and put into operation, its main effect would be to weaken or even cut off the Central Asian and the Caucasian states' economic and transportation dependence on Russia. Azerbaijan, Kazakhstan and Turkmenistan would appear as new competitors to Russia in the export of oil and gas to the world market, and would use the money thus obtained to enhance their political independence from Russia. The role of the Western states, whose oil and gas companies would eventually provide the necessary investment, would increase, as would the role of Turkey. On the other hand, the perceived decrease in Russian influence or outside attempts to isolate or eliminate Russia in the Caspian region could easily become counter-productive, and may quickly encounter an asymmetric response potentially destructive to the stability of regional security.

Finally, in addition to the bilateral rivalries between Russia, Turkey and Iran, at a more general level, we are witnessing the emergence of two rival groups or loosely defined political alliances in the region. They are the Russian Federation, Armenia and Iran on the one side and the United States, Azerbaijan and Turkey on the other, while Georgia, though leaning towards the second group, fears Russian reprimand and refrains joining them openly. When considered with the Turkish-Israeli alignment, and Iranian distaste for its military and economic implications, the long-term significance of this kind of confrontation might have extended affects throughout Eurasia and the Middle East.

On the other hand, environmental questions surrounding the Bosphorus in particular and the Black Sea in general have also begun to weigh heavily in the choice of export routes for Caspian oil. The ports of the Black Sea, along with those in the Baltic Sea, were the primary oil export routes for the former Soviet Union, and the Black Sea remains the largest outlet for Russian oil exports. Exports through the Bosphorus have grown since the break-up of the Soviet Union in 1991, and there is increasing concern that projected Caspian Sea export volumes will exceed the ability of the Bosphorus to accommodate the tanker traffic.[63] To resolve the anticipated problems in the Bosphorus, Turkey declared new navigational rules in November 1998 and plans to install a new radar and navigation system to improve safety and operations in the Turkish Straits. However, these precautions would not be sufficient to protect the environment and provide for navigational safety through the Bosphorus in view of the expected increase in tanker traffic.[64] For this reason, the only way to avoid further congestion and environmentally hazardous accidents in the area would be the development of alternative export routes that bypass the Straits.[65]

Conclusions

The first conclusion that presents itself is the fact that the collapse of the Soviet power and the disintegration of the Soviet Union have been a mixed blessing for Turkey. While the century-old Soviet/Russian threat to Turkey's security has disappeared, the vacuum created by this departure in the CA&C has become the breeding ground on Turkey's borders for potential risks and threats for regional security because of the deep tensions between mixed national groups, contested borders, economic difficulties, and competition of outsiders for influence.

Yet, Turkey is cited as an important stabilizing actor in this emerging new order, or disorder, because of its strong historical, cultural, ethnic and linguistic bonds with the newly independent states. Thus, the positive role Turkey may play in this region has been extensively discussed not only within Turkey but also in the West, whose fear that radical Islam might fill up the power vacuum created by the collapse of the USSR, led to strong encouragement to these states to adopt a 'Turkish model' of secular democracy combined with liberal economy.

While Turkey has traditionally avoided such involvement in regional politics, it has already been unavoidably drawn into the volatile new politics of the Caucasus, where Armenia and Azerbaijan are locked in a potentially expandable war, where Georgian politics are highly unstable, and where other Muslim peoples agitate to break away from the new Russian Federation. For its part, Turkey, mindful of the disruptive impacts of sub-nationalism and ultra-nationalism, has been eager to promote the positive aspects of national formation in Central Asia and the Caucasus. Accordingly, Turkey has already made clear that transitional concepts based on Islam or pan-Turkism are not part of its policy *vis-à-vis* the states in the region, but 'linguistic and cultural links are significant and can benefit these republics in a number of practical fields' and 'cultural ties can also be a guarantee for a long term and easier cooperation.'[66]

In the meantime, a new and ever-deepening Turkish rivalry with Iran and the Russian Federation over influence in the new states of Central Asia and the

Caucasus presents potential new risks and difficult policy choices for Turkey. On the other hand, Turkey has attempted to play down the importance of these potentially threatening tendencies, instead emphasizing its moderate secular character, which could help direct the newly independent Turkic states towards a moderate and secular direction, thereby playing a moderating role in the Muslim regions of the former USSR, supporting secular government, and seeking closer relations with both Russia and Iran as well as with the Turkic republics. It should not be forgotten that Turkish-Russian mutual interest in maintaining peace in the Caucasus and Central Asia, and in regional cooperation in the Black Sea is considerable, and the importance of these states to each other could prove to be greater than that of their bilateral ties to the other Turkic states.

Finally, we can now clearly foresee that Turkey is currently undergoing a dramatic shift away from its traditional policy of isolationism, and that Turkish foreign policy in the future will increasingly focus on Central Asia, alongside the Balkans, and the Middle East. It is too early, however, to judge to what degree military developments in or tensions between the Soviet successor states in Central Asia and the Caucasus will be contributing factors for Turkish security planning in the early part of 2000s. Although Turkey has disavowed any intention of intervening militarily in inter-republican clashes in former Soviet territory, it is still conceivable that Turkish forces might be invited by these states to play the role of peace-keepers between or within them. In this context the Armenian-Azerbaijani conflict has already presented Turkey with a sense of the difficulties that it might encounter in the near future if it chooses to engage in ethnic and nationalist conflicts in the region.

On the other hand, while Turkey's new policy initiatives regarding the Turkic ethnic peoples in former Soviet Central Asia and Azerbaijan have the potential to fulfill its economic and political expectations, they are also, as we have elaborated earlier, likely to pose new challenges and problems. Thus, in short, Turkey's interest in developing closer economic and political ties with the Turkic republics carries with it the danger of Ankara's involvement in ethnic and nationalist conflicts in the region. On the other hand, though Turkey's influence in the region is limited by its own modest economic and industrial resources, the strengthening of a nationalist leadership in the region will most probably benefit Turkey over the long run, even though Turkey's initial expectations from its 'Central Asian brothers' have been disappointed. To be sure, the emergence of independent Turkic republics in Central Asia and the Caucasus represented a turning point in Turkey's regional role and policies. Turkey has become one of the important players in a region where it previously had only a marginal influence and no active involvement. Although economic and political conditions in the region are unlikely to stabilize for some years, it is almost certain that Turkish policymakers will continue with their efforts to create new networks of interdependency between Ankara and the regional capitals. Also, it is without doubt that other regional players, especially Russia and Iran, will continue to view these policies with suspicion and mount challenges to them.

Even if Turkey's initial vision proved somewhat unrealistic, the effects it generated did set the tone for Turkish policy for the rest of the 1990s and early 2000s. While Turkey has not necessarily become the model to which the new states of the Caucasus and Central Asia aspire, its thriving private sector, its secular approach toward Islam and its (usually) well-functioning democracy continue to have their appeal in the region. Meanwhile Turkey had learned two important lessons *vis-à-vis* its relationship with Russia. The first was the understanding that Russia was as important as or more important than its southern neighbors as an economic partner for Turkey. The second was that an overly aggressive foreign policy in CA&C was not advisable, given the risk of escalation into direct confrontation with Russia.

Although Turkey appears to have clear advantages as of today, no outside power has yet emerged as a leader in the competition for influence in the Central Asian and Caucasian countries, all of which have significant Muslim populations, who have shown no haste in choosing the path that each nation must take. Further, as there is not likely to be one model for all these countries, and all of the competitors have political and economic constraints on their activities, it still remains to be seen whether there is as much interest among the Central Asians in a 'Turkish Model' of secular democracy as some western strategists had hoped.

Notes

1 This chapter is substantially revised and updated version of Aydın, M. (1996), 'Turkey and the Central Asia; Challenges of Changes', *Central Asian Survey*, vol.15, no.2.

2 See Hussain, M. (1993, February 19), 'Iran and Turkey in Central Asia; Complementary or Competing Roles?', *Middle East International*; and Henze, P.B. (1992), *Turkey: Toward the Twenty-First Century*, A RAND Note.

3 Brown, J.M. (1991, May 20), 'Isolated and Suspicious', *Financial Times Special Report*, p. 4.

4 *Milliyet*, 12 December 1991.

5 During this period (from early 1989 to mid-1990), which covers the years before national sovereignty when the Republics were strictly tied to Moscow under the central government, initial steps towards establishing contacts were taken by private companies and individuals rather than the Turkish government, and Turkey established official ties with only Azerbaijan when the Azerbaijani president visited Turkey on 5-10 January 1990. Even then he was not accorded full protocol as president but hosted at ministerial level and the Soviet flag was flown next to the Azeri flag.

6 More importantly, Özal stressed the differences between the Azeris and the Turks, saying that the Azeris are Shias, and although the Azeri dialect is close to Turkish they are separate. He also alienated Azeris by saying that the Azeris, being Shia, were more the concern of Iran. See 'Flaş Ülke Oluruz', *Cumhuriyet*, 19 January 1990.

7 Turkey was the first country to recognise the independence of new republics, Azerbaijan on 9 December, and the rest on 16 December. After the recognition, Turkey also signed protocols with each of them, except Armenia, initiating diplomatic relations at ambassadorial level. See *Turkey Confidential*, December 1991, pp. 11-12; *Newspot*, 14 November 1991, pp. 2-3. Even prior to their independence, Turkey had exchanged high

level visits and signed various agreements with the then Soviet Republics after they declared sovereignty one after the other between June and October 1990, though their foreign relations were still under the surveillance of Moscow. See Şimşir, B. (1992, Summer), 'Turkey's Relations with Central Asian Turkic Republics', *Turkish Review Quarterly Digest*, vol.6, no.28, pp. 14-5.

8 President Niyazov of Turkmenistan arrived in Turkey on 2 December, President Kerimov of Uzbekistan came on 16 December, and Akayev of Kyrgyzstan landed on 22 December 1991. They were all preceded by an Azerbaijani delegation which came in November, and by February 1993, Turkey and the five Turkic Republics had signed more than 140 bilateral accords on a variety of different subjects. See Robins, Between Sentiment and Self Interest.

9 The former Turkish State Minister Kamran İnan, in an interview to *Los Angeles Times*, 16 March 1991.

10 Prime Minister Süleyman Demirel's speech at Johns Hopkins University, Bologna, Italy, 14 May 1992, *Turkish Review Quarterly Digest*, vol.6, no.28, Summer 1992, p. 89.

11 In the spring of 1992 Demirel was quick, after the declaration of independence by the Central Asian and Caucasian states, to offer Turkey's services to the West in the form of comprehensive proposal submitted to President Bush of the US as a conduit for channelling funds and ideas to the new republics. See 'Ankara'dan Yardım Hamlesi', *Milliyet*, 24 March 1992.

12 According to the Turkish premier Tansu Çiller, by 1995, Turkey's private and public investment in Central Asia, approximated $4 billion. See the text of her speech at the Centre for Strategic Studies (CSIS), Washington, D.C., 19 April 1995. Also see *Yeni Yüzyıl*, 30 July 1995, p. 8, which argued that the undertakings of Turkish construction firms alone in the region reached $3.7 billion, excluding Russia whose contracts to Turkish construction firms was worth another $6 billion.

13 Sayarı, *Turkey: The Changing European Security Environment*, p. 15; Henze, *Turkey: Toward the Twenty-First Century*, p. 9.

14 One of those who objected following 'pan-Turkic' policy, warned that such a policy 'would not only be a futile attempt, but also one to further polarise the region on ethnic and religious lines and thus sever the painstakingly established organic ties with Europe'. See Sander, O. (1994), 'Turkey and the Turkic World', *Central Asian Survey*, vol.13, no.1, p. 42.

15 Turkey's obligations to the region in two years totalled several billion dollars and it became the fourth largest provider of aid to the Turkic Republics, the largest donors being Japan, the EU, and the US. See Abramowitz, M.I. (1993, Summer), 'Dateline Ankara: Turkey After Özal', *Foreign Policy*, vol.91, p. 197.

16 Hussain, *Iran and Turkey in Central Asia*, p. 14.

17 *Le Figaro* argued that with this meeting the Turkish world was about to be officially born, and indicated that it was the first time a meeting had taken place among Turkic states in history. Similarly, *Nezavisimaya Gazeta* argued that the Ankara meeting was an indicator of the Central Asian states' decision to choose Turkey rather than Iran as a partner. Both reports were quoted in *Dünya*, 6 November 1992. Seven summits have taken place thus far. The last summit was held in April 2001 in İstanbul, at the end of which the presidents of Azerbaijan, Kazakhstan, Kyrgyzstan, Turkey, Turkmenistan and the chairmen of the Uzbek parliament adopted the İstanbul Declaration, highlighting the importance of bilateral and multilateral relations among Turkic countries. The

presidents have also reaffirmed their adherence to the observance of human rights and social justice principles, and pledged to put collective pressure to combating terrorism, drug trafficking, condemning separatism that jeopardizes territorial integrity, sovereignty and security of Turkic countries. The next summit will be held in Turkmenistan in 2002 and will mainly focus on economic cooperation.

18 *The Times*, 17 February 1992, observed that the 'fear of fundamentalism spreading in the Central Asia has in turn prompted Washington to encourage Turkey in its approaches towards the region'. *The Daily Telegraph* of 22 February 1993 quoted the US Secretary of State James Baker as urging Turkmenistan 'to follow Turkey, rather than Iran'. Also see 'The go-between, Turkey: Islam's Link to the West', *Time*, 19 October 1992, pp. 34-5.

19 See his speech at Johns Hopkins University, *Turkish Review Quarterly Digest*, pp. 88-9.

20 *Newspot*, 21 May 1992, p. 2.

21 Following the collapse of the USSR, some of its former Republics continued to use the Ruble as a currency in their economies. These economies were dubbed the 'ruble zone'.

22 For description of the new 'Great Game' and the policies and aims of its players see Ahrari, M.E. (1994), 'The Dynamics of the New Great Game in Muslim Central Asia', *Central Asian Survey*, vol.13, no.4, pp. 525-39.

23 Kimura, Y.T. (1993), 'Central Asia and the Caucasus; Nationalism and Islamic Trends' in Ş.S. Gürel and Y.T. Kimura, *Turkey in a Changing World*, Tokyo, Institute of Developing Economies, p. 196.

24 Fuller, G.E. (1993), 'Turkey's New Eastern Orientation', in G. Fuller and I.O. Lesser, *Turkey's New Geopolitics, From the Balkans to Western China,* Boulder, Westview Press, p. 75.

25 Ibid.

26 For a discussion of this view see Gürel, Ş.S. (1993), 'Turkish Foreign Policy in a Changing World', in Gürel and Kimura, *Turkey in a Changing World*, pp. 21-3.

27 Sander, 'Turkey and the Turkic World', p. 40.

28 For an attempt to explain the Turkish model, see Mango, M. (1993, October), 'The Turkish Model', *Middle Eastern Studies*, vol.29, no.4.

29 It should be mentioned here that none of the Turkic languages, including Turkish, have a word corresponding to 'Turkic' in English. Therefore, even speaking in English, the Turkish leaders during the early 1990s usually referred to all the Turkic-speaking peoples as simply 'Turks'. To overcome this problem, a new word, 'Türkî', has since been created in Turkey, but does not sit very comfortably with the logic of the language.

30 Kesic, O. (1995, Winter), 'American-Turkish Relations at a Crossroads', *Mediterranean Quarterly*, vol.6, no.1, p. 101. This resentment was clearly elucidated by president Nazarbaev of Kazakhstan while visiting Turkey in December 1991; 'In this part of the world pan-Turkism becomes a political current only as a reaction to the Soviet rule and 70 years of neglect. (...) I am against the idea of putting people into solid frames by espousing the cause of pan-Turkism or pan-Islamism. These have no chance of success. What we are witnessing now is a Turkic rapprochement, due to the fact that sharing common values is easier among the Turkic-speaking peoples. But this cannot lead to dangerous chauvinism.' *Cumhuriyet*, 16 December 1991.

31 Kimura, 'Central Asia and the Caucasus', p. 194.

32 For an early exploration of Russia's interests in its 'near abroad' see Blank, S. (1994), 'Russia, The Gulf and Central Asia in New Middle East', *Central Asian Survey*, vol.13, no.2.
33 For early Russian complaints on the issue of 'Turkic-Unity' see *FBIS-SOV*, 20 January 1995, p. 59.
34 This statement was made by the Russian Frontier Forces Commander in August 1994, see Migdalowitz, C. (1995, April 12), 'Armenia-Azerbaijan Conflict', *CRS Issue Brief*, The Library of Congress, Foreign Affairs and National Defence Division, Washington, D.C., p. 13. For a Turkish view that Russia was making political mischief in Azerbaijan and Kazakhstan to persuade them to oppose the Turkish option in exporting their oil, see *Briefing*, 6 February 1995, No 1027, pp. 7-9; and 20 March 1995, No 1033, p. 13.
35 For example see 'Turkish PM Demirel Visits Moscow: Useful, Constructive Talks Expected', *FBIS-SOV*, 27 May 1992, pp. 15-16.
36 Fuller, 'Turkey's New Eastern Orientation', p. 86.
37 The existing Turkish-Armenian border was determined by a peace treaty signed between Turkey and the short-lived independent Armenian Republic in 1921, and the Soviet-Turkish treaty of 1921 that confirmed all the borders between the Soviet Union and Turkey. After the collapse of the Soviet Union, as Turkey no longer shared a border with Russia, the validity of that treaty and its provisions for local borders with former Soviet Republics became questionable. The problem became imminent when the Armenian Parliament announced that it did not recognise those borders established by Moscow between Armenia and Turkey. Thus, in the spring of 1992, Turkey stipulated that it would not proceed to formalise diplomatic relations with Armenia until Armenia provided formal written recognition of existing borders. As of now, it has not done so. See *Briefing*, 19 March 1991, p. 3; Ç. Kırca, 'The Only Hope for Armenia', *Turkish Daily News*, 12 February 1991.
38 Especially during the first half of 1992 there were calls within Turkey for at least a veiled military intervention on the Azeri side. Right wing groups organised public rallies, and even some influential people (among them was the then president Turgut Özal) argued that Turkey 'had the right to intervene'. See *Financial Times Report on Turkey*, 7 May 1993, p. 5.
39 The BSEC was founded 25 June 1992 when the eleven original signatories met in İstanbul. The summit declaration on the BSEC was a multinational organization composed of member states: Albania, Armenia, Azerbaijan, Bulgaria, Georgia, Greece, Moldova, Romania, Russia, Turkey and Ukraine.
40 On 10 March 1993, after a visit by the then foreign minister Hikmet Çetin to Moscow, it was announced that 'Turkey and the Russian Federation will jointly act as moderators between Azerbaijan and Armenia'. *TRT News*, 16 March 1993. For earlier calls on Russia to end the conflict see *Newspot*, 25 January 1990.
41 See *Milliyet*, 25 February 1995, p. 17; and 8 May 1995, p. 13.
42 The Gagauz are a Turkic people who are Orthodox Christians and live in southern Moldova on the Ukrainian border. There are some 27,000 Gagauz across this border in the Odessa oblast of Ukraine (this portion was formerly a part of Bessarabia – the predecessor to Moldavia – occupying the land between the Prut, Dniester and Danube Rivers).
43 For a view that Turkey's Chechnya policy is marked by dilemmas see *Briefing*, No 1023, 9 January 1995, pp. 7-8; and No 1024, 16 January 1995, p. 10.

44 For public accusation from the Head of Russian Federal Counterintelligence Service on December 20, 1995, that volunteer fighters from Turkey were discovered in the Northern Caucasus, mainly in Chechnya, see *FBIS-SOV*, 3 February 1995, p. 71.

45 *Briefing*, 1 May 1995, No 1039, p. 13; 19 June 1995, No 1045, p. 13.

46 Fuller, 'Turkey's New Eastern Orientation', p. 81. For an evaluation of Turkey's options and dilemmas regarding ethnic conflicts within Russia see 'How to Handle Post-Chechnya Crisis Moscow', *Briefing*, No 1029, 20 February 1995, p. 10.

47 For further elaboration of this point see Colarusso, J. (1994), 'Abkhazia', *Central Asian Survey*, vol.13, no.1; and Hostler, C.W. (1993), *The Turks of Central Asia*, London, Praeger.

48 Fuller, 'Turkey's New Eastern Orientation', p. 84.

49 Velayeti's speech in a conference, cited in Haktanır, K. (1992, June), 'Developments in Central Asia and Turkish-Iranian Relations', *Middle East Business and Banking*, p. 11.

50 Diuk N. and Karatnycky, A. (1993), *New Nations Rising: The Fall of the Soviets and the Challenge of Independence*, New York, John Wiley, p. 132.

51 On this subject, see Blandy, C.W. (1997, February), 'Oil is Not the Only Stake', *CSRC Report S28*, Royal Military Academy Sandhurst, Surrey; and Aydın, M. (2000), *New Geopolitics of Central Asia and the Caucasus; Causes of Instability and Predicament*, Center for Strategic Research, Ankara, pp. 56-71.

52 For discussion of American policy towards CA&C, see United States House of Representatives, Committee on International Relations, Staff Report, *Major Setbacks Looming for American Interests in the Caucasus Region*, 6 September 1996. Also see Cohen, A. (1997, July 24), 'United States Policy in the Caucasus and Central Asia: Building a New 'Silk Road' to Economic Prosperity', *Heritage Foundation Backgrounder*, no.1132.

53 For a view that the US has became more active in the region, see 'US Squeezes Turkey on Pipeline Deal', *Stratfor Commentary*, 17 August 1999, at http://www.stratfor.com/MEAF/commentary/m9908170045.htm.

54 Shimizu, M. (ed.), (1998), *IDE Spot Survey: The Caspian Basin Oil and Its Impact on Eurasian Power Games*, Institute of Developing Economies, Tokyo, p. 30.

55 For full text of the 'Ankara Declaration' see http://www.mfa.gov.tr/default2.asp?param=/GRUPH/ Release/1998/Ankara.htm.

56 *Milliyet*, 2 November 1998.

57 See the text of the speech delivered by the Special Advisor to the US President for Caspian Basin Energy Diplomacy, Ambassador Richard Morningstar, at the CERA Conference, Washington D.C., 7 December 1998, p 1. Also see remarks by Jan Kalicki, US Ombudsman for Energy and Commercial Co-operation with the Newly Independent States, for the Conference 'Caspian Pipelines: Building Solutions', Washington D.C., 9 December 1998, pp. 2-3.

58 S. Kinzer, *New York Times*, 22 October 1998.

59 T. Marshall, 'Route of Caspian Sea Oil Pipeline Debated', *Los Angeles Times*, 3 December 1998.

60 See 'United States Bolsters a Nervous Georgia', *Stratfor Commentary*, 6 January 2000, at http://www.stratfor.com/CIS/commentary/c000161955.htm.

61 For details see: 'Caucasian Strife and Caspian Oil', *CSIS Caspian Energy Update*, 24 November 1999, at http://www.csis.or/Turkey/CEU991124.html; and 'Caucasian Strife and Caspian Oil–II', *CSIS Caspian Energy Update*, 14 January 2000, at http://www.csis.org/turkey/CEU000114.html.

62 For a summary of recent developments on the pipeline issue, see: 'The Eurasian Energy Corridor Turning into a Cul-de-sac?', *CSIS Caspian Energy Update*, 25 February 2000, at http://www.csis.org/Turkey/CEU000116.html; and 'The Geopolitics of Caspian Oil', *Stratfor Special Report*, 26 January 2000, at http://www.stratfor.com/CIS/specialreports/special20.htm; Lelyveld, M. (2000, March 9), 'Caspian: Russia Softens Opposition To Baku-Ceyhan Pipeline', *RFE/RL Report*, at http://www.rferl.org/nca/features/2001/03/06032001112931.asp; 'Oil Executive Explores Baku-Ceyhan Pipeline Prospects: Interview with Howard Chase, Director of International Affairs for BP Amoco', *EurasiaNet*, 9 March 2002, at http://www.eurasianet.org/departments/qanda/articles/eav031501.shtml; Killgore, A.I. (2002, March), 'The Great Caspian Sea Oil Pipeline Game-Part II', *Washington Report on Middle East Affairs*, vol.21, no. 2.

63 Already 60 per cent of the 50,000 ships a year that pass through the Straits are tankers. If Novorossiysk is chosen for the main AIOC line, this will add to the oil already coming from Kazakhstan by road and the CPC line between Tengiz and Novorossiysk. Taken together with the Baku-Supsa line, the number of tankers will increase sharply causing more risks and delays. See, Crow, P. (1998, March 16), 'Pipeline Politics', *Oil and Gas Journal*, vol.96, no.11. Also see Alirıza, B. (2000, February 3), 'Clear and Present Danger in the Turkish Straits', *CSIS Caspian Energy Update*, at http://www.csis.org/turkey/CEU000115.htm.

64 For examples of recent serious accidents with possible environmental hazards within the Straits area, see Aybay G. and Oral, N. (1998, June-August),'Turkish Authority to Regulate Passage of Vessels Through the Turkish Straits', *Perceptions*, vol.3, no.2, p. 105.

65 One of the problems in the Bosphorus is that it is suitable only for ships of less then 150 meters in length, while the most used tankers for oil transportation nowadays is somewhere between 250-300 meters. If Turkey tries to decrease the number of ships passing through the Straits, then the size of the ships will increase, causing repeated closure to the other traffic. Naegele, J. (1998, June 23), 'Turkey: Caspian Oil Presents Challenge to the Straits', *RFE/RL Newsline*.

66 Haktanır, 'Developments in Central Asia and Turkish-Iranian Relations', p. 11.

Chapter 9

Cycles of Tension and Rapprochement: Prospects for Turkey's Relations with Greece

Tozun Bahcheli

Introduction

In recent decades it has not been unusual for Turkey and Greece, approximately every ten years, to become involved in a showdown and reach the brink of war. However, in almost every instance, the easing of tensions and salutary diplomatic initiatives to achieve better relations have soon followed these dangerous confrontations. Thus, the threat of resorting to war in the Aegean in 1976 (sparked by their dispute over continental shelf entitlements) ultimately led to sober diplomatic moves that yielded the Berne agreement later that year, ushering in a decade of stability in the Aegean Sea. When the next crisis broke out in the Aegean in 1987, also over the continental shelf issue, even more promising diplomatic exchanges ensued once Ankara and Athens withdrew from the brink of conflict when Turkish Prime Minister Turgut Ozal and Greek Prime Minister Andreas Papandreou decided to launch negotiations to settle their bilateral disputes following their meeting in Davos 1987. The failure of the 'Davos process' meant that Ankara and Athens would remain susceptible to future hazards in their relations. This became evident in 1996 when the two countries nearly went to war over the sovereignty of Imia/Kardak, an uninhabited Aegean islet near the Turkish coast. The transition from crisis to diplomatic dialogue took longer this time. However, in the wake of the favourable atmosphere created by the mutual aid given when both countries experienced earthquakes within weeks of each other in late 1999, Ankara and Athens wasted little in assuming conciliatory stances.

Turkey and Greece have entered the new century with an apparent resolve to bring about lasting improvements in their relations. At the same time, as commentators and officials in both countries have cautioned, a wide divergence of interests continues to exist between the two countries. Without success in the bridging of differences in key areas of contention such as Cyprus and the Aegean, what has been dubbed the 'seismic diplomacy' that began following the earthquakes in Turkey and Greece risks suffering the same fate as previous diplomatic initiatives.

Between War and Managed Rivalry

Turkey and Greece have been adversaries for long periods in their history and this has deeply influenced their relationship and also their leaders' reactions to disputes. Indeed, the mistrust traditionally exhibited is a product of an acrimonious historical legacy. Nevertheless, Greeks and Turks have shown that they are not entirely prisoners of the past. Their history of conflict has not ruled out periods of peace and reconciliation and even close and interdependent relations. Only eight years after their last war (1919 to 1922), which was fought with great ferocity and bitterness, Greece and Turkey, began a period of détente.

Greek-Turkish reconciliation was initiated in 1930 by two powerful, visionary leaders, Kemal Atatürk and Eleftherios Venizelos and yielded agreements in the political, economic, and security spheres that weathered occasional irritants. In the post-World War II era, prospects for closer relations were further enhanced when, in 1952, both Turkey and Greece joined the Western alliance system and simultaneously became NATO members.

Despite these auspicious developments, beginning in the mid-1950s Cyprus emerged as a major arena where Greek and Turkish interests clashed. Turks insist their policy in Cyprus (and the Aegean) was merely reactive. From their viewpoint, it was Greece and the Greek Cypriot leadership that repeatedly reopened the issue of sovereignty over the island, even after the Zurich-London agreements created Cypriot independence in 1960. Later, however, with its position on the island strengthened by its military intervention in 1974, Ankara – together with the Turkish Cypriot leadership – sought fundamental changes to the terms of the independence agreements by creating an exclusive Turkish Cypriot state in north Cyprus. In the Aegean, Ankara accused Athens of wanting to bring about unilateral changes to the status quo by claiming the right to extend its territorial seas from six to twelve miles. It has warned Athens against extending its territorial seas in this way by threatening that it would consider such action as *casus belli*, a justification for war.

Turkish Interests and Approach in the Aegean

It is conceivable that without the legacy of past conflicts and the poisoning effect of the on-going Cyprus issue, Ankara and Athens would find reasonable compromises to resolve their Aegean disputes. On the other hand, it is useful to remember that even the best of neighbors are often enmeshed in sovereignty issues involving such complex areas. The willingness of both Turkish and Greek leaders to consider war on three occasions in the last quarter of the 20th Century attests to the enormity of the two states' stake in the Aegean, as well their deep mistrust. For Turkey, the key concerns are access to its Aegean ports and sovereign control of significant maritime and air space. These are matters of great strategic consequence, but they also relate to the important question of how to share the resources of the Aegean.

The Aegean issues that divide Turkey and Greece are: limits on maritime territoriality, sovereignty over the continental shelf and airspace, management of military and civil air-traffic control zones, and the militarization of Greek islands in the eastern Aegean. Turkey is seriously disadvantaged in pressing its claims by the fact that the great majority of Aegean islands and islets (which number more than two thousand) are Greek; some of these are very close to the Turkish coast and this contributes to the Turks' perception that they are 'hemmed in.'

To the great disappointment of Turkish leaders, international maritime laws have been modified, seemingly in Greece's favor, in recent decades. Article 3 of the 1982 Law of the Sea (LOS) Convention provides for the right of states to establish territorial seas of 'a maximum breadth of twelve miles from the baselines.'[1] Greece was one of the first LOS signatories; Turkey has not signed LOS and does not intend to do so. Nevertheless, Greece thus far has refrained from extending its territorial sea in the Aegean beyond six miles.

While most Aegean contentions have centered on the issues surrounding the continental shelf, the territorial sea issue is the one that is most vital for Turkey. The two issues are not unrelated, since all of the shelf claimed by Greece would accrue to it automatically, were it able to implement a twelve-mile territorial claim. Greek extension of its Aegean territorial waters would make Turkey's access to its major ports, İstanbul and İzmir, more difficult. As Andrew Wilson pointed out in his 1980 study, *The Aegean Dispute*, 'Already the application of the six-mile limit restricts Turkey to only three places where shipping may enter or leave Turkish territorial waters from international waters.'[2]

If the territorial sea claimed by both countries were increased to twelve miles, the Greek share of the Aegean would go up to 64 per cent, whereas Turkey's share would increase to less than 9 per cent.[3] The proportion of international waters would drop from 56 percent to 26 percent.[4] Athens has tried to alleviate Ankara's concerns about port access by arguing that Turkish shipping would be fully protected by the right of innocent passage however, Turkish leaders find such assurances inadequate. Ankara has repeatedly declared that an extension to twelve miles would constitute a *casus belli*. After the Greek parliament ratified the International Law of the Sea on 1 June 1994, the Turkish parliament followed on June 8 with a resolution authorizing the government to use all measures – widely understood to include force – to protect Turkey's rights in the Aegean, if necessary.

The access issue applies also to aircraft, as Turkey feels similarly confined by the airspace of Greece's islands. It has rejected the ten-mile airspace claimed by Athens by arguing that Greece is entitled to exercise sovereignty only over six miles, corresponding to its territorial seas – a position also taken by the US and all NATO countries aside from Greece. Ankara challenges the claimed airspace by regularly sending its military aircraft to a distance of six miles from Greek island coasts. Typically Athens responds to what it considers violations of its airspace by sending its own aircraft to intercept. These aerial challenges have long worried their NATO allies, but Athens and Ankara thus far have managed to prevent mock dogfights from escalating into more serious exchanges. In addition, Ankara has occasionally quarreled with Athens over lesser issues related to flights in the Aegean, repeatedly accusing Greece of abusing its purely technical Flight Information Region (FIR) responsibilities to try to gain sovereign rights. Again, like the US and other NATO states, Turkey does not accept the Greek claim that it is obliged to notify Greek authorities when its military aircraft enter Aegean airspace. Turkey has much regretted its acceptance in 1952 – when Greek-Turkish relations were harmonious – of International Civil Aviation Organization (ICAO) arrangements that assigned FIR responsibilities in the Aegean to Greece. While the FIR issue has been an irritant, the stakes for both Turkey and Greece have been greater in the Aegean continental shelf. The shelf – comprising the seabed and subsoil of the submarine area beyond the territorial sea, to the point where the land mass is deemed to end – has proved to be one of the most difficult and potentially explosive issues facing the Aegean neighbors.

Athens has long held that delimitation of the continental shelf is the sole Aegean issue requiring formal resolution and that the problem must be adjudicated by the International Court of Justice (ICJ) at The Hague. Greek leaders assert that their islands are surrounded by the continental shelf beyond that of the Greek mainland. In the Turkish view, the Greek Aegean islands lie within Turkey's continental shelf as a natural extension of the Anatolian peninsula. According to Wilson, application of Greece's formula would confer on it about 97 per cent of the Aegean seabed, leaving Turkey with less than 3 percent, specifically a narrow strip off Anatolia.[5] It is obvious even to Greek officials that Turkey would reject any such apportionment. Turkish leaders assert that 'equity' should be the key principle in finding solutions for all Aegean problems. In accordance with this position, Ankara has proposed –and Athens has rejected– drawing a median line through the Aegean archipelago, leaving each side with roughly half of the sea's continental shelf.

Unlike Athens, which apparently feels confident about its legal position, Ankara fears that its case on these issues is legally weak and demurs on Athens's desire to pursue an ICJ decision. However, Turkish leaders feel far more confident on the issue of demilitarization of Greece's eastern Aegean islands, and have periodically brought up the issue to demonstrate Greece's seeming contravention of the treaties of Lausanne (1923) and Paris (1947).

Ankara's approach to resolving the Aegean problems is driven by a general strategy of avoiding the ICJ, or indeed any other third party adjudication or arbitration, except 'as a last resort.' Turkish leaders calculate that they can obtain better terms from Greece through bilateral negotiations. In accordance with this approach, Ankara strongly resists Greek attempts to 'internationalize' (and 'Europeanize') Aegean issues. Turkish leaders traditionally angrily react to Athens's attempts to enlist the support of its EU partners and warn those states not to take Greece's side. On the other hand, Ankara has periodically signaled to Athens that it did not rule out third party mediation, including recourse to the ICJ.

Turkey has periodically tried to induce Greece into bilateral negotiations on Aegean issues. Greece has occasionally accepted these overtures, but the ensuing talks did not yield any significant agreements and were essentially exploratory. For instance, there were intermittent talks on Aegean and other issues, particularly after the adoption of the Berne agreement in 1976. These ended with the election of the first PASOK government under Andreas Papandreou in 1981. Talks concerning Aegean issues were briefly revived during the 'Davos process' in 1988-89, but these too proved inconclusive. The dialogue on Aegean issues between Ankara and Athens – launched in early 2002 – may signal a new determination by the both countries to settle their Aegean disputes.

While both countries have generally avoided serious provocations in the Aegean, mutual suspicions sometimes create tensions and even actual confrontations. A case in point was Ankara's concern about Greek attempts to populate remote Aegean islands in 1995.[6] Athens, on the other hand, accused Ankara of a greater transgression in challenging Greek sovereignty over Imia-Kardak in early 1996. Indicating a hardened policy after that incident, Turkish leaders announced a new position that there are more than a hundred uninhabited Aegean islets whose legal status is unclear, and thus represent 'gray areas' of uncertain sovereignty, a policy departure which sowed new doubts in Greek leaders' minds concerning Turkish intentions. For Ankara the prerequisite of any agreement is that Aegean territorial seas and corresponding airspace must be limited to six miles. Once this principle is accepted, it is conceivable that both negotiations and recourse to the ICJ could be utilized to resolve the continental shelf issue.

The Cyprus Issue

Turkish interests in Cyprus, like those in the Aegean, are primarily strategic, and have been just as difficult to reconcile with those of Greece. On the other hand, whereas a confrontation has been avoided in the Aegean, Turkish and Turkish Cypriot (as well as Greek and Greek Cypriot) blood has been spilled on the island. The Greek military junta's coup against Greek Cypriot President Makarios in July 1974 provoked Turkey's military intervention. Before this major war, Cyprus had witnessed periodic fighting between the Turkish and Greek communities. The emotions created by these events in the not-too-distant past have left their mark in the psyche of both Turks and Turkish Cypriots and Greeks and Greek Cypriots.

It is worth recalling that Cyprus first became a disputed Turkish-Greek issue in 1955, eighteen years before the continental shelf issue first emerged in the Aegean in 1973. Consequently, as Turkish-Greek relations had suffered over Cyprus during the preceding years settlement prospects for the Aegean problems were considerably complicated. On the other hand, Turkey's relations with Greece were tranquil when Greek Cypriot leaders began their *Enosis* (union with Greece) campaign in the mid-1950s against the British administration on the island. At the time both Ankara and the Turkish community in Cyprus were content to see a continuation of British rule. The presence of a sizeable Turkish community, and the legacy of three centuries of Ottoman rule (1570-1878) in Cyprus, made it almost certain that Turkish interest would be aroused by any developments affecting its kinsmen. More problematic for Turkish leaders, however, was the fact that Greek Cypriots and Greece contested the sovereignty of the island. In spite of the post-war improvements in Turkish-Greek relations, Turkish leaders continued to have strategic concerns vis-a-vis Greece. Already feeling hemmed in by Greek islands in the Aegean, Turkish leaders have felt that Greece's sovereignty over Cyprus – forty miles from its southern coast – would enable Athens to control access to its southern ports of Mersin and İskenderun and this concern was at the heart of Turkey's objection to *Enosis*.

In the mid-1950s, Greek backing for the Greek Cypriot insurgency for union with Greece, and Turkish backing for the Turkish Cypriot struggle against *Enosis* seriously strained Turkish-Greek relations. To counter *Enosis*, Ankara adopted partition as a goal, though it was rejected by Greek Cypriots. Subsequent clashes between Turkish and Greek Cypriots claimed hundreds of lives, and have poisoned the relationship of the two communities, making it difficult for future communal relations on the island. Three years of Cypriot disturbances (1955-58) and the clash of goals about the future of Cyprus undid the progress that Ankara and Athens achieved in their relations during the preceding thirty years.

Nevertheless, Turkish and Greek diplomacy has succeeded in preventing their relations from deteriorating further, by taking the lead in drawing up a settlement based on independence for Cyprus. In negotiating the Zurich-London agreements that created the Republic of Cyprus, Ankara did well in securing Turkish Cypriot and Turkish rights. The agreements created a power-sharing constitution for the island, providing numerous safeguards for the protection of the Turkish community from the more numerous Greek Cypriots. The principal benefits for Turkey were that, in accordance with the treaties of Guarantee and Alliance, it became a guarantor of Cypriot independence (along with Greece and the United Kingdom), and was authorized to station a small number of troops on the island.

However, Turkish satisfaction turned to disenchantment and dismay as the Turkish and Greek communities began to quarrel over the application of the constitutional provisions, particularly those related to separate municipalities and the 30 percent Turkish Cypriot representation at every grade of civil service employment. From Ankara's and the Turkish Cypriot point of view, the Greek Cypriot leadership had refused to apply the provisions of the 1960 Constitution, and violated the independence agreements by reviving the *Enosis* call.

Both Turkish Cypriots and Turks view the period between the collapse of the bi-communal government on the island in late 1963, up to the Turkish military intervention of 1974 as a period of great adversity for the Turkish community. Greek Cypriot successes in the civil war that began in 1963 had reduced the Turkish community from the status of partner-in-government to a harassed community, with Turkey hard-pressed to intervene without provoking a war with Greece. Ankara was not only angered by the Greek Cypriot abuse of Turkish Cypriots, but also at the support Greek governments gave Makarios while the latter unilaterally altered the constitutional order that Turkey and Greece had bequeathed for the island. Turkish anger turned to outrage when Greek leaders lent their support to the resurrected call for *Enosis*. It was one thing to want *Enosis*, however, and another to achieve it in the face of a threat of war from Turkey. This was well understood by Makarios and most Greek leaders who were careful not to provoke Turkey's intervention. However, in an unexpected twist of events, Greek junta leader Brigadier Ioannidis unwittingly handed Ankara the pretext for military intervention on the island. This happened when Ioannidis engineered a coup against Makarios in July 1974, in an apparent bid to bring Cyprus under Greece's control.

When Ecevit dispatched Turkish troops to Cyprus in July 1974, he did so by citing Turkey's rights of intervention as provided by the 1960 Treaty of Guarantee.[7] By aborting the Greek junta's attempt to unite the island with Greece, Turkey had acted in accordance with treaty requirements. But the Treaty of Guarantee authorized the three guarantor powers (Turkey, Greece, and Britain) to intervene in order to restore the 1960 constitution that established the island's independence and the Ecevit government had no intention of allowing that. Instead, using Turkey's new position of strength, and working closely with Turkish Cypriot leader Rauf Denktash, Ecevit helped create the basis of a new settlement on the island based on the physical separation of the two communities. As a consequence of the war of 1974, 160,000 Greek Cypriots (a third of the Greek community) became refugees, as did 45,000 Turkish Cypriots (representing nearly 40 percent of the Turkish community). This forced movement of people resulted in the creation of two homogeneous ethnic entities on the island, as most Greek Cypriots fled or were forced to leave the Turkish Cypriot-administered area in the north and moved to the south; virtually, all Turkish Cypriots moved from the south to the north. In a bid to enhance the demographic balance in favour of Turkish Cypriots, Ankara arranged for tens of thousands of Turkish citizens to settle in northern Cyprus.[8]

Turkish leaders have exploited the Greek junta's blunder in 1974, and turned the tables against Greek Cypriots and Greece on the island. With 37 percent of the island's territory under their control, including some (such as the uninhabited resort town of Varosha) that could be bargained away in a settlement, Turkish Cypriots are in a position to negotiate from a position of strength. For almost two decades, the Turkish Cypriot leadership called for the creation of a loose federation, and argued in favour of retaining Turkey's rights as a guarantor as well as the indefinite stationing of Turkish troops on the island. By about the mid-1990s this position hardened with the demand that Greek Cypriots recognize Turkish Cypriots right to self-determination. Later, in 1999, with Ankara's support, the Turkish Cypriot leadership called for a confederation based on the union of two sovereign states, one Turkish Cypriot and the other Greek Cypriot.

Greek Cypriot leaders have rejected these demands, arguing instead for a centralized federation and for safeguards against Turkey's intervention. In spite of the island's *de facto* partition for more than a quarter century, and Turkey's undoubted military superiority, Ankara has been unable to compel the Greek Cypriots to accept Turkish/Turkish Cypriot terms as, in spite of their considerably weakened position in 1974, Greek Cypriots, bolstered by Greece, have enjoyed several advantages. First, even though a separate Turkish Cypriot state, the Turkish

Republic of Northern Cyprus (hereinafter TRNC) was established in 1983 and recognized by Ankara, the international community has continued to recognize the Greek Cypriot-controlled Republic of Cyprus as the legitimate government of the whole island. Acting in tandem with Athens, the Greek Cypriot leadership has used this legitimacy advantage by internationalizing the dispute and putting pressure on Turkey to withdraw its troops. Second, the Greek Cypriot government has succeeded in imposing an economic embargo on the Turkish Cypriot-administered area since 1974. As a result of successful Greek Cypriot pressures, European governments do not permit scheduled flights to the TRNC, thus handicapping the promising tourism sector in the Turkish Cypriot economy. Thirdly, Greek/Greek Cypriot lobbying in Washington has regularly caused headaches for Ankara by generating critical Congressional resolutions, and impeding United States arms transfers to Turkey. In Europe, as well, European parliament resolutions criticizing Turkey's Cyprus policy have been commonplace. In a major blow to Ankara, in a ruling dated 28 July 1988, the European Court of Human Rights held Turkey (rather than the Turkish Cypriot government) responsible for barring a Greek Cypriot refugee's access to her property in northern Cyprus, and ordered the Turkish government to pay compensation.

Moreover, Athens has used its EU membership to exert pressure on Turkey. Until the warming of Greek-Turkish relations in the latter half of 1999, Athens repeatedly vetoed the release of aid that the EU agreed to provide Turkey as part of the association and customs union agreements. More importantly, it persuaded its EU partners for Brussels to commence accession negotiations with the Greek Cypriot-controlled Republic of Cyprus, in spite of Turkish objections. While releasing its veto on granting of EU membership status to Turkey at the Helsinki summit in 1999, Greek lobbying secured an apparent pledge that Cyprus' accession to the EU would proceed even without a prior settlement between Greek and Turkish Cypriots. The Republic of Cyprus' EU accession negotiations have made impressive progress, with 24 of the 31 chapters of the *acquis communitaire* completed by December 2001,[9] leaving Cyprus ahead of the other eleven countries with which the EU is engaged in accession talks. Greek Cypriots appear confident that, in spite of Turkish Cypriot and Turkish objections, Cyprus will be included in the next round of enlargement in 2004.

Ankara has been exceedingly frustrated with, and resented these Greek and Greek Cypriot successes. Similarly, it has been angered by the conclusion of a defense agreement between Athens and Greek Cyprus in 1993, which brought the Republic of Cyprus under the defense umbrella of Greece. On the other hand Ankara could enhance its considerable military position on the island in response to accelerated Greek Cypriot arms procurement. Indeed, in a demonstration of its military muscle, Ankara forced the Greek Cypriot government to cancel its proposed deployment of Russian surface-to-air missiles (apparently capable of reaching southern Turkey) in late 1998 by threatening to remove them by force.

Turkish leaders have regularly complained of being surrounded by Greek islands in the Aegean. Consequently, they have suspected that the bolstering of Greek Cypriot/Greek military capabilities on Cyprus is aimed at creating an additional front against Turkey. Also, with an eye on the projected construction of oil pipelines from the Caucasus to Turkey's Mediterranean coast, many Turkish leaders have argued that Cyprus' strategic importance for Turkey has been enhanced.[10] Ankara views the maintenance of Turkish military superiority on Cyprus (and safeguarding Turkey's rights as a guarantor of the Cyprus Republic) as vital Turkish interests. Accordingly, Turkish leaders have rejected any proposal for a settlement that either calls for a total Turkish withdrawal of troops and/or removes or weakens Turkey's right (or perceived right) to intervene in Cyprus unilaterally under the terms of the 1960 Treaty of Guarantee.

Progress on Other Fronts

Apart from Cyprus and the Aegean, Ankara's major grievance against Greece in recent years has been the latter's alleged support for the separatist PKK (Kurdistan Workers Party) insurgency in southern Turkey. The discovery that Greece had sheltered PKK leader, Abdullah Öcalan in its embassy in Nairobi, Kenya, enraged the Turks, whose leaders had long accused Athens of supporting PKK terrorism against Turkey. Turkish threats of retaliation in early 1999 during the Öcalan debacle seem to have had a sobering effect on the Simitis government, and future Greek governments may be wary of provoking Turkey on an issue of existential importance to Turkey. If the PKK armed struggle does come to an end, as its leadership has pledged, the Kurdish issue will likely fade as a bilateral bone of contention.

Compared to the PKK controversy, which became an explosive issue for a short period of time, Greek treatment of the Turkish community in Western Thrace (numbering an estimated 125, 000) has been a long-standing irritant in Turkey's relations with Greece. Thracian Turks have long accused the Greek government of neglecting their economic and educational needs, as well as restricting their rights in a number of areas, including the freedom to choose their *muftis* (religious leaders).[11] Until 1999, Athens refused even to call this group 'Turks,' insisting instead on the terminology of the 1923 Lausanne Treaty, which designates them merely as 'Muslims.'

The Greek government has generally denied that it applies a policy of discrimination against its Turkish minority. Moreover, it accuses Turkey, with justification, of having forced out most of the Greek minority in Istanbul. Whereas the population of the Turkish community in Thrace has been constant, that of the Greek community in İstanbul has diminished drastically over the decades, from roughly 120,000 in 1923 to about 3,500 in 1999. Ankara has found that the virtual disappearance of the İstanbul Greeks substantially reduced its leverage *vis-à-vis* Athens regarding the Thracian Turks. Still, the discriminatory treatment meted out to this community is widely reported in the Turkish media. Ironically, while resisting pressures from several EU countries regarding its own human rights practices, Turkey has sought additional leverage against Greece by using European forums such as the Council of Europe to publicize the plight of Thracian Turks. To some extent, this approach has worked. It was European, rather than Turkish, pressure that prompted Greece, on 11 June 1998, to abolish the controversial Article 19 of its constitution which had effectively deprived many Thracian Turks of their Greek nationality when they traveled to Turkey or to other countries.[12]

In recent years Athens has taken numerous measures to improve the economy of Greek Thrace, which remains the country's poorest region. With the help of EU funds, investments were made in large projects to boost employment prospects, thus benefiting the Turkish community. Members of the Turkish minority in western Thrace welcomed the end of official restrictions on assertions of Turkish ethnicity, as of July 1999. However, both the Thracian Turks and Ankara contend that the Greek government should adopt further measures to improve the minority's economic status and educational opportunities and allow it to elect its own *muftis*.

Domestic Factors

For Turkish policymakers, Greece is one of a number of states, including Syria and Iraq that pose a security threat to Turkey. This helps explain the ease with which nationalist feelings were mobilized during the Imia-Kardak episode. When the issue of contested sovereignty over the uninhabited islet first emerged, both Ankara and Athens discussed the matter quietly for weeks. However, once the story was leaked to the Greek press, both countries' media turned it into a *cause celebre*. Aroused public opinion constrained both governments, making it difficult for the leaders to end the confrontation without losing face.

Given the vital security issues involved in disputes between Ankara and Athens, key matters relating to Greece and Cyprus are deliberated within Turkey's National Security Council (NSC), whose membership includes the top military officers. During the 1990s, particularly with short-lived coalitions serially serving in office after 1991, military influence in Turkish decision-making increased. Turkey's senior military establishment is obviously keen to influence the Greek-Turkish military balance. While Middle Eastern adversaries such as Syria and Iraq became weaker, Greece has continued to use its diplomatic and military assets, as well the Greek lobby in Washington, to check Turkish power.

Policies toward Greece and Cyprus ordinarily enjoy considerable support in Turkey across the political spectrum, but governments that take the public for granted risk much unwelcome criticism. Such was the case in early November 2001 when prime minister Bülent Ecevit and foreign minister İsmail Cem warned that Turkey was prepared to make 'great sacrifices' if the EU proceeded to admit Cyprus, against Turkey's wishes.[13] These remarks unleashed a remarkable and often critical debate in Turkey regarding official policy on Cyprus. Fearing that Ankara might forsake Turkey's EU membership for the sake of its Cyprus policy, many Turkish columnists and media commentators, together with some non-governmental groups, questioned the wisdom of the government's approach to the issue. In particular, critics took Ecevit's coalition government to task for backing

Denktash's policy of boycotting UN-sponsored talks, and called for greater flexibility. Widespread domestic criticism, along with international pressures, prompted Ankara to persuade Denktash to end his boycott of talks in December 2001, and launch direct negotiations with his Greek Cypriot counterpart in January 2002.

During the 1990s in Turkey, weak coalition governments shuffled in and out of office at the average rate of one per year. Eleven governments, including nine coalitions and eleven different foreign ministers held office in Ankara during the decade. This made any major policy changes toward Greece most unlikely, since only a strong government could undertake bold policy departures. Thus, it is not a coincidence that one recent major effort for rapprochement took place during the leadership of Turgut Özal, whose party enjoyed a solid majority in Parliament during 1983-91. Keen on securing Turkey's accession to the EU, for which his government applied in 1987, Özal initiated the 'Davos process' together with Greek prime minister Andreas Papandreou following their meeting in Davos, Switzerland, in early 1988. The Davos initiative however, failed to yield any major breakthroughs, and momentum was lost by 1989, and the domestic political weakening of both leaders soon afterwards spelled the end of the 'Davos spirit.'[14]

The Davos initiative failed in part because public opinion in both countries did not appreciate the 'top-down' approach of their leaders. By contrast, after the Turkish and Greek earthquakes of August and September 1999, public opinion in both countries displayed greater receptivity for improved relations. This augurs well, as do the activities of an impressive number of non-governmental groups that have sought to promote better understanding between Turks and Greeks.[15]

The US Factor and NATO

The United States has long been involved in managing Greek-Turkish differences, particularly since the onset of civil strife on Cyprus in 1963. This has not been an easy task, and US actions have caused major strains in Washington's relationship with both countries, sometimes simultaneously. The arms embargo the US Congress imposed on Turkey in 1975 is a case in point, as is the famous letter from President Lyndon B. Johnson to Prime Minister İsmet İnönü in 1964, warning him against a military intervention in Cyprus. Both caused much bitterness in Turkey and strained Turkish-US relations for several years.

Adding to its anger over the effect of anti-Turkish lobbies in Washington, Ankara resented the 7:10 ratio applied by Congress (usually against White House wishes) to aid provided to Greece and Turkey, respectively, since 1980. At sixty-five million, Turkey's population is six times that of Greece and its armed forces are considerably larger.[16] Turkish leaders contend that Turkey offers more strategic assets to the US and NATO than does Greece. The military aid program ended in the 1999 fiscal year, but Ankara continues to be unhappy about the activities of pro-Greek groups in Washington, including some Greek-American legislators and others with large Greek-American constituencies.

Turkey faces more obstacles in Washington than those posed by lobbies and the US Congress. Successive US administrations have routinely called upon Ankara to remain committed to solving its problems with Greece and to helping settle the Cyprus issue. In Turkish eyes, the handling of these issues by Washington is less offensive than that of European governments, but still unwelcome. In spite of these difficulties, Turkish leaders attach great importance to relations with the US Defense and political cooperation with Washington remains as much a core interest for Turkey as it was during the Cold War. Ankara appreciated US efforts to help bring Turkey closer to Europe, particularly representations of Washington to the EU states in favor of Turkish membership. Turkish initiatives to transport oil from the Caucasus have been bolstered by US support for the proposed Baku-Ceyhan pipeline in preference to proposals favored by Russia, Iran, Greece, and Bulgaria.

In many important respects Turkey needs the US to cope with the Greek 'threat' as well. Eighty percent of Turkey's military weapons are of US manufacture.[17] Ankara also counts on Washington's reliance on Turkey in pursuit of policies in the regions abutting Turkey (such as containing the Saddam Hussein regime in Iraq) and on White House help in neutralizing the pro-Greek tilt in Congress. Unlike the EU, which is often beholden to Greece and takes positions on Greek-Turkish issues that upset Ankara, the US has pursued a more nuanced policy on such disputes. This evokes more respect among Turkish leaders than do the policies of EU states. In some respects, US policy on a number of Aegean issues lends indirect support to Turkey. A case in point is the US position that the sovereign airspace of a state corresponds to its territorial seas, which is identical to the Turkish position. Moreover, by discouraging any unilateral move to alter the territorial *status quo* in the Aegean, Washington may also be said to bolster indirectly the Turkish position on the six-mile territorial-sea limit.

Washington's close relations with both Ankara and Athens, together with the NATO link, have given the US considerable leverage in stabilizing the Turkish-Greek relationship and in exploiting opportunities to help resolve disputes. There is, after all, a shared general interest between Washington, Ankara and Athens in avoiding crises and confrontations in the Aegean. But moving beyond crisis prevention to the settlement of disputes has been a daunting task. Moreover, since the mid-1990s, US leverage has been eclipsed by that of the EU on account of Brussels' decision to proceed with Cypriot accession negotiations without requiring a prior political settlement on the island. As United States diplomat James Wilkinson has argued, 'The EU actions on Turkish and Cypriot membership issues from 1995 to 1998 turned US presidential envoys into paper tigers and vitiated the UN negotiating process.'[18]

Since Ankara and Athens have rejected US involvement in the possible resolution of their Aegean disputes, Washington has expended a good deal more effort in trying to settle the Cyprus issue. It has been hoped in Washington – indeed in many capitals in the West – that a breakthrough in Cyprus would pave the way for substantially improving Turkish-Greek relations and enhance the prospects for settling Aegean disputes.

A recurring concern for the US and its allies has been the perennial threat that Turkish-Greek tensions pose to NATO cohesion, even to the point of potential collapse of the southern flank. Indeed, NATO has been preoccupied with these quarrels throughout much of its existence. Ankara and Athens have regularly brought their quarrels to NATO councils and occasionally used their veto or delaying powers to stall alliance plans.[19]

It is hard to assess the contribution of NATO, especially as distinct from that of the US, in moderating Greek-Turkish conflicts over the years, though it seems logical to credit NATO with a moderating role. NATO meetings have afforded opportunities for Ankara and Athens to discuss their problems in a forum where their allies have encouraged them and offered ideas for the bridging of their differences. Greece and Turkey have reached numerous agreements pertaining to NATO arrangements within alliance councils. Despite occasional setbacks, NATO has persevered in promoting a series of confidence-building measures in the Aegean. On the other hand, it has been argued that the alliance has unwittingly exacerbated conflicts between Greece and Turkey. According to political scientist Ronald Krebs, their membership in the alliance has destabilized relations by, in effect, contracting out their national security and thus allowing each power to pursue its regional interests with reduced vulnerability.[20]

The EU Factor

The Turkish secular establishment has pursued closer European ties for many years. Turkey's associate EU membership – attained in 1963, a year later than Greece – envisioned eventual full membership. Although Turkish leaders did not apply for membership when Greece did in 1975, they sought and received assurances from the EU that Turkish interests and membership prospects would not be affected by Greece's full membership.[21] These assurances proved hollow. In the eyes of Turks as well as many EU members, Greece for years has used its membership to impede progress in EU-Turkish relations.

In the aftermath of the EU's Luxembourg summit of December 12-13, 1997, which rejected Turkey's bid to be included among the countries eligible for EU membership, Ankara vented its anger toward Greece (and Germany) for their active role in the decision. Turkish bitterness was compounded by the EU's decision to bend to Greek pressure and place Cyprus on a fast track for EU accession, in spite of Ankara's insistence on a prior settlement between Greek and Turkish Cypriots. Turkish leaders were additionally upset that, instead of placing the onus for settlement of bilateral problems jointly on Athens and Ankara, EU members called upon Turkey to settle its disputes with Greece 'in particular by legal process, including the International Court of Justice.'[22]

From the Turkish point of view, the EU's Helsinki summit of December 1999, although more acceptable than Luxembourg in its acceptance of Turkey as an EU membership candidate, nevertheless was similarly problematic in endorsing recourse to the ICJ and for its statement on Cyprus. In the words of the Helsinki communiqué:

> The European Council stresses the principle of peaceful settlement of disputes in accordance with the United Nations Charter and urges candidate states to make every effort to resolve any outstanding border disputes and other related issues. Failing this they should within a reasonable time bring the dispute to the International Court of Justice.
>
> The European Council will review the situation relating to any outstanding disputes, in particular concerning the repercussions on the accession process and in order to promote their settlement through the International Court of Justice, at the latest by the end of 2004.
>
> The European Council underlines that a political settlement will facilitate the accession of Cyprus to the European Union. If no settlement has been reached by the completion of accession negotiations, the Council's decision on accession will be made without the above being a precondition. In this the Council will take account of all relevant factors.[23]

Some Turkish officials considered these statements troublesome enough that they counseled the rejection of the EU's offer of candidate status. However, others argued that the benefits of Turkish candidacy and prospective membership in the EU far outweighed the handicaps posed by these statements, and ultimately their counsel prevailed.

While tilting toward Greece, the Helsinki summit communiqué also seemed to acknowledge Turkish interests somewhat. Thus, the EU statement called for the resolution of 'any outstanding border disputes and other related issues,' in seeming acknowledgment of Ankara's position that there are Aegean issues unrelated to maritime boundaries (e.g., the militarization of Greece's eastern Aegean islands) that require resolution. Moreover, the communiqué called on all candidate states to make 'every effort' to resolve disputes; Ankara argues that this underscores the necessity for bilateral negotiations in the resolution of its Aegean disputes with Greece prior to any recourse to the ICJ.

As much as Ankara has been upset by the EU states' episodic involvement in Greek-Turkish disagreements, it should be recognized that European governments have usually preferred to steer clear of Greek-Turkish disputes, as well as the Cyprus issue. Most EU countries prefer that Greek Cypriot leaders, who have ardently pursued EU membership, reach a settlement with the Turkish Cypriots before Cyprus becomes an EU member. However, Greece's membership has made this position very difficult to maintain. When its EU partners have disagreed with its policies, Athens has often used its veto powers, as shown by its blocking of EU aid earmarked for Turkey under the 1963 association agreement and the 1995 customs union agreement. Athens lifted its veto in 1995 against the customs union, but only as a *quid pro quo* for the EU to begin negotiations with Cyprus for full membership. As noted, Greece secured a similar trade-off (concerning Cyprus and the Aegean) in December 1999 at the Helsinki summit when it lifted its veto to allow the EU's assignment of candidate status to Turkey.

Even though the EU partners defer to Athens in many instances, they also have resisted Greek pressure on several major issues. In one area of paramount concern to Turkish security, the EU's security arm, the Western European Union (WEU), in 1992 'declared Greek-Turkish differences to be beyond its scope.'[24] Furthermore, Greece's EU partners rejected its attempts to include a commitment to EU 'territorial integrity' in the Amsterdam Treaty of June 1997,[25] a gambit that was intended to drag the EU into bilateral Greek-Turkish territorial disputes. Similarly, in December 2001, EU states agreed to accommodate Turkey's concerns regarding the proposed European rapid reaction force that the European Security and Defense policy (ESDP) is planning to establish in 2003.[26] In this negotiation, Turkey secured the commitment that the force would not be involved in the Aegean and Cyprus when Turkey threatened to use its NATO membership to veto the ESDP's planned access to NATO assets.

In comparison to this issue, the question of Cyprus' EU membership will be more difficult to resolve. Ankara and the Turkish Cypriots have bitterly complained that, with EU membership seemingly assured regardless of a political settlement, Greek Cypriots need make no significant concessions in the inter-communal negotiations conducted under United Nations auspices. Instead, as Ankara sees it, the EU has saddled Turkish Cypriots and Turkey with the burden of making concessions to Greek Cypriots and Greece. Turkish leaders fear greater Turkish Cypriot isolation should the EU make good on its declared intention to admit a divided Cyprus (in effect, the Greek Cypriot-controlled Republic of Cyprus) if a political settlement does not emerge on the island. In a bid to deter the EU states from admitting Cyprus prior to a political settlement, Ankara has warned that it would strengthen its already close links with the TRNC, and possibly annex it, thus ending any hope of reunifying the island. Few doubt the serious damage such an eventuality would inflict on the overall Turkish-Greek relationship.

Conclusions

As much as Ankara has matched Athens's interest in improving bilateral relations since 1999, Turkish officials display considerable mistrust of Greece. Most Greeks consider that Greece has made concessions to Turkey (viz. endorsing Turkey's candidature for EU accession in Helsinki in 1999) without any reciprocity. But to Turks, Greece is merely 'righting a wrong' by abandoning its obstructionist policy against Turkey in the EU, and assuming a more cooperative stance towards Ankara. In any case, Greek policy in the Aegean remains the same, and Athens has been determined to push for Cyprus' EU accession over Turkish objections. Moreover, there are no assurances that the current and future governments in Athens will not resort to old methods, linking progress in the EU's future relations with Turkey (including Turkey's membership) to conditions which Turkey would find unpalatable.

It is for these reasons that Turkish, Greek, and other observers have been cautious regarding the prospects of the Turkish-Greek rapprochement that began in late 1999. There is no assurance that this new détente will succeed where other such initiatives (most recently Davos) failed. Since 1999, Turkey and Greece have signed more than a dozen agreements on largely non-controversial issues related to economic and cultural ties, border security, terrorism, and cross-border crime. As important as these agreements in stimulating cooperation and improving the climate of Turco-Greek relations, Turkey's rapprochement with Greece is bound to be flounder if no settlements emerge in the Aegean and, especially, Cyprus.

Numerous writers have suggested principles that could serve as the bases of compromise agreements for Turkey and Greece in both the Aegean and Cyprus. Theodore Couloumbis, a prominent Greek academic with links to the Greek political establishment, has argued as follows:

> For the benefit of Turkey, it must be made clear that the Aegean will not be transformed into a 'Greek lake.' For the benefit of Greece, it must also be made clear that the Aegean cannot be partitioned or subdivided in a way that encloses Greek territories such as the Dodecanese and eastern Aegean islands in a zone (or zones) of Turkish functional jurisdiction.[27]

This, and similar arguments made by some Greek writers, suggest a Greek willingness to forsake a blanket extension of the territorial sea in the Aegean from the current six to twelve miles,[28] thus satisfying a basic Turkish demand. As a *quid pro quo*, Ankara needs to acknowledge greater Greek entitlement to the Aegean continental shelf (than Turkey's), and be prepared to have this adjudicated by a third party, possibly by the International Court of Justice at The Hague. Turkey's contention that it is entitled to half of the continental shelf is a maximalist claim. It has long been understood that Ankara would be prepared to settle for a lesser share (than Greece) of the Aegean's continental shelf,[29] even as it argues that the Aegean islands are not entitled to generate their continental shelf on the same basis as the Greek mainland.

There are, to be sure, numerous other issues of contention in the Aegean, such as the limits of sovereign airspace, but the territorial sea and continental shelf issues will form the foundation of a historic compromise that the two adversaries may yet reach. It is even remotely possible that Ankara and Athens, faced with the prospect of stiff domestic opposition to major concessions, might defer an agreement on the Aegean issues to a later date, without necessarily impeding further progress in their relations.

On the other hand, it is improbable that Turkey's relations with Greece could make major progress short of a Cyprus settlement. However much Ankara has endeavoured to de-link the Aegean and Cyprus issues in dealing with Athens, domestic political considerations in Greece would discourage a sustained Greek commitment to détente with Turkey without an anticipation or achievement of progress in re-unifying the island.

Should the communal leaders in Cyprus overcome the legacy of past failures and reach a compromise settlement, Turkey's relations with Greece would improve greatly. Since the beginning of talks in January 2002, Denktash and Clerides have been wrestling with difficult issues that have been impossible to reconcile in the past. These include the size of territorial adjustments that Turkish Cypriots will make as part of a settlement (perhaps reducing Turkish Cypriot control from 37 to less than 30 percent of the island's territory); the status and powers of the federated states in relation to a central government in which both communities would be represented; security arrangements, including the stationing of Turkish troops (a major Turkish Cypriot demand) following a settlement; and, the entitlement of refugees to return and claim their homes and properties (a major Greek Cypriot demand).

In the past, the failure of one set of negotiations regarding the Cyprus issue merely meant that another round of talks would be arranged at a future propitious time. However, the EU has committed itself to decide which countries will be invited for the next round of EU accession by December 2002. Even with a postponement of such determination, the EU is poised (with Greek prodding) to decide on Cyprus' accession sooner rather than later, raising the possibility of a crisis in Turkish-EU (and Turkish-Greek) relations should accession occur without a prior settlement on the island. With the EU clock ticking for Cyprus, the statesmanship of Turkish and Greek, as well as the Cypriot leaders will be tested, as they wrestle with the difficult issues in the Aegean and Cyprus respectively.

Notes

1 Bahcheli, T. (1990), *Greek Turkish Relations since 1955,* Westview Press, Boulder, Colorado, p. 142.
2 Wilson, A. (1980), *The Aegean Dispute,* International Institute of Strategic Studies, London, p. 27.
3 Ibid.
4 Ibid.
5 Ibid.
6 *Country Report, Turkey,* 1st quarter 1996 (1997), Economist Intelligence Unit, London, p. 17.
7 The Turkish government relied on the following provision of the Treaty of Guarantee: 'In the event of any breach of the provisions of the present Treaty, Greece, the United Kingdom, and Turkey undertake to consult together, with a view to making representations, or taking the necessary steps to ensure observance of those provisions. In so far as common or concerted action may prove impossible, each of the three guaranteeing Powers reserves the right to take action with the sole aim of re-establishing the state of affairs established by the present Treaty'. For the text of the Treaty of Guarantee, see Conference on Cyprus: Documents Signed and Initialed at Lancaster House on 19 February 1959, (1964), H.M. Stationery Office, London.
8 Although there are no reliable figures on the number of Turkish settlers, many observers estimate that they constitute about half of the population in north Cyprus.
9 *Cyprus Mail*, 13 December 2001.
10 One observer wrote: 'With effective control over Northern Cyprus because of its troops based there, control of the passage to and from the bay of Iskenderun and Mersin by Turkey is also assured. Such control is important in ensuring the security of southern Turkey. This area would gain additional importance if Turkey's aspirations for an oil pipeline from the Caspian region to Ceyhan harbour materialize. It is quite unlikely,

therefore, that the Turkish military leadership would approve any solutions to the Cyprus question that would undermine this strategic advantage.' Kramer, H. (1997), 'The Cyprus Problem and European Security' *Survival*, vol. 39, no. 3, p. 24.

11 *Destroying Ethnic Identity: The Turks of Greece*, Helsinki Watch Report (1990), Human Rights Watch, New York.

12 Bahcheli, *Greek-Turkish Relations*, p. 182.

13 *Middle East International*, 23 November 2001.

14 Pridham, G. (1991), 'Linkage Politics Theory and the Greek-Turkish Rapprochement,' in D. Constas (ed.), *The Greek-Turkish Conflict in the 1990s: Domestic and External Influences,* Macmillan, Houndmills and London, pp. 84-6.

15 The authors of a recent book on Greek security issues reported as follows: 'A prominent Turkish observer told the author in the fall of 2000, 'If one has not been to a meeting with Greeks in the past week, one is not 'in' in Istanbul'.' See Lesser, I.O., Larrabee, S., Zanini, M., and Vlachos-Dengler, K. (2001), *Greece's New Geopolitics*, Rand, Santa Monica, p. 23.

16 See *The Military Balance*, published annually by the Institute of International Strategic Studies in London.

17 Makovsky, A. 'The New Activism in Turkish Foreign Policy,' *SAIS Review*, vol.19, no.1, p. 106.

18 Wilkinson, M.J. (2000), 'The United States, Turkey, and Greece-Three's a Crowd' in M. Abramowitz (ed.) *Turkey's Transformation and American Policy,* The Century Foundation Press, New York, p. 215.

19 L. Bezanis, *OMRI*, 18 May 1995.

20 Krebs, R.R. (1999, Spring), 'Perverse Institutionalism: NATO and the Greco-Turkish Conflict,' *International Organization*, vol. 53, no.2, p. 369.

21 Stephanou, C. and Tsardanides, C. (1999, Spring), 'The EC Factor in the Greece-Turkey-Cyprus Triangle, *International Organization*, vol. 53, no.2, p. 210.

22 Luxembourg European Council, *Presidency Conclusions,* 12 and 13 December 1997, paragraphs 31-36, http://www. europarl.eu.int/dg7/summits/en/lux1.htm.

23 Helsinki European Council, *Presidency Conclusions*, 10 and 11 December 1999, http://www.europa.eu.int/council/off/conclu/dec99/dec99/_en.pdf.

24 Stearns, M. (1997), 'Greek Security Issues,' in G.T. Allison and K. Nicolaidis (eds.), *The Greek Paradox: Promise vs. Performance,* MIT Press, Cambridge and London, p. 71.

25 Gordon, P.H. (1998, February), 'Storms in the Med Blow towards Europe,' *World Today*, vo.54, no.2, p. 43.

26 *Financial Times*, 11 December 2001.

27 Couloumbis, T. and Klaveras, L. (1998), 'Prospects for Greek-Turkish Reconciliation in a Changing International Setting' in T. Bahcheli, T. Couloumbis and P. Carley, *Greek-Turkish Relations and U.S. Foreign Policy: Cyprus, the Aegean, and Regional Stability,* Peaceworks no. 17, United States Institute of Peace, Washington, DC, p. 37.

28 Couloumbis has suggested that 'Both Greece and Turkey agree to twelve-mile limits (for both territorial waters and airspace) for their mainland territory, and to six-mile limits for Aegean islands belonging to Greece and Turkey (with the exception of Euboea and Crete, which would enjoy the twelve-mile limit because of their size and distance from Turkey.' *Ibid.*, p. 38.

29 Author's interviews with two retired Turkish diplomats with considerable experience in dealing with Turkish-Greek issues in May and November 2001. Another retired Turkish diplomat, Yalım Eralp, underscored the critical importance of Athens and Ankara

reaching agreement on a *compromis* to be submitted to the ICJ at the Hague, and speculated that Turkey would be entitled to roughly twenty percent of the Aegean continental shelf. See *Haberturk*, Internet edition, 10 March 2002.

Chapter 10

Turkey's Relations with Iran in the Post-Cold War Era

Bülent Aras

There is widespread agreement among Turkish academics and in the media that Turkey and Iran have several difficult problems to be resolved in their bilateral relations. This article seeks to outline what these problems are and what has caused these problems in relations between the two countries, as well as critically analyzing the nature and severity of these problems. Of especially critical importance, is the extent to which domestic pressures have been influential in the development of Turkey's foreign policy towards Iran. Do Turkish decision-makers decide who their rivals are on the basis of intrinsic national interests; or have they merely been reacting to images projected by self-interested politicians and external actors? Is Turkey drifting into a potentially dangerous rivalry without sufficient reason to see Iran as a primary opponent? In this paper, it is argued that Turkey's policy towards Iran has become hostage to the worldview of Turkey's governing elite, one that has demonstrated itself to be increasingly unable to successfully cope with political change on domestic, regional, and international levels.

Of course, it is necessary to put the relationship between Turkey and Iran, in historical perspective. The Ottoman State and Iran pursued a long-term rivalry based on sectarian ideological differences. The Turco-Iranian rivalry became most intense during the Safavid period (1486-1722); Iran remained in turmoil throughout the rest of the 18th century, following the overthrow of the Safavid dynasty. For hundreds of years, Turkish-Iranian relations have been characterized by controlled tensions, which, ironically, have served to stabilize the Iranian-Turkish border throughout this period.

The Qajar dynasty, established around 1797, had a positive attitude towards the Ottoman dynasty, and, by 1850, Turkish-Iranian relations were very much improving, as both empires came to increasingly see themselves as victims at the hands of Russia and other European powers. With the Pahlavi dynasty succeeding the Qajars in 1925, good relations continued between Turkey and Iran. Indeed, positive Turkish-Iranian relations reached their peak during the Pahlavi regime, although there were some minor tensions. These were related to the transport passage and the opium trade, and also Pahlavi administration was uneasy about Turkey's close ties to the West.[1] It was at this time that Iran and Turkey, along with Pakistan, formed the Central Treaty Organization (CENTO), as well as the first regional organization for economic cooperation in this part of the world, the Regional Cooperation for Development (RCD). After the triumph of the Islamic Revolution in 1979, Iranian-Turkish relations were once again made uneasy due to the different systems of government in Tehran and Ankara.

Following the 1979 revolution, Turkey pursued, in effect, a two-track policy towards Iran. Using its secular system as a pretext, and fearing the export of the Iranian revolution, it kept its distance from Iran politically, at the same time that it tried to develop its economic relations with Iran, especially during the Iran-Iraq war. Former Turkish President Turgut Özal, in particular, believed that close economic relations with Iran were important for Turkish interests and opposed the isolation of Tehran – even during those periods when the entire world stood strongly opposed to Iran.[2] In return, Iran showed a clear preference for Turkey as an economic partner, especially when Özal was in power.[3] During Özal's prime ministry, the RCD was revived as the Economic Cooperation Organization, or ECO; later, Afghanistan and, after the collapse of the Soviet Union, the Muslim states of the former Soviet Union, came to be included as members.

Methodologically, this study will analyze relations in a wide geopolitical context in order to provide a comprehensive picture. Only an analytical framework that integrates domestic and international politics and identities has the potential to explain both the material and non-material considerations that determine Turkish foreign policy towards Iran. At each level of relations, according to this framework, Turkish foreign policy directly reflects the interest of domestic actors; and therefore, it is set according to the hegemonic concerns of Turkey's ruling elite. For this reason, Turkish foreign policy lacks the flexibility to successfully adapt to changing domestic and international scenarios.

Foreign Policy through the Lens of Domestic Politics

Turkish diplomacy towards Iran has followed a cyclical pattern. After the escalation of a crisis, such as an accusation of spying or interference in each other's domestic affairs, the Turkish side decides to expel the Iranian ambassador and/or other officials. Following the retaliatory expulsion of Turkish officials from the Turkish embassy or consulates in Iran, Turkey recalls official(s) for 'consultation.' Soon thereafter, a Foreign Ministry spokesman says that the Foreign Ministry is taking care not to let the crisis affect its pattern of relations with Iran. In the last phase, the length of time depending on the severity of the crisis, Turkey and Iran decide to once again raise their diplomatic relations to the ambassadorial level. The major crises that emerged between Turkey and Iran, in 1985, from 1988 to 1990, from 1993 to 1994, and in 1997, followed this pattern.

A close look at several concrete issues may help to better understand the reasons behind this cyclical pattern of crises in relations. The most serious problems in the eyes of Turkish foreign policy-makers have been Iranian support to the PKK, Tehran's attempts to spread Islamic ideas in Turkey, and competition with Iran in the Caucasus and Central Asia.

Islam and the Kurdish Question in Bilateral Relations

It has almost become a truism among Turkish foreign policy decision makers that Iran has long continued a campaign to export Islamic revolution in Turkey by all possible means at its disposal, including support of illegal, 'overt Islamist,' groups.[4] According to this line of reasoning, the peculiarly religious nature of the Iranian regime prevents the reaching of an understanding with Turkey's democratic secular regime.

In the eyes of Turkish decision-makers, for example, the Baqeri crisis was part of a broader campaign launched against Turkey, calling on Islamic Turks to embrace a regime similar to the one in Iran. The Iranian ambassador Mohammad-Reza Baqeri addressed a group of people amidst chants of 'God is Great' *(Allah-u Ekber)*, marking the anniversary of Jerusalem Day in February 1997, in Sincan (a district of Ankara). Speaking under posters of Palestinian Islamic Jihad and Hizballah leaders, Baqeri conveyed the message that those who sign agreements with the United States and Israel will, sooner or later, be penalized. He used the ceremony to outline Iran's approach toward 'fundamentalism' and the Shari'a system. Baqeri's speech strengthened the contention that Iran was attempting to influence Turkish domestic affairs and led to his expulsion. An editorial reflected the official view of the Baqeri crisis, in a highly exaggerated form, as follows: 'The people of Turkey who believe in democracy and a contemporary way of life, will not allow individuals like you [Baqeri] to darken the bright future of humanity by creating a situation similar to that which existed in medieval times.'[5] This quotation accurately reflects the passionate sentiment in this regard of the mainstream Turkish media. According to the same line of thought, another source of Turkish resentment in the case of Baqeri was the Iranian official's reluctance to visit the Atatürk Mausoleum. The secularist elite saw this as a foreign policy priority in its relations with Iran; this has often caused a crisis between the two countries, as was the case during Iranian President Rafsanjani's 1996 visit.

One example of the 'threat' posed by Iran in the eyes of the Turkish military, was a brochure entitled, 'Spread of Political Islam' (1997), distributed to all participants at a series of briefings organized by the National Security Council to 'awaken' certain sections of Turkish society, ranging from bureaucrats to media personnel. The brochure suggested that Turkey's democratic and secular structure was the only obstacle preventing Iran from turning the Islamic world into a single *Shari'a*-based bloc.[6]

The Turkish military elite has expressed its view that the banned *Refah* (Welfare) Party and some other Islamic groupings, in collaboration with the Iranian mullahs, wish to combine Turkey and Iran into one Islamic state.[7] This view suggests that a military coup is a morally legitimate means of bringing down these 'reactionary activities,' if it is necessary for the preservation of Turkish integrity. It is worth mentioning that the crisis involving the Iranian ambassador was so important in the eyes of the ruling secular elite that it became a key factor in the military's decision to bring down the *Refahyol* government.

The Foreign Ministry prefers to play down conflicts related to this issue and follows a more pragmatic policy than that of the military elite. After then deputy chief of staff General Çevik Bir accused Iran of supporting militant Islamicist groups in Turkey, Turkish ambassador Osman Korutürk responded to Iranian protests by declaring: 'It is the Foreign Ministry that announces the Turkish Government's policies. What other circles say are their own personal views. The Iranian side must base its policy on the official pronouncements of the Foreign Ministry.'[8]

There is a tendency among those inclined to disregard historical differences between Turkey and Iran to be ignorant of Turkey's unique and original tradition of Sufism. As one editorial writer suggested: 'Do not be surprised if we become "Iranized" as a result of a venture that was undertaken in order to avoid "Iranization".'[9] Turkey's domestic security problems prevent the governing elite from accepting the way in which Turkey is now part of a world where pluralist democracy has become the only acceptable system. They regard Iran as a monolithic entity consisting of a nation of mullahs; this long-standing bias prevents them from responding to changes in Iran in constructive ways.

The second major problem in relations between Turkey and Iran is Turkish foreign policy makers' continuous claims that Iran allows the PKK (Workers' Party of Kurdistan) to use its territory. These claims has been repeatedly endorsed by high level figures in the government, such as former Defense Minister Turhan Tayan, who charged that, 'Iran provides support to the PKK and our security services have confirmed this on many occasions.'[10] In January 1997, PKK militants – who infiltrated into Turkey from their camps in northern Iraq to attack Turkish border posts – used heavy arms and Katyusha rockets. The Turkish foreign ministry charged that the PKK had acquired the arms from Iran and Russia in order to reinforce its military strength.[11] In the wake of this crisis, the military blamed the foreign ministry for not being sufficiently aggressive in the diplomatic war against these two states.

Although this problem is not as severe as is suggested by the foreign ministry and the military, it was also a concern of the then-ruling Islamist *Refah* Party. Abdullah Gül, known as the head of the foreign affairs department of *Refah*, which aimed to improve relations with Iran, argued that 'we cannot say that the problem has been completely solved, but we are working with goodwill to solve it. The number of incidents on our common border has decreased. A struggle is being waged in Iran against the PKK, similar to the one in Turkey. We are cooperating on various issues. In fact, we are very hopeful.'[12] Turkey's decisive policy forced Iran to begin to cooperate in the fight against the PKK. Their agreement to share in these operations, however, was regarded as Iranian admission of the presence of terrorists on its soil. Developments on this front are seen as insufficient, and the Turkish side is asking for the right of hot pursuit into Iran as well as joint operations with Iran.[13]

After the 1990–1991 Gulf crisis, the situation changed as the problem increasingly came to be seen as one that involved all of the countries that have a Kurdish population. The emergence of a Kurdish region with limited autonomy, the convening of a Kurdish parliament, the breakout of fighting between rival Kurdish groups, and the PKK's use of Iranian and Syrian territory in its attacks against Turkish military units and villages led Turkey, Iran, and Syria to adopt a common stance towards the problem. These three countries also met routinely to coordinate policies that would help to maintain the territorial and political unity of Iraq.[14] The problematic situation – in particular during the Asad regime's ousting of PKK leader, Abdullah Öcalan, from Syria – between Damascus and Ankara, blockaded the formulation of an effective policy in this regard. Given the PKK leader's departure from Syria, however, a more pragmatic approach may lead to a rapprochement between Ankara and Damascus.

It is interesting to note that the PKK, in addition to using Iranian territory, is also using Iraqi, Syrian, Armenian, Russian, and Greek territories, and even United States, French, German, and Dutch territories for the organization of its political activities, in the different forms in which they occur. In the case of Iran's, it should be taken into consideration that there is no acceptance of a Kurdish state, or even the presence of Kurdish activists, according to Iran's official 'security doctrine'.[15] Furthermore, Iran does not support the PKK ideologically. Tehran handed over 35 PKK militants to Turkish authorities, and more than 20 simultaneous anti-PKK operations were conducted in 1996 by Iranian security forces.[16] Kamal Kharrazi, the Iranian Foreign Minister, in the meeting of the Foreign Ministers of the Organization of the Islamic Conference (OIC) in March 1998, said that productive cooperation can be made on the 'Neighbourhood Forum' which was prepared by Turkey to normalize the situation in Iraq.[17] This landmark development demonstrated that there was a solid base for security cooperation to handle the Kurdish question as it was related to Iran.

Iran may usher in a new initiative, which would revive the tripartite coordination committee, thus providing a forum for Ankara, Tehran, and Damascus to discuss the situation with respect to northern Iraq and to coordinate the three countries' positions on Iraq's political future. For example, during the October 1998 crisis, after Turkey's threats of military strike, then President Hafez Assad unexpectedly agreed to sign a security agreement with Ankara on 20 October 1998, in the Turkish town of Adana. With the Adana Accord, Damascus agreed to recognize PKK as a terrorist organization, pledged to cease all logistical and financial aid to terrorists and shut down existing PKK camps in the country. Consequently, as a notable first step, Damascus expelled the PKK leader Abdullah Öcalan, whose presence in Syria had always been denied by the Assad administration. Turkey's new 'Neighborhood Forum' approach, initiated by Foreign Minister İsmail Cem in January 1998, targets the same result with other regional countries. His ideas immediately found a receptive audience in both Jordan and Iran. It goes almost without saying that these three countries began to show increasing willingness for cooperation to deal with the challenges posed by a post-PKK period.

Most of the problems between Ankara and Tehran, however, have little to do with Turkey's intrinsic national interests. Rather, they are the results of internal disputes and domestic security problems in Turkey. In the 1990s, Turkey has witnessed the emergence of new identities based on ethnic and cultural diversity. Islamists and Kurds have constituted the most dynamic sectors of these cultural spheres. The Turkish State has attempted to stall or resist increasing levels of demand for greater levels of democratic participation and respect for human rights.

From the perspective of the ruling elite, 'the production of differences and the making of distinctions which transcend official state ideology represent an enemy within.'[18] The media also works towards the homogenization of Turkish society, with networks devoted to the creation of images representing 'oneness' and 'otherness' – us and them. The State elite has sought to play upon this nationalistic sentiment by suggesting that internal challenges are the product of conspiracies from Iran and Syria, especially with respect to the rise of Islamic and Kurdish demands.

The nationalist discourse of the foreign policy elite is by nature exclusionist and constantly seeking to justify itself by, among other things, dramatizing the dangers posed by enemies. As in the case of relations with Iran, perceived or alleged threats to national interest may not be simply imaginary, but they are frequently subject to manipulation at the hands of the ruling elite.[19] Over time, this exclusionist policy has become disconnected from its origins; the initial contexts that gave rise to it, and have come to have a life of its own, accepted as an integral part of the general state of affairs. Thus the ruling elite has consistently held Turkey's foreign policy hostage to domestic politics. A study of the motivations and fears that drive Iranian policy towards Turkey might very well illuminate interesting similarities in terms of the relationship between perceived threats and the development of foreign policy.

It is clearly the case that there is some division or tension between the military and the foreign ministry with respect to the formulation of policy towards Iran, and the increasing role enjoyed by the military over foreign policy decision making decreases prospects for progressive change. The ideological sharpening of Turkish foreign policy that has accompanied the increasing role of the military in Turkish politics has had a direct impact on the conduction of foreign policy, increasing the likelihood of a misinterpretation of Iran's behavior or intentions. This has also led to seeing foreign relations as a function of domestic politics, turning foreign policy into an internal game – namely, as the logic goes, if Islam is a domestic threat, Iran also constitutes a threat since it has an Islamic regime. According to this line of reasoning, improving relations with Europe and more recently with Israel will help Turkey to develop along the path of the Western democracies, while the development of relations with Iran might enhance the role of Islamist in Turkey, thus relegated into a secondary importance.

Rivalry in Central Asia and the Caucasus

Another prominent issue on the agenda of Turkish foreign policy towards Iran has to do with the competition that exists between the two countries for influence in the Caucasus and Central Asia. The appearance of new Islamic states in Central Asia and the Caucasus following the collapse of the Soviet Union, according to Kirişci, caused a shift in the foreign policy priorities of Turkey and triggered a search for a means of tactical political-economic penetration into these countries.[20] Turkey's efforts in this regard were motivated by a desire to spread the Turkish model of government and society – consisting of parliamentary democracy, relatively free-market economy, and secularism in a Muslim society – as well as taking advantage of the mutual development opportunities that regional cooperation could create. From the perspective of Turkish diplomacy, these opportunities included guaranteed access to vital energy resources and lucrative oil transport revenues, as well as increased diplomatic clout and strategic importance.

Iran has made serious initiatives towards these states as well, using its geographic advantage by offering them free passage through its territory and by providing an alternative model to governments and opposition groups. Tehran is aware of the fact, however, that its economic resources, especially with respect to transportation, are insufficient for financing Central Asia's needs. Consequently, Iran sought to gain a partnership with Russia, with whom it has developed a tactical friendship with respect to the Central Asian states.[21]

Following the dissolution of the Soviet Union, especially foreign academics have put forward the idea that a geo-political vacuum had emerged in this region and that Turkey and Iran would be among the major competitors seeking to fill it.[22] This model of a political 'vacuum' in the Caucasus and Central Asia was not originally generated by Ankara's or Tehran's think tanks. It was the result of a handful of articles and papers penned by well-known American specialists (like those at *Rand* and *Heritage*), which were quickly picked up and repeated by influential press organs such as the *New York Times*, and the *Washington Post.*[23] A variety of new strategies – with a multitude of objectives, such as rewarding Turkey, acknowledging the role of language and history, as well as thwarting real or perceived Islamic threats in the region – were being embraced in Europe, the United States and, of course, Turkey itself. Official Ankara grabbed onto it and ran as fast and far as it could, hoping and expecting that the rhetoric was going to soon turn cold cash, not to mention the benefits of a long-term influence in the region.

At that time, the Western media often published articles on various alliances designed to discourage the extension of Iranian influence into Azerbaijan and the new republics of Central Asia. Those articles argued that several pro-Western Islamic countries – most notably Turkey, Pakistan, Egypt, and Saudi Arabia – appeared to have undertaken significant efforts to establish ties with the newly independent Islamic countries to counter Iranian influence.[24] In this sense, the development of Turkish policy towards Central Asia and Azerbaijan has been aimed at preventing the spread of 'fundamentalist' Islamic ideas. Turkey's willingness to accept this role as regional promoter of a secular-democratic model in the area came to serve as a model of 'cultural correctness,' the mainstream political strategy. The articles and policy statements that served to emphasize Turkey's 'Western identity' were encouraging to foreign policy makers as they were seen as an endorsement of the success of Turkey with respect to its Westernization. The new policy line was also in conformity with the ideology of the Turkish establishment in its understanding of Islam as the primary social force to be feared in the domestic political domain. Ironically, the main success that Turkey has so far enjoyed in this newly emerging area is the presence and activities of its civil society organizations and businessmen, who have been motivated by the desire to rejuvenate Ottoman-Islamic consciousness.

Both Turkey and Iran have limited levels of understanding of and capabilities to assist these newly emergent 'kindred' countries; therefore, both their expectations and objectives are limited. There is very little that Iranians are able to do with respect to spreading their message of Islam outside of Tajikistan. All the states of Central Asia have governments with anti-Islamicist postures – with the single exception of Tajikistan – still in a state of civil war, in which Islamic groups are participating. In other words, the primary arena of competition between Iran and Turkey are in the areas of trade and commerce and not in exporting, or preventing the dissemination of Islam to Central Asia. Ignoring their weaknesses and overestimating their strengths, both Tehran and Ankara have committed major mistakes with respect to the former Soviet south. As Igor P. Lipovsky has pointed out, 'neither Turkey nor Iran have been able to take on Russia's previous role in the region.'[25] The new states of Central Asia and Azerbaijan turned their attention towards Europe and the United States and to some extent the Far Eastern countries.[26] Therefore, even if there was a foundation for competition between Turks and Iranians, they may not be able to find a willing audience.

The dissolution of the Soviet Union brought several other issues onto the regional agenda. Due to their importance to relations between Tehran and Ankara, discussions centering on Azerbaijan and the Caspian Sea deserve special attention. The ongoing crisis between Armenia and Azerbaijan over the Nagorno-Karabakh region, initiated a new crisis in the Caucasus. Turkey and Iran sought separate mediatory roles between the fighting states. Iran is home to around 20 million Azerbaijani in its northern regions, and the earlier statements of Azeri officials with respect to a possible 'Greater Azerbaijan' uniting Azerbaijanis on both sides of the Aras River raised serious concerns in Tehran. Malik Mufti's argument that, 'Turkish nationalism in Azerbaijan threatens Iran's very existence' may seem rather exaggerated,[27] but it reflects the feelings of ruling circles in Iran. According to Gussein Baguirov, rector of Baku's Western University, 'Tehran is not honest in its relations with Baku and regards it as a big headache.'[28]

After the removal from office of the pro-Turkish and pro-Western President Abulfaz Elchibey, Tehran had a short-lived honeymoon with Azerbaijan's new Heydar Aliyev administration. However, Azerbaijan accepted a US decision to exclude Iran from a Caspian oil project known as the 'deal of the century,' in January 1995, which rapidly changed the Iranian stance. Soon after, Iran formulated a new policy that involved much closer relations with Russia, increasing political and economic relations with Armenia, and a cautious policy toward Azerbaijan. With the tacit support of the United States, Turkey and Azerbaijan created a counter-alliance. Turkey's relations with Azerbaijan are likely to develop further in coming years, but the prospect for Tehran to do likewise seems limited by the problems discussed so far.

Turkey initiated a Black Sea Economic Cooperation Zone, while Iran created a grouping of Caspian Sea littoral states. Neither of them participated in the other's initiative. Tehran efforts were less ambitious but it has benefited from a well-coordinated policy with Moscow with respect to the new republics. Both Turkey and Iran had timid reactions to the Chechen crisis and demonstrated their inability to contribute to a solution to the Karabakh problem; despite domestic pressures for more active policies, both nations have found it difficult to challenge the influence of Russia over its former satellites.

In general, the Caspian region has gradually been gaining in importance with respect to both regional and international politics. Iranian analysts are quick to point out that Iran can serve as a bridge between the Caspian Sea and the Persian Gulf, which are the two major energy producing regions of the world.[29] Iran adjoins an area of the Caspian with relatively meager mineral deposits, however, and, not surprisingly, its position on the exploitation of resources in this basin has been very close to that of Russia. Tehran has supported the Russian suggestion that the U.N. Law of the Sea Convention has no jurisdiction in this area, adding that all issues related to the Caspian's exploitation should be settled by the five states that touch its shores, without any external interference at all.[30] Moscow, however, began to give signals that it might compromise on this issue. The deal between Russia and Kazakhstan made in July 1998, on dividing the seabed of the northern Caspian is a landmark development. Turkey almost always backs Azerbaijan in Caspian oil controversies and has great prospect for benefiting from the development of Azerbaijani oil reserves; the state-run Turkish oil company, TPAO, received a 6.75 per cent share in the consortium developing the Azeri, Chirag, and Guneshli oil fields and a 9 per cent stake in the consortium developing the Shah-Deniz field. However, Turkey's strongly pro-Azerbaijani stance has not yielded results for Turkey, aside from the possibility of the Baku-Ceyhan pipeline project. The much-debated pipeline was backed by the Clinton administration and adopted by the Bush administration as a way to diversify the transportation routes for the vast amounts of oil that have been discovered in the Caspian Sea region, and avoid having to transport all of it through Russia or Iran.[31]

Cooperation Prospects: Domestic Contentions Still Matter

Despite the fact that there are serious problems in Turkish-Iranian relations, there are also several prospects for cooperation. The first and foremost is natural gas and pipeline projects. Contrary to press reports that the former leader of the *Refah* Party, Necmettin Erbakan, initiated these projects for the sake of improving relations with Tehran, such projects had been on the agenda of the foreign ministry for some time.[32] In March 1995, the Iran-Turkey-Europe natural gas pipeline project was taking shape, involving the shipment of Iranian natural gas to Europe via Turkey. Talks on the subject are expected to continue and, in the short-run, the two sides have already signed a separate agreement that envisages Iran selling 2 billion cubic meters of natural gas to Turkey annually.[33] In 1997, talks on two new projects were added to the earlier discussions. The first calls for the transportation of Turkmenistan's natural gas to the Turkish port of Iskenderun through Iran. The second is in the form of a protocol for the transportation of oil, extracted in southern Iran, to Ceyhan in Turkey.

Commercial relations, however, have been heavily influenced by Turkish foreign policy-makers' fear of Iran, and rumors have occurred concerning the cancellation of these projects on the part of Turkey. Former Iranian Foreign Minister Ali Akbar Velayati arrived in Ankara following the spread of these rumors in 1997. The Iranian administration, fearing that the agreement that Turkey and Iran had reached concerning the sale of natural gas worth $21 billion might be cancelled because of the tensions between the two countries and the pressure the United States has put on Ankara, called for 'moderation' between the two sides.[34] Turkey declared that it started the construction of a 300-kilometer pipeline from Erzurum to the Iranian border in July 1997, and it has given an international tender for the construction of a pipeline from Erzurum to Sivas and thence to Ankara. According to the proposal, once the pipeline grid becomes operational, Tehran will initially supply Turkey with over 2 billion cubic meters of natural gas annually, with the quantity increasing to 10 billion cubic meters of gas within five years.

With respect to the Turkmen project, Askhabat had in mind transiting between 16 to 28 billion cubic meters of gas annually to Turkey and thence to Europe. This high quantity must be conveyed through a complex network, and the present gas pipeline grid has been designed only to meet domestic needs. Some negotiations have been conducted, however, with respect to laying a gas pipeline network through Iran, from Turkmenistan to Turkey. For both projects, the most important challenge will be to find the necessary funds.

Despite its ups and downs, ECO has continued to be important in terms of promoting regional cooperation. ECO was founded in 1985 by Iran, Pakistan, and Turkey to promote economic, technical, and cultural cooperation among the member states. As noted above, ECO is the successor organization to the Regional Cooperation for Development (RCD), which functioned from 1964 to 1979; its basic charter was the Treaty of İzmir, originally signed in 1977. All of this has resulted from geo-strategic concerns, and later on, economic dimension became integrated. In 1992 ECO added seven new members, Afghanistan, Azerbaijan, Kazakhstan, Kyrgyzstan, Tajikistan, Turkmenistan and Uzbekistan. The enlarged body's members represent 325 million people spread out over almost eight million square kilometers. ECO also enjoys a certain cultural cohesion, incorporating all of the non-Arab Islamic countries of Western and Central Asia.[35] In May 1997, Turkish President Süleyman Demirel called for the restructuring of ECO and claimed that cooperation between member countries would help boost the living conditions of the people of the entire region. Praising the Mashhad-Sarakhs-Tajan railroad link, he stressed the need for improving the connection of Turkey's railroad network to the Central Asian countries.[36] From Turkey's perspective, ECO is a forum for the discussion of regional disputes and for the development of peaceful cooperation between the original members and the newly independent member countries.

The Relevance of Turkey's Relations with Israel, the US and the EU

Another issue that has had considerable relevance to Turco-Iranian relations is the Middle East peace process and, more specifically, the increasing level of relations between Turkey and Israel. The peace process, especially in the aftermath of the Oslo agreement, helped Iran to recognize regional realities in the development of its foreign policy, radicalizing political discourse in domestic politics. While declaring its reluctance to impede the peace process, Tehran also underlined the impossibility of endorsing it. According to Mahmood Sariolghalam of Tehran's

Shehid Behesti University, this stance represents a 'demonstration of a compromise between maintaining a domestic ideological constituency and projecting moderate behavior abroad.'[37] R. K. Ramazani goes even further, arguing that with their policy against the peace process, 'Iranian extremists sound more Catholic than the pope.'[38]

The Madrid Framework created a suitable international environment for Turkey to improve its relations with Israel and reaping the potential fruit of a regional economic cooperation scheme. On the other hand, signs that Baku might side with Israel and Turkey in regional politics has increased the suspicions and worries of the Iranian administration. Although Turkey looks primarily to Syria with respect to improving security relations with Israel, the Israeli side also seeks to utilize cooperation against Iran.

Turkey and Israel still have serious differences over this contentious, conflict-prone region and the further development of their relations offers as many challenges as it does opportunities. From the Israeli perspective, cooperation with Turkey may accelerate the acceptance of its geo-cultural integration into the region. In addition, it might aid Tel Aviv's attempt to penetrate the markets of the former republics of the Soviet Union. A flurry of high level visits since 1993 are evidence of the increasing intensity of relations between Tel Aviv and Ankara. From the Turkish perspective, closer relations with Israel might facilitate access to Israeli technology and industrial intelligence, and, most importantly, may serve to address Turkish security concerns, upgrading weaponry systems and monitoring PKK activities. The potential areas of economic cooperation that have the most appeal are water, agriculture, and tourism. Moreover, there is a widespread belief that friendship with Israel would mean greater support from the United States. However, it is doubtful whether Jewish lobbies in Washington, whose support is particularly important to military circles, would use their influence to protect Turkish interests. Among the leading Jewish lobbying groups that have actively contributed to the development of Turkish-Israeli relations are AIPAC (the American-Israeli Public Affairs Committee), JINSA (the Jewish Institute for National Security Affairs), and WINEP (the Washington Institute for Near East Policy).[39] Although their activities include some initiatives that overlap with Turkish interests, these initiatives are mainly the policies of American right-wing conservatives, and the lobbies themselves do not put them forward. From time to time, it is also seen that conservative organizations such as the Center for Strategic and International Studies and the Heritage Foundation take braver attitudes in Turkey's favor.[40] In short, the pro-Israeli lobbies are making efforts to steer US policies toward the Middle East and Turkey in a way that serves Israeli interests and that maximizes Tel Aviv's regional benefits.

On the negative side, Greece and Armenia condemned Israel for improving relations with Turkey, and the PKK threatened to attack Israeli units. On the Turkish side, Ankara was criticized severely at the OIC meeting held in December 1997 in Tehran. The burgeoning of Turkish-Israeli relations has come at a time when the peace process between the Palestinians and Israel has turned into a cold peace. Iran, on the other hand, by the end of 1997, hosted an Islamic summit and restored relations with those Arab countries from which it had been excluded.

Therefore, in terms of regional politics, there is more reason for cooperation than for conflict with Iran; Turkey should not let its relations with Tehran be held hostage to the interests of other countries. Otherwise, the losing side will be Turkey, especially as one considers the clear signs of an emerging Arab-Iranian entente among Iran, Egypt, Syria, and Saudi Arabia. The Turkish foreign policy elite should not turn a blind eye to this new development in the region. Under the current conjuncture, Iran is the only state in the Middle East that opposes Israeli expansion in Jerusalem; this represents a major problem for Tel Aviv. Iran's opposition to the Middle East peace process is basically due to Iran's fear that an end to the Arab-Israeli conflict will lead to the outbreak of an Arab-Iranian conflict, and might raise sensitive Arab-Iranian issues that have remained suspended – most importantly, the issue of the three islands in the Gulf.

Iran sees Turkey as a 'Westoxicated' regime, subservient to the United States, and serving as its representative in the region clearly. Turkey received a full endorsement early on from the US administration in the so-called Turkish-Iranian competition and was clearly acknowledged to be serving as a vanguard against the spread of 'Islamic fundamentalism' among the newly independent Caucasian and Central Asian countries.[41]

In essence, Turkish foreign policy-makers follow an Iranian policy close to the one adopted by the European Union, i.e., 'critical dialogue' and engagement with Iran. Turkey refused, for example, to abide by the US sanctions against Iran in the wake of the embassy crisis in 1979 and benefited greatly from this decision throughout the 1980s by increasing its trade with Iran.

This paper has assumed that state identity in world politics is mostly a product of domestic political contentions and social practices that both enable and restrain a state's interests and actions with respect to its foreign policy. It has also held that inter-subjective relations – interactions and dialogue – in international politics are important in terms of identity formulations with both material and discursive impressions. Accordingly, Turkish foreign policy-makers pay special attention to the roles that are attributed to them and show an open willingness to reshape Western-constructed images in the process of reproducing Turkish identity through social practices and political-ideological contests at home. This will to manifest identity underlines the importance of the opinions of others for Turkish self-understanding; which seems all the more relevant given the oscillating relations with the European Union.

Conclusion

The Turkish establishment's representation of Iran is tainted by its tendency to see all Islamists (and Kurds) as 'other' in domestic politics. The Turkish state aims to legitimize itself by opposing external others, especially, Iran, and aligning itself with like-minded actors, especially the European Union and Israel. Availing itself of both negative and positive reference groups has allowed the Turkish regime 'to maintain a domestic, social and political order characterized by international validity.'[42]

This analysis challenges the dominant view held by both neo-liberalism and neo-realism that 'policy modifications are a matter of rational adaptation to changes in the prevailing opportunity structure, a mechanical response largely devoid of cognitive content or political-ideological contestation.'[43] As Micheal Barnett has argued: 'Identity is not a static construct but, rather, is socially constructed, and this social construction process can be used to good effect for understanding alliance dynamics and changes in security patterns. To understand the social construction of state identity, however, requires examining not only interstate interactions but also state-society relations.'[44] In Turco-Iranian relations, non-material aspects and ideological orientations have held priority and led to abnormal foreign policy behavior. The nature and focus of current Turkish policy towards Iran obscures recognition of actual and potential shifts in the regional and international position of Iran as well as the internal transformation of the Iranian state.

The Turkish State needs to widen its legitimacy base to include the discourses of the new identities based on ethnic, ideological, and cultural diversity. Turkey is a culturally diverse land, and this diversity should be seen as a source of strength rather than a challenge to existing institutions. It is useless to resist the demands of pluralistic society, which go far beyond what Turkey's secular-nationalist Westernizers have been prepared to tolerate. As Soli Özel argued: 'The problem today is how to accommodate the desires of Turkey's citizens to express their particularities. This new development reflects the richness of the country's heritage and its culture.'[45] A new understanding based on a great leap forward, which aims at reconciling the discourses of the new ethnic and cultural identities with the state's official modernization program has some potential for harmonizing and integrating – rather than ignoring, assimilating and silencing – this historically diverse land.

The exclusionist nature of Turkey's current foreign policy vision may be minimized in the future; there is no need or rational basis for over-dramatizing the dangers posed by real or perceived enemies. This may also help foreign policy to escape the constraints of domestic politics and encourage the formulation of national interests that are based on new Turkish realities.

Turkish-Iranian relations are important for the domestic, regional, and international politics of Turkey. Iran's new president, Khatami, in accordance with his other current signs of moderation in Tehran's international relations, has declared that he plans to adopt a 'more active and fresh' approach to foreign policy. Of course, Iran's poor relations with the United States and Europe are a factor of primary importance. Nor can Tehran be said to maintain favorable relations with other countries in the region. A constructive Turkish approach may lead Khatami to improve Iran's relations with its closest neighbors first, including Turkey. According to Prime Minister Ecevit, 'The new President of Iran is opening a new era. The normalization of relations between Turkey and Iran is the right move within this context. Naturally, however, whether or not President Khatami uses his powers is another question.'[46] He clearly acknowledged the positive steps being taken in Iran to strengthen the hands of the moderates.

The United States may not welcome closer Iranian-Turkish ties; but it realizes that Turkey needs to have relations with its neighbors (especially for purposes of getting natural gas). The United States may begin to worry, however, if Turkish-Iranian rapprochement should coincide with a relative withdrawal from European interests on the part of Turkey. From whatever perspective one looks at the issue, close relations between Turkey and Iran are highly meaningful from both commercial and security standpoints. Developments in Iran and Turkey will have a lasting impact on regional politics as well, and the fate of the Islamic world in general. A failure to cooperate on the part of these two states must be understood as resulting from a mutual perception of each other's national interests and available options in the international arena. Foreign policy elites should be aware of the fact that the policy formulation process includes multiple identities, and any *a priori* and exogenous attribution of state identity is invalid; and in turn, it serves to restrain their ability to cope with change in the context of international politics.

After analyzing bilateral, regional, and international contexts, this study has argued that Turkey has drifted into an unproductive rivalry without actually deciding that Iran represents a prime opponent. In addition to domestic actors, the ideology and worldview of Turkey's ruling elite has determined foreign policy behavior towards Iran. The typical cyclical pattern of ruptures in Iranian-Turkish relations, characterized by severe crises involving ideologically driven incriminations, and, at times the recall of diplomats – generally followed by periods of pragmatic relations. If foreign policy makers could move beyond a mere reaction to images projected by self-interested politicians, and formulate a new policy paying attention to changing domestic, regional and international politics, the typical cyclical pattern might well become part of the past.

There are many similarities between Turkey's secular-nationalist establishment and Iran's hard-core religious ruling elite. Liberal-minded mayors have been prosecuted in both İstanbul and Tehran. Whereas Iranian society is sending signals that it wants more liberal rule at home, and is showing moderation in its foreign policy, Turkish society is remembering its Ottoman-Islamic past. This process is consistent with the idea of legitimacy crisis defined by Jurgen Habermas, which determines the limits beyond which a system can no longer find a solution to its problems without losing its identity.[47]

Turkey is on the threshold of a transformation that will open new horizons for both domestic and foreign politics. More and more emphasis will be placed on encouraging links with the Balkans, the Middle East, and the ex-Soviet, Turkic republics, rather than insisting on the idea of a 'Fortress Turkey.' The current mentality – based on the early 20th century European model of the nation-state – does not seem especially relevant for the coming century. In order to secure a leadership role for itself in the 21st century, Turkey's establishment will have to cultivate the ability to recognize the need for progressive changes and take a great leap forward with respect to the dynamism of its own society. Otherwise, Turkish foreign policy will continue to be held hostage to domestic political considerations, and have little opportunity to play a constructive role in regional or international politics.

Notes

1 Bishku, M.B. (1999, Spring), 'Turkey and Iran During the Cold War,' *Journal of Third World Studies*, vol. 16, no.1, pp.13-28.
2 See, Gözen, R. (1996), 'Turgut Özal and Turkish Foreign Policy: Style and Vision,' *Foreign Policy* (Ankara), vol.20, no.3-4.
3 Confidential interviews with research staff at Center for Scientific Research and Middle East Strategic Studies in Tehran, August 2001.
4 For a similar approach see Kongar, E. (2000), *28 Şubat ve Demokrasi,* Remzi Kitabevi, İstanbul.
5 *Sabah,* 2 February 1997, p. 19.
6 *Hürriyet*, 26 April 1997.
7 Ibid.
8 *Anatolia*, 24 February 1997.
9 *Zaman*, 6 March 1997.
10 *Foreign Broadcast Information Service*-West Europe (*FBIS*-WEU), 97-184, 7 July 1997.
11 *Milliyet*, 7 January 1997, p.10.
12 *Milliyet,* 13 January 1997, p 12.
13 *Milliyet,* 6 August 1997.
14 For more information see Özdağ, Ü. (1996, Spring), 'Kuzey Irak ve PKK,' (Northern Iraq and PKK), *Avrasya Dosyası*, vol.3, no.1.
15 Confidential interviews with research staff at Center for Scientific Research and Middle East Strategic Studies in Tehran, August 2001.
16 *Anatolia*, 20 September 1996: Olson explains both countries' policies regarding trans-state Kurdish questions with omni-balancing, which 'emphasizes that where external threats are significant and internal ones manageable, priority may tilt toward external threats.' See Olson, R. (1998), *The Kurdish Question and Turkish-Iranian Relations: From World War I to 1998*, Mazda Publishing, Costa Mesa, CA, p. 85.
17 *BBC*, Summary of World Broadcasts, 18 March 1998.
18 Väyrynen, T. (1997, December), 'Securitised Ethnic Identities and Communal Conflicts,' *Peace and Conflict Studies*, vol.4, no.2, p. 24.
19 Aral, B. (1997, Winter), 'Turkey's Insecure Identity from the Perspective of Nationalism,' *Mediterranean Quarterly*, vol.8, no.1, p. 91.
20 For more detailed information on new trends in Turkish foreign policy, see Kirişci, K. (1995), 'New Patterns of Turkish Foreign Policy Behavior,' in Ç. Balım et al. (eds), *Turkey: Political, Social and Economic Challenges in the 1990s,* E.J.Brill, Leiden.
21 *Zaman*, 22 August 2001, p.8.
22 For a few example see, Smolansky, O.M. (1994), 'Turkish and Iranian Policies in Central Asia,' in H. Malik, (ed.), *Central Asia: Its Strategic Importance and Future Prospects,* St. Martin's Press, New York, pp. 283-310; Winrow, G. (2000), 'Turkish Policy toward Central Asia and the Transcaucasus,' in Alan Makovsky and Sabri Sayari, (eds), *Turkey's New World. Changing Dynamics in Turkish Foreign Policy*, pp. 116-30; and Robins, P. (1993, Autumn), 'Between Sentiment and Self-Interest: Turkey's Policy Toward Azerbaijan and the Central Asian States,' *Middle East Journal*, vol.47, no.4, pp. 593-610.
23 For example see, Mary Beth Sheridan, 'Turkey, Competing with Iran and Saudis, Embraces Soviet Republics,' *The Associated Press*, 27 February 1992; Blaine Harden, 'Turkish Premier Voices Worries,' *The Washington Post*, 19 March 1992, p. A17; Strobe Talbott, 'An Ally Deserves Better,' *Time*, 28 January 1991; William Drozdiak,

'Iran and Turkey,' *The Washington Post,* 24 November 1991, p. A27; Tom Hundley, 'Futures to be Written in Choice of Alphabet,' *Chicago Tribune,* 24 November 1991, p. 25; 'Woerner Says Turkey could be Model to Republics,' *The Reuter,* 20 March 1992; 'Turkey Holds Key to Power in Asia,' *The Sunday Telegraph,* 25 December 1991, p. 15; William Drozdiak, 'Iran and Turkey Vie for Political, Economic Influence in Soviet Muslim States,' *The Washington Post,* 24 November 1991, p. A27; Hugh Pope, 'Turkey's Star Rises over the New Azerbaijan,' *The Independent,* 13 June 1992, p. 13; Blaine Harden, 'Turkey Pushing Eastward by Satellites,' *The Washington Post,* 22 March 1992, p. A1.

24 Ironically, when Turkey was surfacing as a model for other Turkic republics, the most secular and westernized Islamic population of Europe (Bosnian Moslems) was facing onslaught due to its Ottoman-Islamic heritage by anti-Western and anti-secularist Serbs. For more information, see Khan, M. (1996), 'External Threats and the Promotion of a Trans-National Islamic Consciousness: The Case of the Late Ottoman Empire and Contemporary Turkey,' *Islamic World Report,* vol.1, no.1.

25 Lipovsky, I.P. (1996, Spring), 'Central Asia: In Search of a New Political Identity,' *Middle East Journal,* vol.50, no.2, p. 223.

26 Aras, B. (1998, March 13), 'Azerbaijan's Far Eastern Friends,' *Middle East International,* no. 570, p. 16.

27 Mufti, M. (1998, Winter), 'Daring and Caution in Turkish Foreign Policy,' *Middle East* Journal, vol.52, no.1.

28 Personal Correspondence, Gussein Baguirov, Rector of Baku West University, Azerbaijan, 15 April 1998.

29 *FBIS*-NES, 95-238, 14 December 1995.

30 Shoumikhin, A. (1996, November), 'Economics and Politics of Developing Caspian Oil Resources,' *Perspectives on Central Asia* http://www.cpss.org/casianw/novpers.html.

31 Frantz, D. 'Oil Pipeline to Turkey Backed by Chief of BP,' *New York Times,* 21 June 2001,

32 For detailed information see, Iskit, T. (1996, March-May), 'Turkey: A New Actor in the Field of Energy Politics,' *Perceptions,* vol.1, no. 1.

33 *Nokta,* 5-11 March 1995, pp. 22-4.

34 *Hürriyet,* 11 March 1997, p.17.

35 Pompfret, R. (1997, June), 'The Economic Cooperation Organization: Current Status and Future Prospects,' *Europe-Asia* Studies, vol.49, no.4.

36 *FBIS*-NES, 97-134, 15 May 1997.

37 Sariolghalam, M. (1996), 'The Future of the Middle East: The Impact of the Northern Tier,' *Security Dialogue,* vol.27, no.3, p. 314.

38 Ramazani, R.K. (1992, Summer), 'Iran's Foreign Policy: Both North and South,' *Middle East Journal,* vol.46, no.3, p. 412.

39 For detailed activities by these lobbies, see the Internet addresses http://www.jinsa.org, http://www.aipac.org and http://www.washingtoninstitute.org, respectively. Particularly, WINEP has established a section entitled Turkish Studies managed by Alan Makovsky and has hosted a large group of people including top state officials, academicians, military staff and journalists.

40 For more information about the Heritage Foundation and the CSIS, see the Internet addresses http://www.heritage.org and http://www.csis.org, respectively

41 Aras, B. (1998, Fall), 'Iranian Policy Toward Caspian Sea Basin,' *Mediterranean Quarterly,* vol.9, no.4, p. 88.

42 Dittmer, L. and Kim, S.S. (1993), 'In Search of a Theory of National Identity,' in L. Dittmer and S.S. Kim, (eds), *China's Quest for National Identity* Cornell University Press, Ithaca, p. 16.

43 Herman, R.G. (1995), *Ideas, Identity, and the Redefinition of Interests: The Political and Intellectual Origins of the Soviet Foreign Policy Revolution*, Ph.D. Dissertation, Cornell University, p. 76.

44 Barnett, M.N. (1997), 'Identity and Alliances in the Middle East', in P.J. Katzenstein, (ed.), *The Culture of National Security,* Columbia University Press, New York, p. 447.

45 Özel, S. (1995), 'Of Not Being a Lone Wolf: Geography, Domestic Plays, and Turkish Foreign Policy in the Middle East,' in G. Kemp and J. Gross Stein, (eds), *Powder Keg in the Middle East: The Struggle for Gulf Security,* Rowman & Littlefield, Lanham, p. 182.

46 *Sabah,* 7 September 1997.

47 Habermas, J. (1973), *Legitimation Crisis*, trans. Thomas McCharty, Beacon, Boston.

Chapter 11

Syria, Turkey and the Changing Power Configuration in the Middle East: An Analysis of Political, Economic and Regional Differences

Erik L. Knudsen

Irreconcilable Differences?

Modern Turkey since its creation in the wake of the demise of the Ottoman Empire is an anomaly somewhat out of place in the Middle East. Not only has it been successful in establishing democratic institutions in a region almost void of democracy, but it has also sought to orient itself toward the West. However, within this volatile region Turkey has had the misfortune of being a land bridge between two continents that throughout history has placed it in a precarious position in that it is completely encircled by hostile or potentially hostile states. Of Turkey's less than friendly neighbours, in the Caucasus, the Balkans and the Middle East particularly Syria has proven to be a thorn in the soft underbelly of the Turkish government since the 1950s.

Although Hafiz Assad, a long time antagonist of Turkey, is no longer strongman of Syria and in recent months Turkish-Syrian relations have improved, it can be assumed that there will be obstacles in the near and distant future that Turkish and Syrian diplomats will have to confront. The purpose of this paper is to examine both past and present problems between these two states, as well as, outline what role both Ankara and Damascus play in the ebb and flow of the current opposing power configurations. Since the 1930s Syria and Turkey have been subject to changing variables in the region which have resulted at times in the suspension of diplomatic relations, border tensions and military threats which as late as 1998 almost erupted into war. In part, the reason for diplomatic conflict has been the decision by both the Damascus and Ankara governments to orient their states toward opposing regional blocs (which will be discussed in the context of the paper) that they believed were in their best national interests to pursue.

However, these 'power configurations' in recent years have caused the scope of mutual political and economic difficulties to widen. This in turn, has contributed to even greater regional destabilization in that Syria has expressed suspicion if not outrage with the 1996 Turkish decision to sign a strategic agreement with Israel.

This action has prompted Syria to move closer to states which were real or potential enemies of Turkey.

To fully understand the problems between these two republics particularly since the late 1950s, it is necessary to place political difficulties within the context of international and regional developments that in the past played a role in the foreign policies of these two states. Such pronounced differences as the expansion of the Turkish state at the expense of Syria during the French mandate, Turkey's role in NATO, the question of Syria's orientation toward pan-Arabism, and reliance on the Soviet Union/Eastern Bloc all presented dilemmas which both the governments of Syria and Turkey have had to contend with. Furthermore, tension over the sharing of water resources and Syrian support of groups within Turkey such as the Workers' Party of Kurdistan has added to strained relations.

For alleged national security reasons the Syrian republic has also committed itself to a policy of political/diplomatic support of nations such as Greece, Iran and Armenia. These nations in the past have openly criticized or contributed to the diminishing of Turkish influence in the region. All of these developments have placed both Damascus and Ankara on a collision course that appeared to be unavoidable.

Particularly, initiatives that were viewed by the Syrians as Turkish political objectives in north Iraq, as well as, the Turkish decision to embark on a strategic alliance with Israel have made Syria feel very vulnerable. From the perspective of Turkey, Syria's refusal to accept the present territorial border with Turkey in the southeast and prove that it is willing to live in a state of peace without belligerent intensions has placed Turkey in a difficult military and economic position that it needed to rectify. These ongoing problems avoidable or not will present for both states a lasting impact on their political and socio-economic futures.

The Historical Antecedents of Syrian Mistrust

Since the early twentieth century, Syrian-Turkish differences can be traced to the 'Turkification'[1] policy by the reformists within the Committee of Union and Progress. While Arab nationalist sentiments had been brewing for years, this program very much ignited the Arab nationalist movement and the formation of Arab political interest groups that initially called for autonomy and expanded representation in the Ottoman parliament. However, Arab nationalists ultimately demanded the establishment of an independent Arab state that was quite unacceptable to the ruling 'Young Turk' clique of the Ottoman Empire. After it became evident to the Ottoman authorities that a break away movement was being organized there were reprisals[2] which added to the ongoing animosity between Syrian and Turk.

What fuelled the Syrian-Turkish divide for the future was the fact that conditions in the Turkish controlled *Vilayet* of Syria during the First World War deteriorated and led to great suffering on the part of the inhabitants who directly blamed the Turkish authorities. The economic situation in the province became even more deplorable as the fortunes of combat took a heavy toll on the Ottoman Empire.

While the Syrians had hoped to establish their own state after the conclusion of the war and looked favourably on the Turkish withdrawal from Syrian soil, this was not to be the case. Much to the objections of Syrian nationalists a French mandate, which was approved by the League of Nations in 1922, was created in place of Turkish rule. However with respect to the situation immediately after the war, most Syrians and Turks today are unaware of the fact that actually Mustafa Kemal, father of modern Turkey, attempted to establish a policy of cooperation with the Syrian nationalists during the 1919-1921 period.[3]

Kemal and his nationalist supporters were also locked in a conflict with French forces that sought to have a buffer zone for the French mandate of Syria. Consequently, Kemal militarily assisted the Syrian nationalists led by the Emir Faisal in a losing effort. However, there were Turkish-Syrian Nationalist discussions that suggested power sharing might be considered on the Austro-Hungarian model.[4]

While the Turkish nationalists were victorious against the French, Syrian self-determination was crushed in the Maysulun pass. Unfortunately, Syrian Turkish cooperation was also buried. The French decision to prevent the formation of an independent Syrian state and establish a policy to partition what was left of 'Geographic Syria' played no small role in the demand for Syrian independence.[5] While Turkey achieved success both on the battlefield and at the conference table, Syria was unable to do the same. In fact Syrian dreams of independence would become even more frustrated in the following years.

The quest for an independent Syrian state was exacerbated by the French policy to share influence with Turkey in the province of Alexandretta/Hatay. France based this policy with the concern that Turkey might tilt toward Germany as tensions increased in Europe during the late 1930s. From the perspective of Turkey, Hatay had been under Turkish authority for over 4 centuries and Turks constituted the largest ethnic group in the province.[6]

While Syrian nationalists demanded integration into the mandate of Syria in part because of the port of Alexandretta that the business community of Aleppo was in desperate need of, the Turkish population of the province pressured Turkey to press for unification with the Turkish republic. In 1938 a formal French-Turkish treaty was signed that paved the way for the establishment during the same year of an independent state of Hatay. One year later, the process of integration with Turkey was set in motion which resulted in annexation by Turkey in February of 1939.[7]

While today Hatay is not officially recognized as part of the Turkish republic by Damascus and maps printed in Syria delineate Hatay/Alexandretta as part of Syria, most Syrians realize that this 'lost province' will never be returned. Nevertheless, at the time it inflamed anti Turkish feeling and is currently a very sensitive topic.

To Syrian nationalists the sequence of events from 1918 to the 1930's was almost too much to bear. If political emotions were inflamed by the establishment of the French mandate, they certainly exploded with the partitioning of Syria.

However the final insult and one that Turkey had a direct role in, was the loss of Alexandretta. This embittered Syrians from all political persuasions and was a source of tension between Syria and Turkey for years to come.

Turkey, the Baghdad Pact and Operation Strangle

After the independence of Syria was finally achieved, the future development of the Turkish and Syrian states was vastly different. While Turkey embarked on a program of democratization, as well as, obtaining membership in NATO, Syria confronted political disarray, war with Israel and military intervention that alone in 1949 resulted in three military coups d'état.[8]

Once the Shishakali dictatorship was overthrown in 1954 and free democratic elections took place, changes in the Syrian political system did not improve diplomatic relations with Turkey. During the same year of national elections in Syria, the Ankara government joined the Baghdad Pact in association with Iraq, Iran, Pakistan and Great Britain. This western sponsored alliance system, while claiming to contain communism and particularly Soviet expansionism that threatened Turkey immediately after World War II, was viewed by such countries as Egypt and Syria as just another means of foreign control. So to Damascus their Turkish neighbours had decided on a course of action that placed them firmly in the Western camp. The Syrian and Turkish diplomatic battlelines were being drawn once again.

To fully understand the resulting Turkish-Syrian political tensions, they must be seen within the context of the Cold War and the American obsession with its policy of preventing Soviet penetration, as well as, the fear of a monolithic communist movement, which Washington believed had the goal of world domination. However, there was also an Arab Cold War in progress in which Egypt and Iraq were both trying to impose their influence on Syria. The 1955-1958 period in Syria is very confusing.[9] Nevertheless, it is clear that while Syrian politicians of all political shades tried to find a formula, which would bring stability to the system, the western powers were insistent that intervention was necessary to prevent the Syrian leftist orientated parties from taking power.

With respect to the concern for communist participation in the Syrian government which Turkey shared, the so-called 'Red Millionaire' Defence Minister, Khalid al-Assam did play a significant role in obtaining loans from the USSR. However, what appeared to upset US officials even more was the fact that the Syrian army was now controlled by the leftist oriented Revolutionary Council. Furthermore, a key member of the council was the pro-Communist Chief of Staff Afif al-Bizri. [10] Consequently, Washington had reason to believe that there was a possibility that a communist inspired military coup could oust an already leftist leaning government.

As for the machinations of Moscow and Soviet initiatives, there is not concrete proof to date to suggest that the USSR had any illusions of making Syria a satellite state, yet the Soviet Union did have a great interest in fishing in the troubled political waters of Syria. To leftist and centrist elements in the Syrian government it became all too clear that because military and economic aid was badly needed, the Soviet Union could provide help on reasonable terms. Consequently, in 1954 a Soviet-Syrian arms deal was concluded followed by further Russian economic and military assistance.[11]

As a response to what was perceived as growing communist influence orchestrated by the Soviet Union, in 1957 the American Central Intelligence Agency devised 'Operation Strangle' [12] to prevent what was viewed by Washington as Syria's drift toward the communist camp. While there were probably some Washington insiders who believed that Syria was to be the next Soviet satellite, what peeved many if not most US diplomats in the region was the fact that many moderate Syrian government officials did not seem to be concerned with communist activity.[13]

In this atmosphere of concern for the future orientation of Syria, Washington believed that it was imperative to bring about changes in the Syrian government. Furthermore, it was believed that Turkey could play a key role in this effort. What resulted in this planned attempt to undermine the government of Syria was in essence, a clumsy effort to destabilize a fragile yet democratically elected government. After initial plans had been made during the Summer of 1957 and with instructions from Washington the United States Under Secretary for Middle Eastern Affairs, Loy Henderson went to Ankara[14] to convince the Turkish leadership that it was in their best interests and that of the Western Alliance to cooperate to subvert the Syrian government before it moved further to the left.

From the perspective of the pro American Menderes government that was in power in Ankara at the time, a major concern was the question of Turkey's security. Certainly Ankara was alarmed with the pro-Communist elements in the Syrian government and the flood of Soviet arms into Syria. However, there was also a genuine fear that if Syria went communist, Turkey would be encircled by the Soviet Union and one of its foremost allies Bulgaria, as well as Syria.[15]

It is of interest that in Turkey itself, democracy was breaking down in that the Turkish military was being used by the Menderes government to curb the opposition. Despite these domestic difficulties, Turkey was urged to provoke incidents on the Turkish-Syrian border while British planted agents were assigned to incite the desert tribes of Syria. [16] Meanwhile, the United States was supposed to mobilize combatants that the then right wing Syrian Social Nationalist Party (SSNP) would provide. Furthermore, Turkey's Baghdad Pact partner, Iraq would also be involved.

While Turkey mobilized its army on the Syrian border, the plan started to unravel with the result that the leftist elements which shared power with the Syrian right, used this incident to arrest almost all of the conservative leaders in the Damascus government who they claimed were a party to this conspiracy.[17] To the Syrians, Turkey's action was very provocative and one that could have lead to war given Ankara's membership in two western alliances.

Attempts at Stability and New/Old Regional Differences

With respect to Turkey's role in the region after this event it was one of isolation and in this poisoned political atmosphere the entire Middle East was more conducive to Soviet influence.[18] However, during the next two decades there was a political change of heart coming from Ankara that brought about a more even handed, if not neutral regional policy.

Evidently, Turkish foreign policy analysts had come to the conclusion that given the ebb and flow of the Cold War, and growing insecurity concerning its present and future ties with the US/NATO Turkey should reconsider its policy in the Middle East. Much of the animosity between Ankara and Washington was over the question of Cyprus. Once the Greek dominated Makarios government in the Republic of Cyprus tried to change the constitution in 1963 to the detriment of the Turkish Cypriot population, communal fighting broke out.

This was the beginning of hostilities that Turkey would be drawn into *vis-à-vis* agreements signed during 1959 and 1960 which called for Turkey to be a guarantor power along with Greece and the United Kingdom to maintain the *status quo* in Cyprus.[19] The deterioration of the situation in Cyprus and the belief that the United States and NATO could have better represented the interests of Turkey had a particular bearing on the future orientation of Turkish foreign policy. What further outraged Ankara was an insult to Turkish pride in the form of a tersely worded letter written by the then US president Lyndon B. Johnson. In the Johnson letter the American president threatened the Ankara government, in no uncertain terms, with ending US/NATO protection of Turkey if Turkey took initiatives in Cyprus which might undermine the western alliance.[20]

In the future, Turkish relations would sour even more with Washington over the Turkish view that her interests were not supported by NATO in the United Nations. The final blow to Turkish sensibilities was the US decision to impose an arms embargo because of the 1974 Turkish intervention in Cyprus.

What brought about a more fundamental change in Turkish foreign policy was the fact after the military coup of 1960 that overthrew the Menderes government and the scrapping of the old 1923 constitution for the 1961 Constitution, new political parties and personalities were brought into the Turkish political system. These new elements realized a necessity to revaluate Turkey's relationship with the Arab world as well as Europe in light of East-West detente.[21]

In this new political climate there surfaced a view that political/diplomatic fence mending in the Middle East was long overdue. There were certainly those in Ankara, military and civilian alike, who had come to the conclusion that perhaps Turkey's long term goals were not congruent with that of the Western alliance. Had Turkey finally decided to re-think its Middle East policy in an attempt to sooth the bad relations of the past?

As war clouds spread over the Middle East in May 1967, Turkey faced a dilemma that had the potential to place it at odds with the United States. Although the US was not the major military benefactor of Israel at the time, Washington was certainly a close friend that had sold Israel offensive weapons. Displaying a change of regional attitude, Ankara informed the NATO powers that its bases could not be used if a conflict between the Arabs and Israel erupted.[22] It seemed as if Turkey had defiantly changed course to the approval of its Arab neighbours. The heads of Middle Eastern states again applauded Ankara when after the 1967 war, it criticized the Israeli annexation of East Jerusalem and years later that of the Golan.

Once Egypt and Syria launched an offensive in 1973 against Israel, Turkey was once again confronted with a situation that might cause friction with Washington. However, for a second time Ankara broke ranks and stated that its bases would not be available to the United States for the purpose of supplying Israel.[23]

These decisions were viewed favourably by the Arab states which now started seeing the Turkish Republic in a much different light. Such diplomatic actions in turn allowed Ankara to end its isolation and to play a respected role in the region that it might have fully capitalized on. Unfortunately, this window of opportunity was to close and diplomatic relations with Turkey's neighbours would face new strains. If the question of Cyprus was a key factor in the move away from the Western Alliance toward the Arab world, the hope that the Arab states would politically support Turkey on the Cyprus question was to be an even greater disappointment. Much to the dismay of Ankara, the recurrent Arab theme of showing Muslim solidarity by refraining to support the Turkish agenda in Cyprus [24] was an ongoing problem for warmer Turkish-Middle Eastern relations.

However, this did not prevent Turkey from further improving its standing in the region by establishing relations with the Palestine Liberation Organization in 1979 as well as lending support in calls for the establishment of a Palestinian state. However, while Turkey may have increased its trade with the Islamic world,[25] which benefited the Turkish state, Ankara appeared to have no intension to fully reorient its foreign policy toward its eastern neighbours.

The Turkish proclivity to continue to develop its democratic institutions (although certainly tested), maintain its ties with NATO, and the desire to be accepted as a European state caused Arab states to suspect long term Turkish intensions. Moreover, during the early 1980s changing conditions in the region brought new pressures to bear on Turkey. This presented the Turkish republic with the urgency to re-evaluate its Middle Eastern policy once again. The Soviet invasion of Afghanistan, the Islamic revolution in Iran and the concern with the impact of Iraq's war with Iran,[26] all played a role in future Turkish policy making.

Turkey, Syria and the PKK

Unfortunately, during the late 1980s tensions increased between Turkey and her neighbours; Iran, Iraq and particularly Syria, which seemed to be on a collision course with Ankara over the question of state supported terrorism which was taking a heavy toll of innocent lives in south eastern Anatolia and causing a weak economy to suffer even more. Of course, among these three states Syria was the most involved in the support of groups such as the Workers' Party of Kurdistan (PKK).

It might be pointed out that from the position of Damascus support of the PKK was a result of Turkey's water policy which will be discussed further in the text. While certainly not advocating the establishment of an independent Kurdish state in part because of its own Kurdish minority, a tactic that the Hafiz Assad government traditionally implemented as state policy was the use of proxy elements[27] to do the bidding of Damascus and to send none-too-subtle messages to states with which Syria had problems.

In the judgment of Turkey, it appeared that the Assad government was playing an instrumental role directly pertaining to the conflict in southeast Anatolia.[28] The not unjustified view that Damascus was aiding Kurdish separatists did more to erode Syrian-Turkish relations than any of the previous events. Turkey and Syria were entering a new zone of conflict that neither side seemed willing to halt. A rapid downward spiral of animosity had now been fully set into motion. Consequently, from the belief that Syria was offering significant support for the PKK to the extent that, Kurdish guerrilla chief, Abdullah Öcalan was allowed to establish offices in Damascus,[29] Turkish-Syrian relations were now marked by a new and intense belligerency.

Ankara made it all too clear to those inside and outside of the region that it believed that the Damascus government had the express policy to encourage the PKK to wage an insurgency against Turkey.[30] Furthermore, it seemed that Damascus was about to draw well defined battlelines that Turkey could not accept. The Turkish authorities also claimed that Syria had sought regional allies such as Iran in this well orchestrated policy against the Turkish state.

Ankara pointed out that Syria had supplied a steady stream of arms and logistical support to the Kurdish insurgents. Damascus was further accused of providing sanctuary in this campaign of terrorism against the Turkish state by allowing PKK combatants to use training camps in the Syrian controlled Bekka valley of Lebanon.[31]

The Turkish authorities were further outraged that while in Lebanon, and under the protection of the Syrian army, the PKK militants met with combatants of the Armenian Secret Army for the Liberation of Armenia (ASALA) to coordinate activities against the Turkish army. It was also believed by Ankara that this region of Lebanon was used for the production of drugs,[32] which financed the campaign against Turkey.

With respect to dealing with Syria and their PKK allies, Turkey held the view that if the PKK chief could be separated from his benefactor in Damascus then the movement would collapse. In essence, the Turkish government was convinced that Syria held all the cards in the deck and could with a minimum of effort shut down the PKK and end the insurgency if and when it was pressured into doing so. The Turkish leadership felt it was imperative to apply pressure immediately or it would face more carnage and a further setback to the economy.

Actually, as early as 1987 the Turkish Prime Minister was able to convince his Syrian counterpart to sign an agreement, in which Turkey and Syria would cooperate on security matters and Damascus agreed to clamp down on the PKK.[33] Unfortunately, nothing materialized. The message that Damascus was sending was somewhat different. It became all too apparent that Syria was hardly committed to cracking down on the PKK as long as there were outstanding disputes with Turkey.

By the mid 1990s Turkey was rapidly losing patience with Damascus. In 1996 the Ankara government officially requested that Damascus extradite Öcalan. After this request was ignored, diplomatic contact between Turkey and Syria was suspended altogether. This did not end the frustration felt by the Ankara government which now considered new options in pursuit of the goal to end the conflict with the PKK and prevent Damascus' future ability to exert negative influence on Turkey.

With the Turkish conviction that Syria had a policy to continue to support the PKK in its insurgency against the Ankara government, and given the fact that Israel was involved with a similar campaign against Hezbollah in south Lebanon, which Tel Aviv was certain that Syria was a party to, the Israeli and Turkish governments were drawn closer. Of course, the United States played no small role in this process.

Once the 'new world order' failed to materialize, the Oslo Accords were going no where, dual containment was only a dream and the Syrian-Israeli peace talks were dead in the water, the United States saw it was imperative to strengthen its position.[34]

Turkey's New Found Friend, the Question of Water and North Iraq

The Strategic Agreement that was signed in 1996[35] between Israel and Turkey has a number of clauses which remain secret. However, of the points that were made public, they include such topics as joint naval and air operations, mutual sharing of seaports and permission for the Israeli air force to train over Turkish air space. Furthermore, this arrangement was intended at the time of its signing, as well as now, to be very much directed toward a partnership in combating terrorism.[36] The agreement also allowed Turkey to obtain more influence in the United States Congress and the ability to procure additional weapons from Israel.

This military partnership was not exactly what Syria and for that matter the other states in region had prepared themselves for. Arab states which had hoped for Ankara to be more even handed with respect to relations with its neighbours were disappointed if not threatened.

From the perspective of the Assad regime, the Turkish decision to involve itself in a strategic agreement with Israel coupled with its ongoing ties with the US, imposed on Syria a serious predicament. To the authorities in Damascus, this dilemma carried with it an echo of the 1950s.[37] For Syria, not only was the Turkish-Israeli agreement highly disturbing, but it had in effect placed Syria in a position whereby she was engulfed by one enemy; Israel, another potential enemy; Turkey and a state which it had had long standing disputes – Iraq.

Another issue that was (and continues to be) the potential for conflict is the sharing of water resources claimed by both Syria and Turkey, namely the Euphrates River whose source happens to be located in Turkey. Damascus not only depends heavily on the river for drinking water and agriculture but also claims a need to use the waterway for hydroelectric power.

The Syrians believe that Turkey's policy of hoarding the precious water resources of the river was much to the determent and disregard of Syrian water needs. Indeed, the question of water continued to be a very sore spot in Syrian-Turkish relations. Tensions approached that of a conflict once Turkey established the GAP dam project. The overall scheme of the project that calls for the building of 22 dams and 19 hydroelectric plants,[38] to be completed in 2010, will in affect cut in half the yearly flow of 30 billion cubic metres which Syria had received in the past.[39]

The Syrian authorities made it perfectly clear to Turkey and the international community that the creation of the GAP would lead to something paramount to an environmental, social and agricultural disaster for the Syrian state. While meetings were held to address this problem no solution was agreed upon and to date no final accord has been signed concerning the sharing of water resources. [40] If the mutual concern for state supported terrorism resulted in Turkey moving closer to Israel, the water question and Turkish policy in northern Iraq has similarly drawn the Baghdad government closer to Syria.

Indeed, another point of contention that has caused strained relations between Ankara and Damascus is the question of what Syria views as Turkish foreign policy objectives in Iraq and the deployment of troops 200 kilometres into Iraq on the Iraqi-Syrian border.[41] Because of a growing uneasiness with respect to Turkish policy in Iraq and a concern that Ankara would capitalize on the power vacuum which surfaced there in the wake of the Gulf War, as early as February 1991 talks were held between the Foreign Ministers of Syria and Turkey, in which Syria urged Turkey not to take advantage of the situation in northern Iraq.[42] While Syria and Turkey were a part of the same alliance that went to war against Saddam Hussein, differences were soon to appear. Syria evidently was concerned that Turkey had the intension of establishing a sphere of influence in the most oil rich region of Iraq and may have considered the possibility of annexing the city Mosul in the future.[43]

It was then and is now obvious that the Turkish government views the instability in north Iraq, which emerged after the Gulf War, as a major security problem that Ankara could ill afford to ignore. It is not just the fact that the PKK, although weakened since 1998, has continued to use bases in the area, but the Turkish government is even more concerned with the reality of a Iraqi Kurdish quasi-state that Washington has appeared to stand behind for its own political purposes. [44]

In 1991, Turkish President Turgut Özal encouraged the American president George Bush to support a Kurdish revolt in Iraq in order to oust Saddam Hussein immediately following the Gulf War,[45] probably because he had concerns that a power vacuum would have a negative impact on Turkey. However, the United States at the time opted for a policy of non-involvement. Once the Iraqi Kurdish rebellion without outside support proved to be a failure, Turkey faced not only what Özal feared but also a flood of refugees. Because of the carnage and confusion that was present in North Iraq, 'Operation Provide Comfort' (renamed Northern Watch in 1997) was set in motion. This in turn led to the establishment of safe havens in Iraq that were protected by the United Nations. Soon, cries for statehood could be heard by the many Kurds who started to return to north Iraq from Iran and Turkey. This certainly was not what the Turkish government wanted to hear. Now Turkey had to confront on her border an embryonic Kurdish entity. It was this '...statehood by stealth',[46] encouraged by the United States with the purpose of using it to undermine if not overthrow the government of Saddam Hussein that Turkey would have to confront.[47] This development very much became a source of suspicion and fear with respect to United States intentions.[48]

What made matters even worse, was the fact that slowly PKK bases were being moved into the chaotic safety of north Iraq, which was used as a sanctuary for cross border attacks into Turkey. With this Balkanisation of northern Iraq becoming a reality, Turkish authorities were placed in the unavoidable position of being sucked into the quagmire of a civil war between Mas'ud Barzani's Kurdish Democratic Party and Jalal Talabani's Patriotic Union of Kurdistan which the PKK was playing a role in.[49] A further development that has not been ignored by Damascus as well as Baghdad is that Turkey seemed to pursue a policy of further increasing its influence by becoming a patron if not the protector of the Turkmen minority in northern Iraq that numbers 500,000 or more and inhabits among other places, the oil rich city of Kirkuk.[50]

The Crisis of 1998 and Syrian Diplomatic Fence Mending

By 1998 tensions between Ankara and Damascus were at a fever pitch. It was no longer just a case of Syria supporting the PKK or an outstanding water dispute. What intensified outstanding problems was the Turkish belief that Syria was involved in a full-on propaganda war that had the intended purpose of turning the entire Arab world against the Turkish state. As a consequence of this, Turkey warned Syria to stop supporting the PKK and spreading disquietude throughout the region. On 2 October 1998 the Turkish president, Süleyman Demirel stated: 'This is not a friendly attitude. I declare to the world that our patience is running out and we retain the right to retaliate against Syria, which despite all our warnings and peaceful approaches, has not abandoned its hostile attitude towards Turkey'.[51]

On the same day, the Turkish president stated to the Turkish Grand National Assembly that Syria was trying to '... provoke the Arab world against Ankara using Turkey's relations with Israel as a pretext.' It is believed that at no time since the end of the Second World War (with the exception of the Cyprus conflict) has Turkey come so close to an armed confrontation.

The situation was so grave that the Turkish Chief of Staff General Hüseyin Kıvrıkoğlu was quoted as stating that his country was in a state of undeclared war with Syria.[52] Indeed it appeared that war would soon break out because the Turkish government for a second time in recent memory moved their forces supported by artillery and armour right up to the Syrian border, and seemed to be poised for an attack. There were even reports that Turkish warplanes had entered Syrian airspace.[53] It was clear that Turkish patience had been totally exhausted.

However, at the last moment war was averted. With the help of Egyptian president Husni Mubarak, shuttling between Damascus and Ankara, and assistance from Iran's Foreign Minister Kharazzi,[54] Ankara and Damascus agreed to negotiate and thus the crisis was defused. In reality the Bathist leadership in Damascus had two choices. The first being war which, given the state of the Syrian economy, was out of the question. The second was to close down the PKK once and for all. As a result of these discussions Damascus pledged that it would stop aiding the PKK and prevent Öcalan from using Syria as a base. This led to the signing of the Adana accords that started a normalization of Turkish-Syrian diplomatic relations.[55]

However, in part because of Syrian-Turkish differences and regional mistrust that has engulfed both states, two definite power configurations have slowly yet steadily emerged. These two divergent camps have already made and may continue to make an imprint in the area that might increase the volatility of an already turbulent region.

Once Ankara and Tel Aviv established their strategic agreement that sent shock waves throughout the region, Syria which previously had close ties with Egypt and Saudi Arabia started to normalize diplomatic relations with Iraq. While there had been some Syrian-Iraqi co-operation over objections to Turkey's water policy, after 1996 Damascus and Baghdad realized an even greater necessity to explore common interests in the region.

This move has been somewhat of an extraordinary development. While both Syria and Iraq were committed to the same credo of pan-Arabism and ruled by different branches of the same political party; the Arab Socialist Renaissance Party (*Baath*) starting with 1968 almost no cooperation between Damascus and Baghdad was forthcoming. In fact they frequently conspired to undermine the other.

Syria prevented Iraq from using an oil pipeline running from Iraq to the Syrian coast which had been constructed at a time that Damascus and Baghdad had at least been on speaking terms. Furthermore, Syria supported Iraq's enemy Iran during the eight year war Baghdad fought against Tehran.

However, in recent years some common interests have been realized. Both states have decided to re-establish diplomatic relations, open their borders, and conclude new trade deals. It is interesting that the strengthening of the former Arab Triangle of Egypt, Saudi Arabia and Syria has led to the rehabilitation or at least to the 'de-demonization' of Iraq throughout the region. Arguably this realignment has come in part as a reaction to the agreement between Turkey and Israel.

It should be noted that the Arab camp has been further strengthened by Damascus playing a major role in normalizing diplomatic relations between Saudi Arabia and Syria's long time ally, Iran.[56] If the Syrian-Iraqi rapprochement is a surprising development, then the Riyadh–Tehran improvement of relations must be viewed as achieving almost the impossible, given the fears that the pro-US Saudi Arabia had for the spread of Iran's Islamic revolution.

The Syrian-Egyptian-Saudi camp (possibly supported by Iran and perhaps even tacitly by Iraq) may make its voice heard.[57] It might be speculated the widening Arab Triangle has the potential to have an even greater social and economic impact on the region for Ankara than the Israel-Turkish-American (and perhaps in the future Jordanian) power configuration. This could create a dilemma for Turkey that may be beyond its means to deal with.

Despite Turkish-Syrian problems over the water question, Syrian support of the PKK, and the configurations that have the potential to cause greater tension in the region, a window of opportunity has slowly opened for Damascus and Ankara. In March 1999 Farouk al-Shara, Syrian Foreign Minister, met with his Turkish counterpart İsmail Cem in which both diplomats attempted to work on a declaration of principles that would be a guide to future bilateral relations. Topics such as improving commercial agreements, and the Turkish interest in Syrian gas was discussed.[58]

Later that year meetings were held in both Damascus and New York and it was agreed that working groups should be created to hammer out the details of outstanding disputes particularly the question of water. [59] In early November 2000, Syrian Vice President Abdal Helim Khaddam made an official visit to Ankara with a personal message from president Assad stressing the need for the proposed declaration of principles.

A follow up meeting was supposed to be held in Ankara to sign the agreement. However, there was a last minute snag in that Turkey was not fully convinced that Syria had relinquished all claims on the Turkish province of Hatay believed by many Syrians to be part of 'Geographic Syria' (Greater Syria). Consequently, a meeting that was scheduled for 8-11 December 2001 was cancelled.[60]

Nevertheless, there have been other instances of the warming of diplomatic relations. With the death of Hafiz Assad, and in an obvious attempt to bring a further normalization of relations, the Turkish president Ahmet Necdet Sezer personally attended the funeral of the deceased Syrian president much to the approval of the Syrian population. This was followed by discussions concerning the improvement of trade and a change of border restrictions that would help facilitate this process. During the following months a number of deals were concluded which were not only mutually beneficial to both Syria and Turkey, but also helped the process of normalization.

However, perhaps the most startling development that was almost unthinkable six months ago were military proposals made in May 2001 that could very much end past disagreements and bring about a new era of cooperation. It was reported in the Turkish media that high level political/military discussions were held between Syrian and Turkish officials. After the Syrian Ambassador to Ankara made a number of initial comments to the Turkish press that suggested both states were moving toward a military partnership, Turkish officials affirmed the fact that indeed a military agreement was under consideration. It was reported that the core of what was discussed was the 'mutual exchange of military personnel, invitations for the monitoring of joint war games as well as an exchange of military training'.[61]

Furthermore a proposal was made for Syrian military officers to be invited to the Turkish military academy for instruction. It is interesting that these military discussions prompted both sides to set in motion other aspects of the newly emerging relationship such as the removal of visas, the formation of a free trade zone along the Turkish-Syrian border and a Turkish proposal to clear land mines.[62]

The Future: Are There Really Common Interests?

Despite such a long history of tensions, provocative acts and mistrust, both Turkey and Syria have a number of common interests that should be recognized and taken advantage of in the process to fully normalize diplomatic relations. Not only are Turkey and Syria neighbours who share a common border; they also have similar cultural and family values.

For the most part both states are of the same religion and have similar traditions that were nurtured during the Ottoman centuries. More importantly, both of these states are confronted by some of the same variables and must face similar socio-economic pressures imposed on them from both inside and outside of the region.

With respect to specific common concerns, both countries views on terrorism and specifically Islamic fundamentalist terrorism are similar and Ankara, as well as, Damascus has used counter-terror to solve their perceived problems. In the early 1980s Syria faced the determined wrath of the Muslim Brotherhood[63] and Turkey has had ongoing problems with extremist Islamic organizations such as Hezbollah. However, in light of the NewYork/Washington terrorist attacks, it is apparent that Turkey has opted for a more activist approach. Nevertheless, in the future both Syria and Turkey may realize the need to pool their resources in the conflict against terrorism if the need arises.

It can also be argued that Turkey and Syria have young populations that must be aware of many of the regional social, economic and political problems at hand. Both states have had to deal with minority dilemmas, severe economic setbacks in recent years and criticism of their respective political systems. While certainly Syrian problems are much more advanced than that of Turkey, Ankara because of its successes could very well offer an example that Damascus might emulate.

With respect to the economy, it would seem that in recent months a breakthrough of a sort has taken place with regular meetings between Turkish-Syrian representatives who are determined to revive trade. With the continuing economic downward spiral of the Turkish economy, Turkish business people should recognize that with a strengthened Syrian middle class and a recovering economy, Syria could provide a willing market for Turkish produce.

Another goal shared by both states is that they are equally determined to modernize and although at a different pace both support the globalization of their respective states. Certainly Syria under the helm of Dr. Bashar Assad, a self proclaimed high tech addict, is very much committed to the modernization of his state. Although Turkey may not able to economically afford contributing to the modernization of its southern neighbour, it could none the less provide expertise in an exchange program.

With the passing of Hafiz Assad, the demise of the PKK and discussions between Ankara and Damascus concerning trade, tourism and regional military/political co-operation, a new era in Turkish Syrian diplomatic relations appears to have been set in place. However, the Syrians will have to accept the fact that Turkey will continue to look westward and accept the Turkish obsession with entry into the European Union. This is part of a Kemalist tradition which is not likely to be discontinued. That is not to say that Turkey will always view Europe in such a positive light.

Turkey must be disappointed that the European Union has presented a number of conditions, which, to many Turks, are close to impossible to fulfil. European demands include: solving the Cyprus dispute, dealing with human rights (which the Turkish population is convinced the Europeans do not fully understand), resolving the very complicated issue of the 'Kurdish Question' and of course dealing with an economy that almost faced a collapse during the Winter and Spring of 2001.

Nevertheless, the power elite in Turkey will certainly continue to pursue the quest for European membership and look westward for inspiration as well as acceptance. However, the powers-that-be in Ankara as well as the citizens of Turkey should realize the future role that Turkey has the potential to play in the region as a political/diplomatic, economic and cultural bridge connecting Europe and the Balkans to the Arab East.

In fact, Turkey may have entered a new threshold in that the ushering in of closer relations with Syria could be the beginning of new regional opportunities for the Turkish republic. Turkey is arguably in a unique position to serve as a political role model for other states in the region. This could very much benefit the eastern as well as the western world. On the diplomatic tract, by virtue of it belonging to the western alliance as a Muslim state, it could play a greater role in the Arab-Israeli dispute by either offering peacemaking or peacekeeping troops. Another possibility is providing its good offices in future peace negotiations between the Palestinians and Israelis or perhaps between Syria and Israel. A strengthening of Turkish involvement in the Middle East could only enhance the prestige of the Turkish Republic.

Economically speaking, Turkey should consider the feasibility of fully developing a strategy to tap into markets of the Arab east because it has the ability to provide the raw materials and finished productions to do so. There is also the possibility of providing water, which Turkey has an abundant supply of in exchange for natural resources or other products which Turkey could use.

Culturally, Turkey could also play a significant role. Because of its Ottoman past it may have more common cultural interests with its Arab cousins than it realizes. While Turkey offers scholarships to students from such countries as Albania, Georgia, Uzbekistan and Kyrgyzstan, it has not considered offering educational opportunities in countries such as Syria, Egypt and Jordan. Allowing Arab students to study in the Turkish Republic could only enhance its reputation as a centre of secular education as well as spread Turkish culture. Furthermore, its activities in the Organization of Islamic Conference and the Red Crescent also are well known. However, the full potential of Turkish involvement in non governmental/secular organizations should be further explored.

While integration into Europe may be Turkey's destiny, it is a slow and apparently frustrating process with many pitfalls on the way. A more balanced foreign policy (which seems to have been set in motion with the improvement of Turkish-Syrian relations), and one that features in Arab considerations might prove to be equally beneficial without the potential for disappointment. Turkey is in a very advantageous position as gateway to the Arab world. It would seem that there are few risks in establishing improved relations in the region and much to be gained.

Notes

1 A reference to the *Turkification* program can be found in Goldschmidt, A. (1996), *A Concise History of the Middle East*, Westview Press, Boulder, p. 184.
2 In 1915 and 1916 trials were held and a total of 33 Arab nationalists were convicted of high treason and publicly hanged in Beirut and Damascus. Look at Salibi, K.S. (1990), *The Modern History of Lebanon*, Caravan Books, New York, p.159.
3 An interesting analysis of Kemalist support for the Turkish nationalists can be found in Khoury, P. (1987), *Syria and the French Mandate – The Politics of Arab Nationalism 1920-1945*, Princeton University Press, Princeton.
4 This is discussed in Zeine, Z.N. (1966), *The Emergence of Arab Nationalism With a Background in the Study of Arab-Turkish Relations*, Khayats, Beirut.
5 The French established a policy to divide Syria into a number of mini-states such as Greater Lebanon, a Damascus state, an Aleppo state (which included an autonomous Alexandretta) and an Alawi territory, as well, as, the autonomous district of Dayr al-Zur. Yapp, M.E. (1998), *The Near East Since The First World War*, Longman, London, pp. 88-89.
6 Önder, M. (1994), *Atatürk'le Adım Adım Türkiye*, Ankara, p. 9. For a full analysis of the Hatay question from the Turkish perspective look at, Sönmezoğlu, F. (1994), *Türk Dış Politikasının Analizi*, Der Yayınları, İstanbul, pp. 69-77.
7 Another analysis of the Alexandretta/Hatay question can be found in Muslih, M. (1996), 'Syria and Turkey: Uneasy Relations', in H.J. Barkey (ed.), *Reluctant Neighbour: Turkey's Role in the Middle East*, US Institute of Peace, Washington, pp. 115-16.
8 For a complete analysis of the coups of 1949 look at Haddad, G.M. (1965), *Revolution and Military Rule in the Middle East*, vol. II, George Speller, New York.
9 One of the best sources is Seale, P. (1965), *The Struggle for Syria: A Study in Post War Politics*, Oxford University Press, London.
10 For a comprehensive analysis of communist involvement in the Syrian government look at Ismael, T.Y. and Ismael, J.S. (1998), *The Communist Movement in Syria and Lebanon*, University Press of Florida, Gainsville.
11 Golan, G. (1990), *Soviet Politics in the Middle East: From World War II to Gorbachev*, Cambridge University Press, Cambridge, p. 140.
12 Look at Little, D. (1990, Winter), 'Cold War and Covert Action: The United States and Syria 1945-1958', *Middle East Journal*, vol.44.
13 For a discussion of this view look at Laqueur, W. (1959), *The Soviet Union and the Middle East*, Praeger, New York, p. 138-140.
14 For an outstanding analysis of the American perception of events taking place in Syria look at Mo'az, M. (1995), *Syria and Israel: From War to Peacemaking*, Clarendon Press, Oxford, pp. 54-6.
15 Sönmezoğlu, *Türk Dış Politikasının Analizi*, pp. 79-90.
16 Little, D. op. cit., p. 66.

17 With respect to the arrests George Lenczowski points out the 'roster of the accused read like a "Who's Who" of political conservatism in Syria'. See Lenczowski, G. (1980), *The Middle East in World Affairs*, Cornell University Press, New York, p. 343.

18 Aykan, M.B. (Summer), 'The Turkey–US–Israel Triangle: Continuity, Change and Implications for Turkey's Post-Cold War Middle East Policy', *Journal of South Asian and Middle East Studies*, vol.22, p. 3.

19 For an accurate explanation of the Zurich and London agreements look at Kyriakides, S. (1968), *Constitutionalism and Crisis*, University of Pennsylvania Press, Philadelphia, pp. 171-7.

20 In the Johnson letter the US president questioned whether the US and NATO had an obligation to protect Turkey if Turkish actions in Cyprus brought about a Soviet intervention. In the same document Johnson warned Turkey not to use US-supplied military equipment for a Turkish intervention. A full text of the Johnson letter can be found in *The Middle East Journal* (1996, Summer), pp. 386-393.

21 Look at Yavuz, M.H. (1991), 'Turkey's Relations With Israel', *Foreign Policy*, vol.15, no.3-4, pp. 41-69.

22 Muslih, 'Syria and Turkey: Uneasy Relations', p. 118.

23 Ibid.

24 Makovsky, A. (1996), 'Israeli-Turkish Relations A Turkish 'Periphery Strategy'', in H.J. Barkey (ed.), op. cit., p. 149.

25 Ibid. p. 148.

26 Eralp, A. (1996), 'Facing the Challenge; Post-Revolutionary Relations with Iran', in H.J. Barkey (ed.), op. cit., p. 96.

27 The Assad government in the past has used such proxy forces as Fatah, The Popular Front for the Liberation of Palestine General Command, The Syrian Social Nationalist Party Amal and Hezbollah.

28 Look at Elver, H. (2000), 'Hydropolitics in the Middle East', in T.Y. Ismael (ed.), *The International Relations of the Middle East in the 21st Century*, Ashgate, Hampshire, p. 59.

29 When visiting the Political section of the United States Embassy in Damascus in 1988, I was offered the same information.

30 While Syria did not admit that it was using the PKK to undermine the government of Turkey, in a 1993 security protocol signed with Turkey, Syria called the PKK a terrorist organization and declared that Abdullah Öcalan and other 'terrorists' could not use Syrian territory for operations against Turkey. Found in Olson, R. (1995, Fall), 'The Kurdish Question and Turkey's Foreign Policy, 1991-1995: From the Gulf War to the Incursion into Iraq', *Journal of South Asian and Middle Eastern Studies*, vol.xix, no.1, p. 4.

31 Agha, H.J. and Khalidi, A.S. (1995), *Syria and Iran Rivalry and Cooperation*, Royal Institute of International Affairs, London, p. 84.

32 Although it has not been proven that the Bekaa Valley was the center of drug production for the PKK, in 1994 Drug Enforcement Officers stated that three to five tons of morphine base was transported each month through Turkey by suspected Kurdish insurgents. *BBC World Wide Magazine*, April 1994, p. 26.

33 Robbins, P.J. (1996), 'Avoiding the Question', in H.J. Barkey (ed.), op.cit.

34 Gresh, A. (1988, Spring), 'Turkish-Israeli-Syrian Relations and their Impact on the Middle East', *Middle East Journal*, vol.52, p. 188.

35 Look at Eisenstadt, M. (1997), *Turkish-Israeli Military Co operation: An Assessment*, The Washington Institute for Near East Policy, Washington.
36 Gresh, 'Turkish-Israeli-Syrian Relations and their Impact on the Middle East', p, 189.
37 Seale, P. and Butler, L. (1996, Autumn), 'Assad's Regional Strategy and the Challenge From Netanyahu', *Journal of Palestine Studies*, vol.24, p.38.
38 Elver, 'Hydropolitics in the Middle East', p. 57.
39 Gresh, 'Turkish-Israeli-Syrian Relations and their Impact on the Middle East', p. 196. For another analysis of the water question look at Jouejati, M. (1996), 'Water Politics as High Politics; The Case of Turkey and Syria', in H.J. Barkey (ed.), op. cit.
40 Cited in Jouejati, ibid., p. 141.
41 Gresh, 'Turkish-Israeli-Syrian Relations and their Impact on the Middle East', p. 196.
42 Eppel, M. (1993), 'Syria: Iraq's Radical Nemesis', in A. Baram, and B. Rubin (eds), *Iraq's Road to War*, St. Martin's Press, New York, p. 186.
43 Bengio, O. and Özcan, G. (2000, March-May), 'Changing Relations: Turkish-Israeli-Arab Triangle', *Perceptions*, p. 138.
44 Since the end of the Gulf War the United States has made a concerted effort to play a key role in bringing Jalal Talabani's Patriotic Union of Kurdistan and Massud Barzani's Kurdistan Democratic Party closer together for the purpose of undermining the regime of Saddam Hussein despite the protests of Turkey.
45 Aykan, M.B. (1996, October), 'Turkey's Policy in Northern Iraq, 1991-95', *Middle Eastern Studies*, vol.32, no.4, p. 345.
46 Cuny, F. (1992), *Northern Iraq: One Year Later*, The Carnegie Endowment, Washington, p. 15.
47 Kirişci, K. (1996, Spring), 'Turkey and the Kurdish Safe Haven in Northern Iraq', *Journal of South Asian and Middle Eastern Studies*, vol.xix, no.3, p. 23.
48 Kirişci, K. (2000), 'Turkey and the Muslim East, Turkey's New World', in A. Makovsky and S. Sayari (eds), (2000), Washington Institute For Near East Policy, Washington, p. 45.
49 For good analysis look at Gunter, M.M. (1996, Spring), 'The KDP-PUK; Conflict in Northern Iraq', *The Middle East Journal*.
50 With respect to the Turkmen situation, since the administration of Turgut Özal, Ankara has cultivated close ties with the Iraqi Turkmens to off-set Kurdish separatists. Furthermore, the Iraqi Turkmen party is based in Ankara. See Marr, P. (1996), 'Turkey and Iraq', in H.J. Barkey (ed.), op. cit., p.61.
51 *Turkish Daily News*, 2 October 1998.
52 *Sabah*, 8 October 1998.
53 *Turkish Daily News*, 4 October 1998.
54 Sever, A. (2001, September), 'Turkey and the Syrian Israeli Peace Talks in the 1990s', vol.5, no.3, p. 8.
55 The Adana Accords, singed on 20 October 1998 by Turkish representative Uğur Ziyal and Syrian representative Adan Badr al-Hassan, in effect stopped the PKK operations from Syria. For a full text see *Minutes of the Agreement*, Republic of Turkey, Ministry of Foreign Affairs.
56 For an analysis of Syrian diplomatic activity and what the future might bring for Turkey, see Agha, H.J. and Khalidi, A.S. (1995), *Syria and Iran Rivalry and Cooperation*, Royal Institute of International Affairs, London, pp. 82-88.

57 Another view of the two opposing configurations is that of Turkey-Israel-Jordan-Azerbaijan opposing that of Syria-Armenia-Greece and Russia. See Mufti, M. (1998, Spring), 'Daring and Caution in Turkey's Foreign Policy', *Middle East Journal*, vol.52, no.2, pp. 40-41.

58 *Arabic News-com*, 20 March 1999.

59 Ibid., 25 August 1999.

60 *Turkish Daily News*, 15 December 2000.

61 *Turkish Daily News*, 18 April 2001.

62 *Turkish Daily News*, 3 May 2001.

63 For a full analysis look at Knudsen, E.L. (1994, April), 'Hafiz al-Assad, Islamic Fundamentalism and the Syrian State: An Analysis of Fundamentalist Opposition to the Bathist-Alawite Political/Military Complex', *International Issues*.

Index